LEADERSHIP

LEADERSHIP

●●●●●●●●

Theory and Practice

Peter G. Northouse

●●●●●●●●

SAGE Publications
International Educational and Professional Publisher
Thousand Oaks   London   New Delhi

For information address:

 SAGE Publications, Inc.
2455 Teller Road
Thousand Oaks, California 91320
E-mail: order@sagepub.com

SAGE Publications Ltd.
6 Bonhill Street
London EC2A 4PU
United Kingdom

SAGE Publications India Pvt. Ltd.
M-32 Market
Greater Kailash I
New Delhi 110 048 India

Printed in the United States of America

Library of Congress Cataloging-in-Publication Data

Northouse, Peter Guy.
   Leadership: Theory and practice / author, Peter G. Northouse.
     p. cm.
   Includes bibliographical references and index.
   ISBN 0-8039-5768-8. — ISBN 0-8039-5769-6 (pbk.)
    1. Leadership. 2. Leadership—Case studies. I. Title.
 HM141.N67 1997
 303.3'4—dc21   96-45796

This book is printed on acid-free paper.

       99   00   01   02   03   10 9 8 7 6

Acquiring Editor:	Marquita Flemming
Editorial Assistant:	Frances Borghi
Production Editor:	Sherrise M. Purdum
Production Assistant:	Denise Santoyo
Typesetter/Designer:	Danielle Dillahunt
Indexer:	Teri Greenberg
Cover Designer:	Lesa Valdez

35694533

CONTENTS

To
Laurel, Scott, and Lisa

Preface

This book is about leadership—a subtle, complex, often subjective, but highly valued concept. A great deal has been written about leadership, but it has frequently been presented in a fashion that is either too simplistic or too theoretical and impractical. In an effort to bridge this gap, in this book we review and analyze the research findings of many approaches to leadership, giving special attention to how leadership can be explained and applied in real-world organizations. In essence, we describe how the research on leadership can inform and direct our practical applications of leadership.

The text comprises 12 chapters. The introductory chapter is followed by 9 chapters that present singular approaches. The last 2 chapters deal with multiple perspectives on leadership. In a general way, the chapters follow leadership from the earliest research to the more recent.

More specifically, Chapter 1, "Introduction," provides an overview of leadership that defines leadership and describes its various characteristics. Chapter 2, "Trait Approach," examines the multitude of studies that have been conducted through the years on individuals' personal leadership characteristics and discusses some of the important traits that are consistently identified in the people we call leaders. Chapter 3, "Style Approach," focuses on the behavior of leaders—what they *do* and how they *act* in various contexts. Chapter 4, "Situational Approach," describes a model, one that is used extensively in training and development and that describes how leaders should adapt their styles to the development level of followers and to the demands of various organizational settings.

Chapter 5, "Contingency Theory," based on Fiedler's research, focuses on how effective leadership may result when a leader's style correctly matches the characteristics of a particular situation. Chapter 6, "Path-Goal Theory," examines how leaders can motivate subordinates to be productive and satisfied with their work by selecting a style of leadership that provides "what is missing" for subordinates in a particular setting. Chapter 7, "Leader-Member Exchange Theory," addresses leadership as a process of interactions between leaders and followers, making the leader-member relationship the pivotal concept in the leadership process. Chapter 8, "Transformational Leadership," describes a full range of leadership behaviors, including factors that contribute to transformational, transactional, and nontransactional leadership. Chapter 9, "Team Leadership Theory," focuses on organizational teams, the vital functions of team leadership, and the factors contributing to organizational team effectiveness.

Chapter 10, "Psychodynamic Approach," based on the works of Freud and Jung, focuses on the basic personality of the leader and subordinates and stresses the idea that leaders can become more effective by obtaining insights into their own upbringing, prior relationships, and psychological development. Chapter 11, "Women and Leadership," using women's and feminist theory, explores the relationship between gender and leadership, providing historical, theoretical, and practical perspectives. Chapter 12, "Popular Approaches to Leadership," analyzes the common themes of current leadership approaches typically found in writings intended for a general audience.

Special Features

Although this text presents and analyzes a wide range of leadership research, every attempt has been made to present the material in a clear, concise, interesting, and understandable manner. Initial reviews of early chapters of the book indicated that clarity was one of its major strengths. In addition to the writing style, several other features are provided in the book to help make it user-friendly.

- Each chapter follows the same *format* and is structured to include theory first and then practice.
- Each chapter includes a discussion of the *strengths and criticisms* of the approach and assists the reader in determining the relative merits of each approach.
- Each chapter includes an *application* section that discusses the practical aspects of the approach and how it could be used in today's organizational settings.
- Three *case studies* are provided in each chapter to illustrate common leadership issues and dilemmas. Thought-provoking questions follow each case study, assisting readers to interpret the case.
- A leadership *instrument/questionnaire* is provided in each of the chapters to help the reader apply the approach to his or her own leadership style or setting.
- Throughout the text, many *drawings*, *charts*, *figures*, and *tables* depict the content of the theory and make the ideas more meaningful.

Through these special features, every effort has been made to make this text substantive, understandable, and practical.

Audience

This book provides both an in-depth presentation of leadership theory and a discussion of how it applies to real situations. As such it is intended for undergraduate *and* graduate classes in business, business communication, management, communication, organizational communication, political science, training and development, and health services. It is particularly well suited as a supplementary text for core organizational behavior courses or as an overview text within MBA curricula. This book would also be useful as a text in continuing education, in-service training, and other leadership development programs.

Acknowledgments

I am indebted to many people who helped me in the development of this book. Some of their contributions were large and others were small, but each contribution helped to enhance the overall quality of the book.

First, for their critiques and valuable feedback on individual chapters, I am indebted to Bruce J. Avolio (Binghamton University of New York), Fred E. Fiedler (University of Washington), George B. Graen (University of Cincinnati), Julie Indvik (California State University-Chico), Mary Uhl-Bien (University of Central Florida), and Drea Zigarmi (Blanchard Training and Development). The comments and suggestions made by these leadership scholars strengthened the book and guaranteed that the content was "on mark" with the current thinking about leadership in the field.

Second, the breadth of the text was enhanced by the contributions of four people who wrote individual chapters for the book. These include Mary Ann Bowman (Western Michigan University), Susan E. Kogler Hill (Cleveland State University), Dayle M. Smith (University of San Francisco), and Ernest L. Stech (Chief Mountain Publishing).

Third, I owe a special thanks to the individuals who read selected case studies in the book and made sure the cases were accurate and representative of leadership in real organizations. They include: Greg

Detmer, Bert DeVries, Kathy Drennan, Rodger Jones, Marcy Lindhout, Doug Paine, Jay Pflasterer, Ken Saulter, and Pat Tamblyn.

Fourth, I am grateful to Joan Kmenta for her willing editorial assistance on early drafts of the manuscript.

Fifth, I would like to thank the Leadership 335 students that I have taught through the years. Their ongoing feedback has been helpful in sharpening my thinking about leadership and in encouraging me to make plain the practical implications of leadership theories.

Finally, I would like express my appreciation to all of the staff at Sage Publications. In particular, my appreciation goes to Marquita Flemming, my highly competent editor, who worked with me on this project from acquisition to completion. I would also like to thank Sherrise Purdum for her special efforts during the production phase of the book. The staff at Sage have provided outstanding assistance throughout the duration of this project and have worked hard to assure that this book would meet a high standard.

CHAPTER 1

Introduction

Introduction

In bookstores today there are many publications that have been written for mass consumption on the popular trends in leadership. People
are fascinated with the idea of leadership, and they seek more information on how to become effective leaders. Many individuals believe
that leadership is a way to improve how they present themselves to
others. Corporations want individuals who have "leadership ability"
because they believe these individuals provide special assets to their
organizations. Generally, leadership is a highly sought-after and highly
valued commodity.

In addition to popular books, there are also many publications
about leadership in the research literature. A review of the scholarly
studies on leadership shows that there is a wide variety of different
theoretical approaches to explain the complexities of the leadership
process (e.g., Bass, 1990; Bryman, 1992). Some researchers conceptualize leadership as a trait, or as a behavior, while others view leadership from a political perspective, or from a humanistic viewpoint.
Leadership has been studied using both qualitative and quantitative
methods in many contexts, including small groups, therapeutic groups,

and large organizations. Collectively, the research findings on leadership from all of these areas provide a picture of a process that is far more sophisticated and complex than the often simplistic view presented in some of the popular books on leadership.

The present book will treat leadership as a complex process having multiple dimensions. Based on the research literature, this text will provide an in-depth description and application of many different approaches to leadership. The emphasis in the text will be on how theory can inform the practice of leadership. In the book, we will describe each theory and then explain how the theory can be used in real situations.

Leadership Defined

There are a multitude of ways to finish the sentence, "Leadership is . . . ." In fact, as Stogdill (1974) points out in a review of leadership research, there are almost as many different definitions of *leadership* as there are people who have tried to define it (p. 7). It is much like the words *democracy, love,* and *peace.* Although each of us intuitively knows what he or she means by such words, the words can have different meanings for different people. As soon as we try to define "leadership," we immediately discover that leadership has many different meanings.

In the past 50 years there have been as many as 65 different classification systems developed to define the dimensions of leadership (Fleishman et al., 1991). One such classification system, directly related to our discussion, is the scheme proposed by Bass (1990, pp. 11-20). He suggested that some definitions view leadership as the *focus of group processes.* From this perspective the leader is at the center of group change and activity, and embodies the will of the group. Another group of definitions conceptualizes leadership from *a personality perspective,* which suggests that leadership is a combination of special traits or characteristics that individuals possess and that enable them to induce others to accomplish tasks. Other approaches to leadership have defined it as an *act* or *behavior*—the things leaders do to bring about change in a group.

In addition, leadership has been defined in terms of the *power relationship* that exists between leaders and followers. From this viewpoint, leaders have power and wield it to effect change in others. Still others view leadership as an *instrument of goal achievement* in helping group members achieve their goals and meet their needs. This view includes leadership that transforms followers through vision setting, role modeling, and individualized attention.

Despite the multitude of ways that leadership has been conceptualized, several components can be identified as central to the phenomenon of leadership. They are (a) leadership is a process, (b) leadership involves influence, (c) leadership occurs within a group context, and (d) leadership involves goal attainment. Based on these components, the following definition of leadership will be used in this text. *Leadership is a process whereby an individual influences a group of individuals to achieve a common goal.*

Defining leadership as a *process* means that it is not a trait or characteristic that resides in the leader, but is a transactional event that occurs between the leader and his or her followers. *Process* implies that a leader affects and is affected by followers. It emphasizes that leadership is not a linear, one-way event but rather an interactive event. When leadership is defined in this manner, it becomes available to everyone. It is not restricted to only the formally designated leader in a group.

Leadership involves *influence;* it is concerned with how the leader affects followers. Influence is the sine qua non of leadership. Without influence, leadership does not exist.

Leadership occurs in *groups*. Groups are the context in which leadership takes place. Leadership involves influencing a group of individuals who have a common purpose. This can be a small task group, a community group, or a large group encompassing an entire organization. Leadership training programs that teach people to lead themselves are not considered a part of leadership within the definition that is set forth in this discussion.

Leadership includes attention to *goals*. This means that leadership has to do with directing a group of individuals toward accomplishing some task or end. Leaders direct their energies toward individuals who are trying to achieve something together. Therefore, leadership occurs and has its effects in contexts where individuals are moving toward a goal.

Throughout this text, the people who engage in leadership will be referred to as *leaders* and those individuals toward whom leadership is directed will be referred to as *followers*. Both leaders and followers are involved together in the leadership process. Leaders need followers and followers need leaders (Burns, 1978; Jago, 1982; Heller & Van Til, 1983; Hollander, 1992). Although leaders and followers are closely linked, it is the leader who often initiates the relationship, creates the communication linkages, and carries the burden for maintaining the relationship.

In our discussion of leaders and followers, attention will be directed toward follower issues as well as leader issues. As Burns (1978) has pointed out, discussions of leadership are sometimes viewed as elitist because of the implied power and importance frequently ascribed to leaders in the leader-follower relationship. Leaders are not above followers or better than followers. Leaders and followers need to be understood in relation to each other (Hollander, 1992) and collectively (Burns, 1978).

Leadership Described

In addition to definitional issues, it is also important to discuss several other questions pertaining to the nature of leadership. In the following section we will address questions such as how leadership as a trait differs from leadership as a process; how appointed leadership differs from emergent leadership; and how the concepts of power, coercion, and management differ from leadership.

Trait Versus Process Leadership

We have all heard statements such as "He is born to be a leader" or "She is a natural leader." These statements are commonly expressed by people who take a trait perspective toward leadership. The trait perspective suggests that certain individuals have special innate or inborn characteristics or qualities that make them leaders, and it is these qualities that differentiate them from nonleaders. Some of the personal qualities used to identify leaders include unique physical factors (e.g., height), personality features (e.g., extroversion), and ability characteristics (e.g., speech fluency) (Bryman, 1992). In Chapter 2, we will discuss a large body of research that has examined these qualities.

To describe leadership as a trait is quite different from describing it as a process (see Figure 1.1). The trait viewpoint conceptualizes

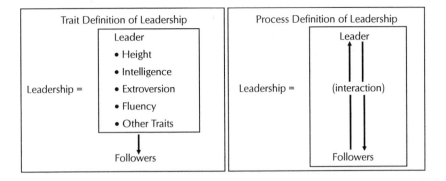

Figure 1.1. The Different Views of Leadership Based on the Trait and Process Definitions

leadership as a property or set of properties possessed in varying degrees by different people (Jago, 1982). This suggests that it resides *in* select people and restricts leadership to only those who are believed to have special, usually inborn, talents. The process viewpoint suggests it is a phenomenon that resides in the context and makes leadership available to everyone. As process, leadership can be observed in leader behaviors (Jago, 1982) and it is something that can be learned. The process definition of leadership is consistent with the definition of leadership that we have set forth in this chapter.

Assigned Versus Emergent Leadership

Some people are leaders because of their formal position within an organization, whereas others are leaders because of the way other group members respond to them. These two common forms of leadership are called *assigned leadership* and *emergent leadership*. Leadership that is based on occupying a position within an organization is called *assigned leadership*. Team leaders, plant managers, department heads, directors, and administrators are all examples of assigned leadership.

Yet the person assigned to a leadership position does not always become the real leader in a particular setting. When an individual is perceived by others as the most influential member of a group or organization, regardless of the individual's title, the person is exhibiting *emergent leadership*. The individual acquires emergent leadership through other people in the organization who support and accept that individual's behavior. This type of leadership is not assigned by position, but rather it *emerges* over a period of time through communication. Some of the positive communication behaviors that account for successful leader emergence include being verbally involved, being informed, seeking others' opinions, initiating new ideas, and being firm but not rigid (Fisher, 1974).

The leadership approaches we discuss in the subsequent chapters of this book apply equally to assigned leadership and emergent leadership. When an individual is engaged in leadership, that individual is a leader, whether or not the individual was assigned to be the leader or the individual emerged as the leader. This book will focus on the leadership process that occurs when any individual is engaged in influencing other group members in their efforts to reach a goal.

Leadership and Power

The concept of power is related to leadership because it is part of the influence process. Power is the capacity or potential to influence. People have power when they have the ability to affect others' beliefs, attitudes, and courses of action. Ministers, doctors, coaches, and teachers are all examples of individuals who have the potential to influence us. When they do, they are using their power, the resource they draw upon to effect change in us.

In organizations there are two major kinds of power: position power and personal power. *Position power* refers to the power a person derives from a particular office or rank in a formal organizational system. Vice presidents or department heads have more power than staff personnel because of the position they have in the organization. *Personal power* refers to the power a leader derives from followers. When leaders act in ways that are important to followers, it gives leaders power. For example, some managers have power because their subordinates find them to be good role models. Others have power because they are viewed as highly competent or considerate by their subordinates. In both cases, these managers' power is ascribed to them based on how they are seen in their relationships with others.

The most widely cited research on power is French and Raven's (1959) work on the bases of social power. In their work, power was conceptualized from the framework of a dyadic relationship that included both the person influencing and the person being influenced. French and Raven identified five common and important types of power: (a) reward, (b) coercive, (c) legitimate, (d) referent, and (e) expert. Each of these types of power increases a leader's capacity to influence the attitudes, values, or behaviors of others.

In discussions of leadership, it is not unusual that leaders are described as wielders of power, as individuals who dominate others. In these instances power is conceptualized as a tool that leaders use to achieve their own ends. Contrary to this view of power, Burns (1978) emphasizes power from a relationship standpoint. For Burns, power is not an entity that leaders use over others to achieve their own ends, but instead it occurs in relationships and should be used by leaders and followers to benefit their collective goals.

In this text, our discussions of leadership will treat power as a relational concern for both leaders and followers. We will pay attention to how leaders work with followers to reach common goals.

Leadership and Coercion

Coercion is one of the specific kinds of power that are available to leaders. Coercion involves the use of force to affect change. It means influencing others to do something by manipulating the penalties and rewards in their work environment. Coercion frequently involves the use of threats, punishment, and negative reward schedules. Classic examples of leaders who used coercion are Adolf Hitler in Germany, Jim Jones in Guyana, and David Koresch in Waco, Texas, each of whom used power and restraint to force his followers to engage in extreme behaviors.

It is important to distinguish between coercion and leadership because it allows us to separate out from our examples of leadership the behaviors of individuals such as Hitler, Jones, and Koresch. In our discussions of leadership, coercive people will not be used as models of what ideal leadership is about. Our definition suggests that leadership is reserved for those individuals who influence a group of individuals toward a common goal. Leaders who use coercion are interested in their own goals and seldom are interested in the wants and needs of subordinates. Using coercion runs counter to working with followers to achieve a common goal.

Leadership and Management

Leadership is a process that is similar to management in many ways. Leadership involves influence, as does management. Leadership requires working with people, which management requires as well. Leadership is concerned with effective goal accomplishment and so is management. In general, many of the functions of management are activities that are consistent with the definition of leadership we set forth in the beginning of this chapter.

But leadership is also different from management. While the study of leadership can be traced back to Aristotle, management emerged around the turn of the century with the advent of our industrialized society. Management was created as a way to reduce chaos in organizations and to make them run more effectively and efficiently. The primary functions of management, first identified by Fayol (1916), were planning, organizing, staffing, and controlling. These functions are still representative of the field of management today.

In a book that compares the functions of management to the functions of leadership, Kotter (1990) argues that the functions of the two are quite dissimilar (see Figure 1.2). The overriding function of management is to provide order and consistency to organizations, whereas the primary function of leadership is to produce change and movement. Management is about seeking order and stability; leadership is about seeking adaptive and constructive change.

The major activities of management get played out differently than the activities of leadership. In planning and budgeting, the emphasis of management is on establishing detailed agendas, setting timetables from several months to a few years, and allocating the necessary resources to meet organizational objectives. In contrast to this, the emphasis of leadership is on direction setting, clarifying the big picture, building a vision that is often long term, and setting strategy to create needed organizational changes.

In organizing and staffing, management focuses on providing structure to the work of individuals, their relationships in the organization, and the physical context in which they work. It includes placing people in the right jobs, and developing rules and procedures for how work is to be performed. For leadership, organizing and staffing take the form of communicating a vision to employees, invoking their commitment, and working with them to build teams and coalitions useful in fulfilling the organization's mission.

MANAGEMENT	LEADERSHIP
"Produces Order and Consistency"	"Produces Change and Movement"
• Planning/Budgeting	• Vision Building/Strategizing
• Organizing/Staffing	• Aligning People/Communicating
• Controlling/Problem Solving	• Motivating/Inspiring

Figure 1.2. Comparison of Management and Leadership
SOURCE: Adapted from John P. Kotter's *A Force for Change: How Leadership Differs From Management* (1990, pp. 3-8).

For the activities of controlling and problem solving, the focus of management is on developing incentive systems to motivate the workforce, problem solving, monitoring progress toward performance objectives, and taking corrective action when performance is off track. In contrast to this, leadership emphasizes motivating and inspiring individuals, empowering them, and energizing them to satisfy their unmet needs.

There have been many scholars, in addition to Kotter, who have argued that leadership and management are distinct constructs (see Bennis & Nanus, 1985; Bryman, 1992; Hickman, 1990; Peters & Austin, 1985). Approaching the issue from a more narrow viewpoint, Zaleznik (1977) goes so far as to argue that leaders and managers themselves are distinct—they are basically different types of people. He contends that managers are reactive and prefer to work with people to solve problems but do so with low emotional involvement. They act to limit choices. Zaleznik suggests that leaders, on the other hand, are emotionally active and involved. They seek to shape ideas instead of responding to them, and act to expand the available options to long-standing problems. Leaders change the way people think about what is possible.

Although there are clear differences between management and leadership, or leaders and managers, there is also a considerable amount of overlap (Yukl, 1989). When managers are involved in influencing a group to meet its goals they are involved in leadership. When leaders are involved in planning, organizing, staffing, and controlling, they are involved in management. Both processes involve influencing a group of individuals toward goal attainment. For purposes of our discussion in this book, we will focus on the leadership process. In our examples and case studies we will treat the roles of managers and leaders similarly and not emphasize the differences between them.

Plan of the Book

This book will be user-friendly. It will be based on substantive theories but written to emphasize practice and application. Each chapter in the book will follow the same format. The first section of each chapter will briefly describe the leadership approach and discuss various research studies applicable to the approach. The second section of each chapter will evaluate the approach, highlighting its strengths and criticisms. Special attention will be given to how the approach contributes or fails to contribute to an overall understanding of the leadership process. The next section will use brief case studies to provide a discussion of how the approach can be applied in ongoing organizations. The final section of each chapter will provide a leadership questionnaire with a discussion of how the questionnaire measures the reader's leadership style. Each chapter ends with a summary and references.

Summary

Leadership is a topic with universal appeal, and in the popular press and academic research literature there is much written about leadership. Despite the abundance of writing on the topic, leadership has presented a major challenge to practitioners and researchers interested in understanding the nature of leadership. It is a highly valued phenomenon that is very complex.

Through the years, leadership has been defined and conceptualized in many ways. The component common to nearly all of the classifications is that leadership is an influence process that assists groups of individuals toward goal attainment. Specifically, in this book, leadership is defined as a process whereby an individual influences a group of individuals to achieve a common goal.

Because leaders and followers are both a part of the leadership process, it is important to address issues that confront followers as well as those that confront leaders. Leaders and followers need to be understood in relation to each other. In prior research, many studies have focused on leadership as a trait. The trait perspective suggests that certain people in our society have special inborn qualities that make them leaders. This view restricts leadership to only those who are believed to have special characteristics. In contrast, the approach in this text suggests that leadership is a process that can be learned and that it is available to everyone.

Two common forms of leadership are assigned and emergent. Assigned leadership is based on having a formal title or position within an organization. Emergent leadership results from what one does and how one acquires support from followers. Leadership, as a process, applies to individuals in both assigned roles and emergent roles.

Related to leadership is the concept of power—the potential to influence. There are two kinds of power: position and personal. Position power, which is much like assigned leadership, refers to the power an individual derives from having an office in a formal organizational system. Personal power comes from followers. It is given to leaders because followers believe leaders have something of value. Treating power as a shared resource is important because it de-emphasizes the idea that leaders are power-wielders.

Leadership and coercion are not the same. Coercion involves the use of threats and punishment to induce change in followers for the sake of the leader. Coercion runs counter to leadership because it does not treat leadership as a process that includes followers, and it does not emphasize working with followers to achieve common goals.

Leadership and management are different concepts that have a considerable amount of overlap. They are different in that management traditionally focuses on the activities of planning, organizing, staffing, and controlling, whereas leadership emphasizes the general influence process. According to some researchers, management is concerned with creating order and stability while leadership is about adaptation and constructive change. Other researchers go so far as to argue that managers and leaders are different types of people, managers being more reactive and less emotionally involved, and leaders being more proactive and more emotionally involved. The overlap between leadership and management is centered on how they both involve influencing a group of individuals in goal attainment.

In this book we will discuss leadership as a complex process. Based on the research literature, we will describe selected approaches to leadership and assess how they can be employed to improve leadership in real situations.

References

Bass, B. M. (1990). *Bass and Stogdill's handbook of leadership: A survey of theory and research.* New York: Free Press.

Bennis, W. G., & Nanus, B. (1985). *Leaders: The strategies for taking charge.* New York: Harper & Row.

Bryman, A. (1992). *Charisma and leadership in organizations.* London: Sage.

Burns, J. M. (1978). *Leadership.* New York: Harper & Row.

Fayol, H. (1916). *General and industrial management.* London: Pitman.

Fisher, B. A. (1974). *Small group decision making: Communication and the group process.* New York: McGraw-Hill.

Fleishman, E. A., Mumford, M. D., Zaccaro, S. J., Levin, K. Y., Korotkin, A. L., & Hein, M. B. (1991). Taxonomic efforts in the description of leader behavior: A synthesis and functional interpretation. *Leadership Quarterly, 2*(4), 245-287.

French, R. P., Jr., & Raven, B. (1959). The bases of social power. In D. Cartwright (Ed.), *Studies in social power.* Ann Arbor, MI: Institute for Social Research.

Heller, T., & Van Til, J. (1983). Leadership and followership: Some summary propositions. *Journal of Applied Behavioral Science, 18,* 405-414.

Hickman, C. R. (1990). *Mind of a manager, soul of a leader.* New York: John Wiley.

Hollander, E. P. (1992). Leadership, followership, self, and others. *Leadership Quarterly, 3*(1), 43-54.

Jago, A. G. (1982). Leadership: Perspectives in theory and research. *Management Science, 28*(3), 315-336.

Kotter, J. P. (1990). *A force for change: How leadership differs from management.* New York: Free Press.

Peters, R., & Austin, N. (1985). *A passion for excellence.* New York: Random House.

Stogdill, R. M. (1974). *Handbook of leadership: A survey of theory and research.* New York: Free Press.

Yukl, G. A. (1989). *Leadership in organizations* (2nd ed.). Englewood Cliffs, NJ: Prentice Hall.

Zaleznik, A. (1977, May-June). Managers and leaders: Are they different? *Harvard Business Review, 55,* 67-78.

CHAPTER 2

Trait Approach

Description

Of interest to scholars throughout the 20th century, the trait approach was one of the first systematic attempts to study leadership. In the early 1900s, leadership traits were studied to determine what made certain people great leaders. The theories that were developed were called "great man" theories because they focused on identifying the innate qualities and characteristics possessed by great social, political, and military leaders (e.g., Thomas Jefferson, Abraham Lincoln, and Mahatma Gandhi). It was believed that people were born with these traits and only the "great" people possessed them. During this time, research concentrated on determining the specific traits that clearly differentiated leaders from followers (Bass, 1990; Jago, 1982).

In the mid-1900s, the trait approach was challenged by research that questioned the universality of leadership traits. In a major review in 1948, Stogdill suggested that no consistent set of traits differentiated leaders from nonleaders across a variety of situations. An individual with leadership traits who was a leader in one situation might not be a leader in another situation. Rather than being a quantity that individuals possessed, leadership was reconceptualized as a relationship between people in a social situation (Stogdill, 1948). Personal factors related to leadership continued to be important, but researchers contended that these factors were to be considered as relative to the requirements of the situation.

In recent years, there has been a resurgence in interest in the trait approach—in explaining how traits influence leadership (Bryman, 1992). For example, based on a new analysis of much of the previous trait research, Lord, DeVader, and Alliger (1986) found that personality traits were strongly associated with individuals' perceptions of leadership. Similarly, Kirkpatrick and Locke (1991) have gone so far as to claim that effective leaders are actually distinct types of people in several key respects. Further evidence of renewed interest in the trait approach can be seen in the current emphasis given by many researchers to visionary and charismatic leadership (see Bass, 1990; Bennis & Nanus, 1985; Nadler & Tushman, 1989; Zaleznik, 1977).

In short, the trait approach is alive and well. It began with an emphasis on identifying the qualities of great persons; next, it shifted to include the impact of situations on leadership; and most currently, it has shifted back to reemphasize the critical role of traits in effective leadership.

Although the research on traits has spanned the entire 20th century, a good overview of this approach is found in two surveys completed by Stogdill (1948, 1974). In his first survey, Stogdill analyzed and synthesized more than 124 trait studies that were conducted between 1904 and 1947. In his second study, he analyzed another 163 studies that were completed between 1948 and 1970. By taking a closer look at each of these reviews, a clearer picture can be obtained of how individuals' traits contribute to the leadership process.

Stogdill's first survey identified a group of important leadership traits that were related to how individuals in various groups became leaders. His results showed that the average individual in the leadership role is different from an average group member in the following ways: (a) intelligence, (b) alertness, (c) insight, (d) responsibility, (e) initiative, (f) persistence, (g) self-confidence, and (h) sociability.

The findings of Stogdill's first survey also indicated that an individual does not become a leader solely because he or she possesses certain traits. Rather, the traits that leaders possess must be relevant to situations in which the leader is functioning. As stated earlier, leaders in one situation may not necessarily be leaders in another situation. Findings showed that leadership was not a passive state but resulted from a working relationship between the leader and other group members. This research marked the beginning of a new approach to leadership research that focused on leadership behaviors and leadership situations.

Stogdill's second survey, published in 1974, analyzed 163 new studies and compared the findings of these studies to the findings he had reported in his first survey. The second survey was more balanced in its description of the role of traits and leadership. While the first survey implied that leadership is determined principally by situational factors and not personality factors, the second survey argued more moderately that both personality and situational factors were determinants of leadership. In essence, the second survey validated the original trait idea that the leader's characteristics are indeed a part of leadership.

Similar to the first survey, Stogdill's second survey also identified traits that were positively associated with leadership. The list included the following 10 characteristics: (a) drive for responsibility and task completion, (b) vigor and persistence in pursuit of goals, (c) venturesomeness and originality in problem solving, (d) drive to exercise initiative in social situations, (e) self-confidence and sense of personal identity, (f) willingness to accept consequences of decision and action, (g) readiness to absorb interpersonal stress, (h) willingness to tolerate frustration and delay, (i) ability to influence other persons' behavior, and (j) capacity to structure social interaction systems to the purpose at hand.

Mann (1959) conducted a similar study that examined more than 1,400 findings regarding personality and leadership in small groups, but he placed less emphasis on how situational factors influenced leadership. Although tentative in his conclusions, Mann suggested that personality traits could be used to discriminate leaders from nonleaders. His results identified leaders as strong in the following traits: intelligence, masculinity, adjustment, dominance, extroversion, and conservatism.

Lord et al. (1986) reassessed the findings put forward by Mann (1959), using a more sophisticated procedure called meta-analysis. Lord and co-workers found that intelligence, masculinity, and dominance were significantly related to how individuals perceived leaders. From their findings, the authors argued strongly that personality traits could be used to make discriminations consistently across situations between leaders and nonleaders.

TABLE 2.1 Studies of Leadership Traits and Characteristics

Stogdill (1948)	Mann (1956)	Stogdill (1974)	Lord, DeVader, & Alliger (1986)	Kirkpatrick & Locke (1991)
Intelligence	Intelligence	Achievement	Intelligence	Drive
Alertness	Masculinity	Persistence	Masculinity	Motivation
Insight	Adjustment	Insight	Dominance	Integrity
Responsibility	Dominance	Initiative		Confidence
Initiative	Extroversion	Self-confidence		Cognitive Ability
Persistence	Conservatism	Responsibility		Task Knowledge
Self-confidence		Cooperativeness		
Sociability		Tolerance		
		Influence		
		Sociability		

Yet another review argues for the importance of leadership traits: Kirkpatrick and Locke (1991) contended that "it is unequivocally clear that leaders are not like other people" (p. 59). From a qualitative synthesis of earlier research, Kirkpatrick and Locke postulated that leaders differ from nonleaders on six traits: drive, the desire to lead, honesty and integrity, self-confidence, cognitive ability, and knowledge of the business. According to these writers, individuals can be born with these traits, they can learn them, or both. It is these six traits that make up the "right stuff" for leaders. Kirkpatrick and Locke contend that leadership traits make some people different from others, and this difference needs to be recognized as an important part of the leadership process.

Table 2.1 provides a summary of the traits and characteristics that were identified by researchers from the trait approach. It illustrates clearly the breadth of traits related to leadership. Table 2.1 also shows how difficult it is to select certain traits as definitive leadership traits; some of the traits appear in several of the survey studies, whereas others appear in only one or two studies. Regardless of the lack of precision in Table 2.1, however, it represents a general convergence of research regarding which traits are leadership traits.

What, then, can be said about trait research? What has a century of research on the trait approach given us that is useful? The answer is an extended list of traits that "would-be" leaders might hope to

TABLE 2.2   Major Leadership Traits

INTELLIGENCE
SELF-CONFIDENCE
DETERMINATION
INTEGRITY
SOCIABILITY

possess or wish to cultivate if they want to be perceived by others as leaders. Some of the traits that are central to this list include the following: intelligence, self-confidence, determination, integrity, and sociability (see Table 2.2).

Intelligence

Intelligence or intellectual ability is positively related to leadership. Having strong verbal ability, perceptual ability, and reasoning appears to make one a better leader. Although it is good to be bright, the research also indicates that a leader's intellectual ability should not vary too much from that of his or her subordinates. In situations where the leader's IQ is very different from that of the followers, it can have a counterproductive impact on leadership. Leaders with higher abilities may have difficulty in communicating with followers because they are preoccupied or because their ideas are too advanced to be accepted by their followers.

Self-Confidence

Self-confidence is another trait that helps an individual to be a leader. Self-confidence is the ability to be certain about one's competencies and skills. It includes a sense of self-esteem and self-assurance and the belief that one can make a difference. Leadership involves influencing others, and self-confidence allows the leader to feel assured that his or her attempts to influence are appropriate and right.

Determination

Many leaders also exhibit determination. Determination refers to the desire to get the job done and includes characteristics such as initiative, persistence, dominance, and drive. Individuals with determination are willing to assert themselves, they are proactive, and they have the capacity to persevere in the face of obstacles. Being determined includes showing dominance at times and in certain situations where followers need to be directed.

Integrity

Integrity is another of the important leadership traits. Integrity is the quality of honesty and trustworthiness. Individuals who adhere to a strong set of principles and take responsibility for their actions are exhibiting integrity. Leaders with integrity inspire confidence in others because they can be trusted to do what they say they are going to do. They are loyal, dependable, and not deceptive. Basically, integrity makes a leader believable and worthy of our trust.

Sociability

A final trait that is important for leaders is sociability. Sociability refers to a leader's inclination to seek out pleasant social relationships. Leaders who show sociability are friendly, outgoing, courteous, tactful, and diplomatic. They are sensitive to others' needs and show concern for their well-being. Social leaders have good interpersonal skills and create cooperative relationships with their followers.

Although our discussion of leadership traits has focused on five major traits (i.e., intelligence, self-confidence, determination, integrity, and sociability), this list is not all-inclusive. There are other traits indicated in Table 2.1 that are associated with effective leadership. Yet the five traits we have identified contribute substantially to whether or not an individual is going to be a leader.

How Does the Trait Approach Work?

The way the trait approach works is very different from the other approaches discussed in subsequent chapters because the trait approach focuses exclusively on the leader, and not on the followers or the situation. This makes the trait approach theoretically more straightforward than other approaches. In essence, the trait approach is concerned with leaders and their traits. It is concerned with what traits leaders exhibit and who has these traits.

The trait approach does not lay out a set of hypotheses or principles about what kind of leader is needed in a certain situation or what a leader should do, given a particular set of circumstances. Rather, this approach emphasizes that having a leader with a certain set of traits is crucial to having effective leadership. It is the leader and his or her personality that is central to the leadership process.

The trait approach suggests that organizations will work better if the people in managerial positions have designated leadership profiles. To find the right people, it is common for organizations to utilize personality assessment instruments. The assumption behind these procedures is that selecting the "right" people will increase organizational effectiveness. Organizations can specify the characteristics or traits that are important to them for particular positions and then use personality assessment measures to determine whether or not an individual fits their needs.

The trait approach is also used for personal awareness and development. By analyzing their own traits, managers can gain an idea of their strengths and weaknesses, and they can get a feel for how others see them within the organization. A trait assessment can help managers to determine if they have the qualities to move up or to move to other positions in the company. It gives individuals a clearer picture of who they are as a leader and how they fit into the organizational hierarchy. In areas where their traits are lacking, leaders can try to make changes in what they do or where they work in order to increase the potential impact of their given traits.

At the end of the chapter a leadership instrument is provided that can be used to assess your leadership traits. This instrument is typical of the kind of personality tests that companies use to assess individuals' leadership potential. As you will find out by completing this instrument, trait measures are a good way to assess your own abilities.

Strengths

The trait approach has several identifiable strengths. First, the trait approach is intuitively appealing. It fits clearly with our notion that leaders are the individuals who are "out front" and "leading the way" in our society. The image in the popular press and community-at-large is that leaders are a special kind of people—people with gifts who can do extraordinary things. The trait approach is consistent with this perception because it is built upon the premise that leaders are different and their difference resides in the special traits they possess. People have a need to see their leaders as gifted people and the trait approach fulfills this need.

A second strength of the trait approach is that it has a century of research to back it up. No other theory can boast of the breadth and depth of studies conducted on the trait approach. The strength and longevity of this line of research give the trait approach a measure of credibility not afforded other approaches. Out of this abundance of research has emerged a body of data that points to the important role of various personality traits in the leadership process.

Another strength, more conceptual in nature, results from the way the trait approach highlights the leader component in the leadership process. Leadership is comprised of leaders, followers, and situations, but the trait approach is devoted only to the first of these, leaders. Although this is also a potential weakness, by focusing exclusively on the role of the leader in leadership the trait approach has been able to provide us with a deeper and more intricate understanding of how the leader and his or her personality are related to the leadership process.

Lastly, the trait approach has given us some benchmarks for what we need to look for if we want to be leaders. It identifies what traits we should have and whether the traits that we do have are the best traits. Based on the findings of this approach, personality and assessment procedures can be utilized to offer invaluable information to supervisors and managers about their strengths and weaknesses and ways to improve their overall leadership effectiveness.

Criticisms

In addition to its strengths, the trait approach also has several weaknesses. First and foremost is the failure of the trait approach to delimit a definitive list of leadership traits. Although an enormous number of studies have been conducted over the past 100 years, the findings from these studies have been ambiguous and uncertain at times. Furthermore, the list of traits that has emerged appears endless. This is obvious from Table 2.1, which illustrates a multitude of traits; and these are only a sample of the many leadership traits that were studied.

Another criticism is that the trait approach has failed to take situations into account. As Stogdill (1948) pointed out about 50 years ago, it is difficult to isolate a set of traits that are characteristic of leaders without factoring situational effects into the equation as well. People who possess certain traits that make them leaders in one situation may not be leaders in another situation. Some people may have the traits that help them emerge as leaders but may not have the traits that allow them to maintain their leadership over time. In other words, the situation influences leadership, and it is therefore difficult to identify a universal set of leadership traits in isolation from the context in which the leadership occurs.

A third criticism, derived from the prior two criticisms, is that this approach has resulted in highly subjective determinations of the "most important" leadership traits. Because the findings on traits have been so extensive and broad, there has been much subjective interpretation of the meaning of the data. This subjectivity is readily apparent in the many self-help practice-oriented management books. For example, one author might identify ambition and creativity as crucial leadership traits, whereas another might identify power and achievement. In both cases it is the author's subjective experience and observations that are the basis for the identified leadership traits. These books may be helpful to readers because they identify and describe "important leadership traits," but the methods used to generate these lists of traits are weak. In our culture, people want to know a set of definitive traits of leaders. To respond to this need, authors have set forth lists of traits, even if the origins of these lists are not grounded in strong reliable research.

Research on traits can also be criticized for failing to look at traits in relationship to leadership outcomes. It has emphasized the identification of traits but it has not addressed how leadership traits affect group members and their work. In trying to ascertain universal leadership traits, researchers have focused on the link between specific traits and leader emergence, but they have not tried to link leader traits with other outcomes such as productivity or employee satisfaction. For example, trait research does not provide data on whether leaders who might have high intelligence and strong integrity have better results than leaders without these traits. The trait approach is weak in describing how leaders' traits affect the outcomes of groups and teams in organizational settings.

A final criticism of the trait approach is that it is not a useful approach for training and development. Even if definitive traits could be identified, teaching new traits is not an easy process because traits are not easily changed. For example, it is not reasonable to send managers to a training program to raise their IQ or to train them to become introverted or extroverted people. The point is that traits are relatively fixed psychological structures, and this limits the value of teaching and leadership training.

Application

Despite its shortcomings, the trait approach provides valuable information about leadership. It can be applied by individuals at all levels and in all types of organizations. Although a definitive set of traits is not provided by the trait approach, the approach does provide direction regarding which traits are good to have if one aspires to take a leadership position. By taking personality tests and other similar questionnaires, individuals can gain insight into whether or not they have select traits deemed important for leadership, and they can pinpoint their strengths and weaknesses.

As we discussed previously, managers can utilize information from the trait approach to assess where they stand within their organization and what they need to do to strengthen their position. It can suggest areas in which their personal characteristics are very beneficial to the company, and areas in which they may wish to get more training to enhance their overall approach. Using trait information, managers can develop a deeper understanding of who they are and how they will affect others in the organization.

Case Studies

In the following section, three case studies (Cases 2.1, 2.2, and 2.3) are provided to illustrate the trait approach and to help you understand how the trait approach can be used in making decisions in organizational settings. The settings of the cases are diverse—from directing a research department, to running a paper supplies business, to being head of recruitment for a large bank—but all of the cases deal with trait leadership. At the end of each of the cases you will find questions that will help in analyzing the cases.

Case 2.1

Sandra Coke is vice president for research and development at Great Lakes Foods (GLF), a large snack food company that has approximately 1,000 employees. As a result of a recent reorganization, Sandra must choose an individual to be the new director of research. The director will report directly to Sandra and will be responsible for developing and testing new products. The research division of GLF employs about 200 individuals. The choice of directors is important because Ms. Coke is receiving pressure from the president and board of GLF to improve the company's overall growth and productivity.

Sandra has identified three candidates for the position. Each candidate is at the same managerial level. She is having difficulty choosing one of them because each of the individuals has very strong credentials. Alexa Smith is a long-time employee of GLF who started part-time in the mail room while in high school and after finishing school worked in as many as 10 different positions throughout the company to become manager of new product marketing. Performance reviews of Alexa's work have repeatedly described her as being very creative and insightful. In her tenure at GLF, Alexa has developed and brought to market four new product lines. Alexa is also known throughout GLF as being very persistent about her work; when she starts a project she stays with it until it is finished. It is this quality that probably accounts for the success of each of the four new products with which she has been involved.

A second candidate for the new position is Kelsey Metts, who has been with GLF for 5 years and is presently manager of quality control for established products. Kelsey has a reputation of being very bright. Before joining GLF, she received her MBA at Harvard, graduating at the top of her class. People talk about Kelsey as the kind of person who will be president of her own company someday. Kelsey is also very personable. On all of her performance reviews she received extra high scores on sociability and human relations skills. There isn't a supervisor in the company who doesn't have positive things to say about how comfortable it is to work with Kelsey Metts. Since joining GLF, Kelsey has been instrumental in bringing two new product lines to market.

Brian Murphy, the third candidate, has been with GLF for 10 years and is frequently consulted by upper management regarding strategic planning and corporate direction setting. Brian has been very involved in establishing the vision for GLF and he is a company person all the way. He believes in the values of GLF and he actively promotes its mission. The one quality that stands out above the rest in Brian's performance reviews is his honesty and integrity. Employees who have worked under Brian's supervision consistently report that they feel they can trust Brian to be fair and consistent with them. Brian is highly respected at GLF. In his tenure at the company, Brian has been involved in some capacity with the development of three new product lines.

The challenge confronting Sandra Coke is to choose the best person for the newly established director's position. Because of the pressures she feels from upper management, Sandra knows she must select the best leader for the new position.

Questions

Based on the information provided about the trait approach in Tables 2.1 and 2.2

- Which candidate should Ms. Coke select?
- In what ways is the trait approach helpful in this type of selection?
- In what ways are the weaknesses of the trait approach highlighted in this case?

Case 2.2

Carol Baines was married for 20 years to the owner of the Baines Company until he lost his life in a tragic car accident. After his death, Carol decided not to sell the business but to try to run it herself. Before the accident, her only involvement in the business was in informal discussions with her husband over dinner, although she has a college degree in business, with a major in management.

Baines Co. was one of three office supply stores in a city with a population of 200,000 people. The other two stores were owned by national chains. Baines Co. was not a large company, employing only 5 people. Baines Co. had stable sales of about $200,000 a year, serving mostly the smaller companies in the city. The firm had not grown in a number of years and was beginning to feel the pressure of the advertising and lower prices of the national chains.

For the first 6 months, Carol spent her time familiarizing herself with the employees and the operations of the company. Next, she did a citywide analysis of those companies that had reason to purchase office supplies. Based on her understanding of Baines's capabilities and her assessment of the potential market for their products and services, Carol developed a specific set of short-term and long-range goals for the company. Behind all of her planning, Carol had a vision that Baines could be a viable, healthy, and competitive company. She wanted to carry on the business that her husband had started, but more than that, she wanted it to grow.

Over the first 5 years, Carol invested significant amounts of money in advertising, sales, and services. These efforts were well spent because the company began to show rapid growth immediately. Because of the growth, another 20 individuals were hired at Baines.

The expansion at Baines was particularly remarkable because of another major hardship Carol had to confront. Carol was diagnosed with breast cancer a year after her husband died. The treatment for her cancer included 2 months of radiation therapy and 6 months of strong chemotherapy. Although the side effects included losing her hair and being very tired, Carol continued to manage the company throughout the ordeal. In spite of her difficulties, Carol was successful. Under the strength of her leadership, the growth at Baines continued for 10 consecutive years.

Interviews with new and old employees at Baines revealed much about Carol's leadership. Employees said that Carol was a very solid person. She cared deeply about others and was fair and considerate. They said she created a family-like atmosphere at Baines. Few employees had quit Baines since Carol took over. Carol was devoted to all the employees and she supported their interests. For example, the company has a softball team in the summer and a basketball team in the winter, and both are sponsored by Baines. Others described Carol as a strong individual. Even though she had cancer, she continued to be positive and interested in them. She did not get depressed with the cancer and its side effects, even though it was difficult. Employees said she was a model of strength, goodness, and quality.

At the age of 55, Carol turned the business over to her two sons. She continues to act as the president but does not supervise the day-to-day operations. The company is presently doing more than $3.1 million in sales and it outpaces both of the other two chain stores in the city.

Questions

- How would you describe Carol Baines's leadership traits?
- How big a part did Carol's traits play in the expansion of the company?
- Would Carol be a leader in other business contexts?

Case 2.3

Pat Nelson is the assistant director of human resources in charge of recruitment for Central Bank, a large full-service banking institution. One of Pat's major responsibilities each spring is to visit as many college campuses as he can to interview graduating seniors for credit analyst positions in the commercial lending area at Central Bank. Although the number varies, Mr. Nelson usually ends up hiring about 20 new people, most of whom come from the same schools year after year.

Pat has been doing recruitment for the bank for more than 10 years and he enjoys it very much. However, for the upcoming spring he is feeling increased pressure from management to be particularly discriminating about who he recommends be hired. Management is concerned about the retention rate at the bank because in recent years as many as 25% of the new hires have left. Departures after the first year have meant lost training dollars as well as excess strain on the staff who remain. Although management understands that some new hires always leave, they are not comfortable with the present rate and they have begun to question the recruitment and hiring procedures.

The bank wants to hire individuals whom they can groom for higher level leadership positions. Although certain competencies are required at the entry level of credit analyst, the bank is equally interested in skills that will allow individuals to advance to upper management positions as their careers progress.

In the recruitment process Pat Nelson always looks for several characteristics. First, individuals need to have strong interpersonal skills, they need to be confident, and they need to show poise and initiative. Next, because banking involves fiduciary responsibilities, individuals need to have proper ethics, including a strong sense of the importance of confidentiality. In addition, to do the work in the bank, individuals need to have strong analytical and technical skills as well as experience in working with computers. Lastly, individuals need to exhibit a good work ethic, they need to show commitment and a willingness to do their job even in difficult circumstances.

Pat is relatively certain that he has been selecting the right people to be leaders at Central Bank, yet upper management is telling him to reassess his hiring criteria. Although he feels he that has been doing the right thing, he is starting to question himself and his recruitment practices.

Questions

Based on ideas described in the trait approach

- Do you think Pat Nelson is looking for the right characteristics in the people he hires?
- Could it be that the retention issue raised by upper management is unrelated to Pat's recruitment criteria?
- If you were Pat, would you change your approach to recruiting?

Leadership Instrument

There are a wide variety of questionnaires that are used by organizations for measuring individuals' personality characteristics. In many organizations it is common practice to use standard personality measures such as the Minnesota Multiphasic Personality Inventory or the Myers-Briggs Type Indicator. These measures provide valuable information to the individual and the organization about the individual's unique attributes for leadership and where the individual could best serve the organization.

In this section, the Leadership Trait Questionnaire (LTQ) is provided as an example of a measure that can be used to assess your personal leadership characteristics. The LTQ quantifies the perceptions of the individual leader and selected observers, such as subordinates or peers. It measures an individual's traits and points the individual to those areas in which he or she may have special strengths or weaknesses.

By taking the LTQ, you can gain an understanding of how trait measures are used for leadership assessment. You can also obtain an assessment of your own leadership traits.

Leadership Trait Questionnaire (LTQ)

INSTRUCTIONS: The purpose of this questionnaire is to measure personal characteristics of leadership. The questionnaire should be completed by the leader and five individuals who are familiar with the leader.

For each adjective listed below, indicate the degree to which you think the adjective describes the leader. Please select one of the following responses to indicate the strength of your opinion.

KEY: 5 = Strongly Agree,   4 = Agree, 3 = Neutral, 2 = Disagree, 1 = Strongly Disagree

1. Articulate - Communicates effectively with others.	1 2 3 ④ 5
2. Perceptive - Discerning and insightful.	1 2 ③ 4 5
3. Self-confident - Believes in oneself and one's ability.	1 2 3 ④ 5
4. Self-assured - Secure with self, free of doubts.	1 2 3 ④ 5
5. Persistent - Stays fixed on the goal(s), despite interference.	1 2 3 4 ⑤
6. Determined - Takes a firm stand, acts with certainty.	1 2 3 4 ⑤
7. Trustworthy - Acts believable, inspires confidence.	1 2 3 4 ⑤
8. Dependable - Is consistent and reliable.	1 2 3 4 ⑤
9. Friendly - Shows kindness and warmth.	1 ② 3 4 5
10. Outgoing - Talks freely, gets along well with others.	1 ② 3 4 5

Scoring Interpretation

The scores you received on the Leadership Trait Questionnaire (LTQ) provide information about how you see yourself and how others see you as a leader. The chart allows you to see where your perceptions are the same as others and where they differ from others.

The example below provides ratings for the first three characteristics, which help explain how the questionnaire can be used. For example, on the characteristic Articulate, the leader rated himself or herself significantly higher than the observers. On the second characteristic, Perceptive, the leader rated him- or herself substantially lower than others. On the Self-confident characteristic, the leader was quite close to others' ratings of his or her leadership.

There are no best ratings on this questionnaire. The purpose of the instrument is to give you a way to assess your strengths and weaknesses and to evaluate areas where your perceptions are congruent with others and where there are discrepancies.

EXAMPLE RATINGS

	R1	R2	R3	R4	R5	AVE	SELF	DIF
1. Articulate	4	3	5	2	5	3.8	5	−1.2
2. Perceptive	3	5	5	5	4	4.4	3	+1.4
3. Self-confident	4	4	5	4	4	4.2	4	+0.2
4. Self-assured	4							
5. Persistent	5							
6. Determined	5							
7. Trustworthy	5							
8. Dependable	5							
9. Friendly	2							
10. Outgoing	2							
Total	39							

Summary

The trait approach has its roots in leadership theory that suggested that certain people were born with special traits that made them "great" leaders. Because it was believed that leaders and nonleaders could be differentiated by a universal set of traits, throughout the century researchers have been challenged to identify the definitive traits of leaders.

Around the middle of the century, several major studies questioned the basic premise that a unique set of traits defined leadership. As a result, attention shifted to incorporating the impact of situations and of followers on leadership. Researchers began to study the interactions that occur between leaders and their context instead of focusing only on leaders' traits. More recently, there are signs that trait research has come full circle, because there is a renewed interest in focusing directly on the critical traits of leaders.

From the multitude of studies that have been conducted through the years on individuals' personal characteristics, it is clear that many traits contribute to leadership. Some of the important traits that are consistently identified in many of these studies are intelligence, self-confidence, determination, integrity, and sociability. These traits, more than many of the others, are characteristic of the people we call leaders.

On a practical level, the trait approach is concerned with which traits leaders exhibit and who has these traits. Organizations employ personality assessment instruments to identify how individuals will fit within their organizations. The trait approach is also used for personal awareness and development, as it allows managers to analyze their strengths and weaknesses and to gain a clearer understanding of how they should try to change to enhance their leadership.

There are several advantages to viewing leadership from the trait approach. First, it is intuitively appealing because it fits clearly into the popular idea that leaders are special people who are "out front," leading the way in society. Second, there is a great deal of research that validates the basis of this perspective. Third, by focusing exclusively on the leader, the trait approach provides an in-depth understanding of the leader component in the leadership process. Lastly, it has provided some benchmarks against which individuals can evaluate their own personal leadership attributes.

On the negative side, the trait approach has failed to delimit a definitive list of leadership traits. In analyzing the traits of leaders, the approach has failed to take into account the impact of situations. In addition, the approach has resulted in subjective lists of the most "important leadership traits," which are not necessarily grounded in strong, reliable research. Furthermore, the trait approach has not adequately linked the traits of leaders with other outcomes such as group and team performance. Lastly, this approach is not particularly useful for training and development because individuals' personal attributes are relatively stable and fixed, and therefore their traits are not amenable to change.

References

Bass, B. M. (1990). *Bass and Stogdill's handbook of leadership: A survey of theory and research*. New York: Free Press.

Bennis, W. G., & Nanus, B. (1985). *Leaders: The strategies for taking charge*. New York: Harper & Row.

Bryman, A. (1992). *Charisma and leadership in organizations*. London: Sage.

Kirkpatrick, S. A., & Locke, E. A. (1991). Leadership: Do traits matter? *The Executive, 5*, 48-60.

Lord, R. G., DeVader, C. L., & Alliger, G. M. (1986). A meta-analysis of the relation between personality traits and leadership perceptions: An application of validity generalization procedures. *Journal of Applied Psychology, 71*, 402-410.

Mann, R. D. (1959). A review of the relationship between personality and performance in small groups. *Psychological Bulletin, 56*, 241-270.

Nadler, D. A., & Tushman, M. L. (1989). What makes for magic leadership? In W. E. Rosenbach & R. L. Taylor (Eds.), *Contemporary issues in leadership* (pp. 135-139). Boulder, CO: Westview.

Stogdill, R. M. (1948). Personal factors associated with leadership: A survey of the literature. *Journal of Psychology, 25*, 35-71.

Stogdill, R. M. (1974). *Handbook of leadership: A survey of theory and research*. New York: Free Press.

Zaleznik, A. (1977, May-June). Managers and leaders: Are they different? *Harvard Business Review, 55*, 67-78.

| # Style Approach

Description

The style approach is very different from the trait approach, which we discussed in the previous chapter. Whereas the trait approach emphasizes the *personality characteristics* of the leader, the style approach emphasizes the *behavior* of the leader. Or, as Fleishman (1973) has noted, "The shift in emphasis . . . was from thinking about leadership in terms of traits that someone 'has' to the conceptualization of leadership as a form of activity" (p. 3). The style approach focuses exclusively on what leaders *do* and how they *act*. In shifting the study of leadership to leader style or behaviors, the style approach expanded the study of leadership to include the actions of leaders toward subordinates in various contexts.

Researchers studying the style approach determined that leadership is comprised of essentially two general kinds of behaviors: *task behaviors* and *relationship behaviors*. Task behaviors facilitate goal accomplishment: They help group members to achieve their objectives. Relationship behaviors help subordinates feel comfortable with themselves, with each other, and with the situation in which they find themselves. The central purpose of the style approach is to explain how leaders combine these two kinds of behaviors to influence subordinates in their efforts to reach a goal.

Many studies have been conducted to investigate the style approach. Some of the first studies to be done were conducted at Ohio State University in the late 1940s, based on the findings of Stogdill's (1948) work, which pointed to the importance of considering more than leaders' traits in leadership research. At about the same time, another group of researchers at the University of Michigan were conducting a series of studies that explored how leadership functioned in small groups. A third line of research was begun by Blake and Mouton in the early 1960s; it explored how managers used task and relationship behaviors in the organizational setting.

Although many research studies could be categorized under the heading of the style approach, the Ohio State studies, the Michigan studies, and the studies by Blake and Mouton (1964, 1978, 1985) are strongly representative of the ideas in this approach. By looking closely at each of these groups of studies, a clearer picture can be drawn of the underpinnings and implications of the style approach.

The Ohio State Studies

Because the results of studying leadership as a personality trait appeared fruitless, a group of researchers at Ohio State began to analyze how individuals acted when they were leading a group or organization. This analysis was conducted by having subordinates complete questionnaires about their leaders. On the questionnaires, subordinates had to identify the number of times their leaders engaged in certain types of behaviors.

The original questionnaire that was used in these studies was constructed from a list of more than 1,800 items describing different aspects of leader behavior. From this long list of items, a questionnaire composed of 150 questions was formulated, and it was called the Leadership Behavior Description Questionnaire (LBDQ) (Hemphill & Coons, 1957). The LBDQ was given to hundreds of individuals in educational, military, and industrial settings, and the results showed that certain clusters of behaviors were typical of leaders. Five years later, Stogdill (1963) published a shortened version of the LBDQ. The new form, which was called the LBDQ-XII, became the most widely used in research. A style questionnaire similar to the LBDQ appears later in this chapter. You can use this questionnaire to assess your own leadership behavior.

Researchers found that subordinates' responses on the questionnaire clustered around two general types of leader behaviors: *initiating structure* and *consideration* (Stogdill, 1974). Initiating structure behaviors were essentially task behaviors, including such acts as organizing work, giving structure to the work context, defining role responsibilities, and scheduling work activities. Consideration behaviors were essentially relationship behaviors and included building camaraderie, respect, trust, and liking between leaders and followers.

The two types of behaviors identified by the LBDQ-XII represent the core of the style approach—these behaviors are central to what leaders do: Leaders provide structure for subordinates, and they nurture them. The Ohio State studies viewed these two behaviors as distinct and independent. They were not thought of as two points along a single continuum, but as two different continua. For example, a leader could be high in initiating structure and high or low in task behavior. Similarly, a leader could be low in setting structure and low or high in consideration behavior. The degree to which a leader exhibited one behavior was not related to the degree to which she or he exhibited the other behavior.

Many studies have been done to determine which style of leadership is most effective in a particular situation. In some contexts high consideration has been found to be most effective, but in other situations high initiating structure has been found most effective. Some research has shown that being high on both behaviors is the best form of leadership. Determining how a leader optimally mixes task and relationship behaviors has been the central task for researchers from the style approach. The path goal approach, which is discussed in Chapter 6, exemplifies a leadership theory that attempts to explain how leaders should integrate consideration and structure into the leader's style.

The University of Michigan Studies

While researchers at Ohio State were developing the LBDQ, researchers at the University of Michigan were also exploring leadership behavior, giving special attention to the impact of leaders' behaviors on the performance of small groups (Cartwright & Zander, 1960; Katz & Kahn, 1951; Likert, 1961, 1967).

The program of research at Michigan identified two types of leadership behaviors called *employee orientation* and *production orientation*. *Employee orientation* describes the behavior of leaders who approach subordinates with a strong human relations emphasis. They take an interest in workers as human beings, value their individuality, and give special attention to their personal needs (Bowers & Seashore, 1966). Employee orientation is very similar to the cluster of behaviors identified in the OSU studies as consideration.

Production orientation refers to leadership behaviors that stress the technical and production aspects of a job. From this orientation, workers are viewed as a means for getting work accomplished (Bowers & Seashore, 1966). Production orientation parallels the initiating structure cluster found in the Ohio State studies.

Unlike the Ohio State researchers, the Michigan researchers, in their initial studies, conceptualized employee and production orientations as opposite ends of a single continuum. This suggested that leaders who were oriented toward production were less oriented to employees, and those who were employee oriented were less production oriented. As more studies were completed, however, the researchers reconceptualized the two constructs, similar to the Ohio State studies, as two independent leadership orientations (Kahn, 1956). When the two behaviors were treated as independent orientations, leaders were seen as being able to be oriented to both production and employees at the same time.

In the 1950s and 1960s, there was a multitude of studies conducted by researchers from both Ohio State and the University of Michigan to determine how leaders could best combine their task and relationship behaviors so as to maximize the impact of these behaviors on the satisfaction and performance of followers. In essence, the researchers were looking for a universal theory of leadership that would explain leadership effectiveness in every situation. The results that emerged from this large body of literature were contradictory and unclear (Yukl, 1994). Although some of the findings pointed to the value of a leader being both high-task and high-relationship oriented in all situations (Misumi, 1985), the preponderance of the research in this area was inconclusive.

Blake and Mouton's
Managerial (Leadership) Grid®

Perhaps the most well-known model of managerial behavior is the Managerial Grid®, which first appeared in the early 1960s and since that time has been refined and revised several times (Blake & McCanse, 1991; Blake & Mouton, 1964, 1978, 1985). It is a model that has been used extensively in organizational training and development. The Managerial Grid, which has been renamed the Leadership Grid, was designed to explain how leaders help organizations to reach their purposes through two factors: *concern for production* and *concern for people*. Although these factors are described as leadership orientations in the model, they closely parallel the task and relationship leadership behaviors we have been discussing throughout this chapter.

Concern for production refers to how a leader is concerned with achieving organizational tasks. It involves a wide range of activities, including attention to policy decisions, new product development, process issues, workload, and sales volume, to name a few. Not limited to things, concern for production can refer to whatever it is the organization is seeking to accomplish (Blake & Mouton, 1964).

Concern for people refers to how a leader attends to the people within the organization who are trying to achieve its goals. This concern includes building organizational commitment and trust, promoting the personal worth of employees, providing good working conditions, maintaining a fair salary structure, and promoting good social relations (Blake & Mouton, 1964).

The Leadership (Managerial) Grid joins *concern for production* and *concern for people* in a model that has two intersecting axes (see Figure 3.1). The horizontal axis represents the leader's concern for production and the vertical axis represents the leader's concern for people. Each of the axes is drawn as a 9-point scale on which a score of 1 represents minimum concern and 9 represents maximum concern. By plotting scores from each of the axes, various leadership styles can be illustrated. The Leadership Grid portrays five major leadership styles: Authority-Compliance (9,1), Country Club Management (1,9), Impoverished Management (1,1), Middle-of-the-Road Management (5,5), and Team Management (9,9).

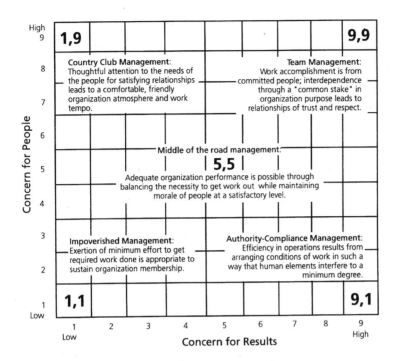

Figure 3.1. The Leadership Grid®: Concern for Results

SOURCE: The Leadership Grid® figure, Paternalism figure, and Opportunism from *Leadership Dilemmas—Grid Solutions*, by Robert R. Blake and Anne Adams McCanse (formerly the Managerial Grid by Robert R. Blake and Jane S. Mouton). Houston: Gulf Publishing Company (p. 29). (Opportunism figure: p. 31). Copyright 1991 by Scientific Methods, Inc. Reproduced by permission of the owners.

Authority-Compliance (9,1)

The 9,1 style of leadership places heavy emphasis on task and job requirements and less emphasis on people, except to the extent that people are tools for getting the job done. Communicating with subordinates is not emphasized except for the purpose of giving instructions about the task. This style is results-driven, and people are regarded as tools to that end. The 9,1 leader is often seen as controlling, demanding, hard-driving, and overpowering.

Country Club Management (1,9)

The 1,9 style represents a low concern for task accomplishment coupled with a high concern for interpersonal relationships. De-emphasizing production, 1,9 leaders stress the attitudes and feelings of people, making sure the personal and social needs of followers are met. They try to create a positive climate by being agreeable, eager to help, comforting, and uncontroversial.

Impoverished Management (1,1)

The 1,1 style is representative of a leader who is unconcerned with both the task and interpersonal relationships. This type of leader goes through the motions of being a leader, but acts uninvolved and withdrawn. The 1,1 leaders often have little contact with followers and could be described as indifferent, noncommittal, resigned, and apathetic.

Middle-of-the-Road Management (5,5)

The 5,5 style describes leaders who are compromisers, have an intermediate concern for the task and an intermediate concern for the people who do the task. They find a balance or mixture between taking people into account while still emphasizing the work requirements. Their compromising style gives up some of the push for production as well as some of the attention to employee needs. To arrive at an equilibrium, the 5,5 leader avoids conflict and emphasizes moderate levels of production and interpersonal relationships. This type of leader is often described as one who is expedient, prefers the middle ground, soft-pedals disagreement, and swallows convictions in the interest of "progress."

Team Management (9,9)

The 9,9 style places a strong emphasis on both tasks and interpersonal relationships. It promotes a high degree of participation and teamwork in the organization, and satisfies a basic need in employees to be involved and committed to their work. Some of the phrases that could be used to describe the 9,9 leader are: stimulates participation, acts determined, gets issues into the open, makes priorities clear, follows through, behaves open-mindedly, and enjoys working.

In addition to the five major styles described in the Leadership Grid, Blake and his colleagues have identified two other styles that incorporate multiple aspects of the grid.

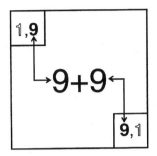

Figure 3.2. Paternalism/Maternalism: Reward and approval are bestowed to people in return for loyalty and obedience; failure to comply leads to punishment.

SOURCE: The Leadership Grid® figure, Paternalism figure, and Opportunism from *Leadership Dilemmas—Grid Solutions*, by Robert R. Blake and Anne Adams McCanse (formerly the Managerial Grid by Robert R. Blake and Jane S. Mouton). Houston: Gulf Publishing Company (p. 30). Copyright 1991 by Scientific Methods, Inc. Reproduced by permission of the owners.

Paternalism/Maternalism

Paternalism/Maternalism refers to a leader who uses both 1,9 and 9,1 styles but does not integrate the two (see Figure 3.2). This is the "benevolent dictator" who acts gracious but does so for the purpose of goal accomplishment. In essence the paternalistic/maternalistic style treats people as if they were disassociated with the task.

Opportunism

Opportunism refers to a leader who uses any combination of the basic five styles for the purpose of personal advancement (see Figure 3.3).

Blake and Mouton (1985) indicate that a person usually has a dominant Grid style, which he or she uses in most situations, and a backup style. The backup style is what the leader reverts to when under pressure, when the usual way of accomplishing things does not work.

In summary, the Leadership Grid is an example of a practical model of leadership that is based on the two major leadership behaviors: task and relationship. It closely parallels the ideas and findings that emerged in the Ohio State and University of Michigan studies. It is used in consulting for organizational development throughout the world.

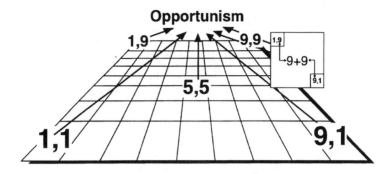

Figure 3.3. Opportunism: In opportunistic management, people adapt and shift to any Grid style needed to gain the maximum advantage. Performance occurs according to a system of selfish gain. Effort is given only for an advantage for personal gain.

SOURCE: The Leadership Grid® figure, Paternalism figure, and Opportunism from *Leadership Dilemmas—Grid Solutions*, by Robert R. Blake and Anne Adams McCanse (formerly the Managerial Grid by Robert R. Blake and Jane S. Mouton). Houston: Gulf Publishing Company, (p. 31). Copyright 1991 by Scientific Methods, Inc. Reproduced by permission of the owners.

How Does the Style Approach Work?

Unlike many of the other approaches discussed in the book, the style approach is not a refined theory that provides a neatly organized set of prescriptions for effective leadership behavior. Rather, the style approach provides a framework for assessing leadership in a broad way, as behavior with a task and relationship dimension. The style approach works not by telling leaders how to behave, but by describing the major components of their behavior.

The style approach reminds leaders that their actions toward others occur on a task and relationship level. In some situations, leaders need to be more task oriented whereas in others, they need to be more relationship oriented. Similarly, some subordinates need leaders who provide a lot of direction, whereas others need leaders who can show them a great deal of nurturance and support. The style approach gives the leader a way to look at his or her own behavior by subdividing it into two dimensions.

An example may help explain how the style approach works. Imagine two college classrooms on the first day of class and two professors with entirely different styles. Professor Smith comes to class, introduces herself, takes attendance, goes over the syllabus, explains the first assignment, and dismisses the class. Professor Jones comes to class and, after introducing herself and handing out the syllabus, tries to help the students to get to know one another by having each of the students describe a little about themselves, their major, and their favorite nonacademic activities. The leadership styles of Professors Smith and Jones are quite different. The preponderance of what Professor Smith does could be labeled task behavior, and the majority of what Professor Jones does is relationship behavior. The style approach provides a way to inform the professors about the differences in their behaviors. Depending on the response of the students to their style, the professors may wish to change their behavior to improve their teaching on the first day of class.

Overall, the style approach offers a means of assessing in a general way the behaviors of leaders. It reminds leaders that their impact on others occurs through the tasks they perform as well as in the relationships they create.

Strengths

The style approach makes several positive contributions to our understanding of the leadership process. First, the style approach marked a major shift in the general focus of leadership research. Prior to the inception of the style approach, researchers treated leadership exclusively as a personality trait (see Chapter 2). The style approach broadened the scope of leadership research to include the behaviors of leaders and what they do in various situations. No longer was the focus of leadership on the personal characteristics of leaders; it was expanded to include what leaders did and how they acted.

Second, a wide range of studies on leadership style validates and gives credibility to the basic tenets of the approach. First formulated and reported by researchers from Ohio State University and the University of Michigan and subsequently in the work of Blake and Mouton (1964, 1978, 1985) and Blake and McCanse (1991), the style approach is substantiated by a multitude of research studies that offers a viable approach to understanding the leadership process.

Third, on a conceptual level, researchers from the style approach have ascertained that a leader's style is composed of primarily two major types of behaviors: task and relationship. The significance of this idea is not to be understated. Whenever leadership occurs, the leader is acting out both task and relationship behaviors; the key to being an effective leader often rests on how the leader balances these two behaviors. Together they form the core of the leadership process.

Fourth, the style approach is heuristic. It provides us with a broad conceptual map that is worthwhile to use in our attempts to understand the complexities of leadership. Leaders can learn a lot about themselves and how they come across to others by trying to see their behaviors in light of the task and relationship dimensions. Based on the style approach, leaders can assess their actions and determine how they may wish to change to improve their leadership style.

Criticisms

Along with its strengths, the style approach also has several weaknesses. First, the research on styles has not adequately shown how leaders' styles are associated with performance outcomes (Bryman, 1992; Yukl, 1994). Researchers have not been able to establish a consistent link between task and relationship behaviors and outcomes such as morale, job satisfaction, and productivity. According to Yukl (1994), the "results from this massive research effort have been mostly contradictory and inconclusive" (p. 75). He further points out that the only strong finding about leadership styles is that leaders who are considerate have followers who are more satisfied.

Another criticism is that this approach has failed to find a universal style of leadership that could be effective in almost every situation. The overarching goal for researchers studying the style approach appeared to be the identification of a universal set of leadership behaviors that would consistently result in effective outcomes. Because of inconsistencies in the research findings, this goal was never reached. Similar to the trait approach, which was unable to identify the definitive personal characteristics of leaders, the style approach has been unable to identify the universal behaviors that are associated with effective leadership.

A final criticism of the style approach is that it implies that the most effective leadership style is the high-high style (i.e., high task and high relationship). Even though some researchers (e.g., Blake & McCanse, 1991; Misumi, 1985) have suggested that high-high managers are most effective, that may not be the case in all situations. In fact, the full range of research findings provides only limited support for a universal high-high style (Yukl, 1994). Certain situations may require different leadership styles; some may be complicated and require high task behavior, and others may be simple and require supportive behavior. At this point in the development of research on the style approach, it remains unclear whether the high-high style is the most preferred style of leadership.

Application

The style approach can be easily applied in ongoing leadership settings. At all levels within all types of organizations, managers are continually engaged in task and relationship behaviors. By making an assessment of their own style, managers can determine how they are coming across to others and how they could change their behaviors to be more effective. In essence, the style approach provides a mirror for managers that is helpful in answering the frequently asked question, "How am I doing as a leader?"

In training and development, there are many programs throughout the country that are structured along the lines of the style approach. Almost all of them are designed similarly, and include giving managers questionnaires that assess in some way their task and relationship behavior toward subordinates. Participants utilize these assessments to improve their overall leadership style.

An example of a training and development program that deals exclusively with leader styles is Blake and Mouton's Leadership Grid (formerly Managerial Grid) seminar. Grid seminars are about increasing productivity, improving morale, and gaining employee commitment. They are offered by Scientific Methods,[1] an international organization development company. At Grid seminars, through self-assessments, small-group experiences, and candid critiques, managers learn how to define effective leadership, how to manage for optimal results, and how to identify and change ineffective leadership behaviors. The conceptual framework around which the Grid seminars are structured is the style approach to leadership.

In short, the style approach applies to nearly everything a leader does. It is an approach that is employed as a model by many training and development companies to teach managers how to improve their effectiveness and organizational productivity.

Case Studies

On the following pages you will find case studies (Cases 3.1, 3.2, and 3.3) that describe the leadership styles of three different managers, each of whom is working in a different organizational setting. The first case is about a maintenance director in a large hospital, the second deals with a supervisor in a small sports store, and the third is concerned with the director of a design department in a large manufacturing company. At the end of each case there are questions that will help you to analyze the case from the perspective of the style approach.

Case 3.1

Mark Young is the head of the painting department in a large hospital and 20 union employees report to him. Prior to coming on board at the hospital, he had worked as an independent contractor. At the hospital he took a position that was newly created because the hospital believed change was needed in how painting services were provided.

Upon beginning his job, Mark did a 4-month analysis of the direct and indirect costs of painting services. His findings supported the perceptions of his administrators that painting services were inefficient and costly. As a result, Mark completely reorganized the department, designed a new scheduling procedure, and redefined the expected standards of performance.

Mark says that when he started out in his new job he was "all task," like a drill sergeant who didn't seek any input from his subordinates. From Mark's point of view, the hospital environment did not leave much room for errors, so he needed to be strict about getting painters to do a good job within the constraints of the hospital environment.

As time went along, Mark relaxed his style and was less demanding. He allocated some responsibilities to two crew leaders who reported to him, but always stayed in close touch with each of the employees. On a weekly basis, Mark was known to take small groups of workers to the local sports bar for burgers on the house. He loved to banter with the employees and could "dish it out" as well as "take it."

Mark is very proud of his department. He says he always wanted to be a coach and that's how he feels about running his department. He enjoys working with people and in particular he says he likes to see that glint in their eyes when they come to the realization that they've done a good job and they have done it on their own.

Because of Mark's leadership, the painting department improved substantially and is now seen by workers in other departments as the most productive department in hospital maintenance. Painting services received a customer rating of 92%, which was the highest of any service in the hospital.

Questions

- From the style perspective, how would you describe Mark Young's leadership?
- How did his style change over time?
- In general, do you think he is more task oriented or more relationship oriented?
- If he took Blake and Mouton's Grid, what score do you think he would get?

Case 3.2

Susan Parks is the part-owner and manager of Marathon Sports, an athletic store that specializes in running shoes and accessories. The store employs about 10 people, most of whom are college students who work part-time during the week and full-time on weekends. Marathon Sports is the only store of its kind in a college town with a population of 125,000 people. The annual sales figures for the store have shown a 15% growth for each of the past 7 years.

Ms. Parks has a lot invested in the store, and she works very hard to make sure the store continues to maintain its reputation and pattern of growth. She works 50 hours a week at the store, where she wears many hats, including those of buyer, scheduler, trainer, planner, and salesperson. There is never a moment when Susan is not doing something. Rumor has it that she eats her lunch standing up.

Employees' reactions to Ms. Parks are strong and quite varied. Some people like her style and others do not. Those who like her style talk about how organized and efficient the store is when she is in charge. Susan makes the tasks and goals for everyone very clear. She keeps everyone busy, and when they go home at night they feel as if they have accomplished something. They like to work for Susan because she knows what she is doing. Those who do not like her style complain that she is too driven. It seems that her sole purpose for being at the store is to get the job done. She seldom, if ever, takes a break or just "hangs out" with the staff. These people say Susan is pretty hard to relate to and as a result it is not much fun working at Marathon Sports.

Susan is beginning to sense that employees have a mixed reaction to her leadership style. This bothers her but she does not know what to do about it. In addition to her work at the store, Susan struggles hard to be a good spouse and mother of three children.

Questions

- According to the style approach, how would you describe Susan Parks's leadership?
- Why does it create such a pronounced reaction from her subordinates?
- Do you think she should change her style?
- Would she be effective if she changed?

Case 3.3

Douglas Ludwig is the director of design services at a large office furniture manufacturing company that employs about 1,200 people. The design department is made up of 80 individuals who are divided into eight working teams, all of which report to Mr. Ludwig. Douglas is relatively new to the company, having been hired away from a smaller competitor where he was vice president for research and development. His reputation as a leader at the previous company was generally favorable.

During his first year, Douglas has spent a lot of time trying to enhance the culture in his department. Unlike the previous director, who had spent a good portion of his time monitoring projects and emphasizing company goals, Douglas has involved himself with the mood, climate, and tenor of the department. To that end, Douglas has instituted a new department meeting schedule for the purpose of allowing everyone to share his or her ideas and concerns. While continuing to do the "nuts and bolts" things, Douglas has tried to promote greater esprit de corps in the department by having brown-bag lunches on Fridays. Each week, Douglas meets informally with the team leaders to get a feel for what they need and how they are doing.

Douglas is also a strong supporter of social events outside of work. In the summer, the design department held an outdoor family barbecue—the first ever for some of the older employees in the company. Over the holidays, Douglas held an open house at his residence that was catered by the company. Employees thought it was "first class" and talked about it for many months. Douglas was also instrumental in getting the company to sponsor a co-ed indoor soccer team, made up completely of employees from the design department.

Most, but not all, of the people in the department give Douglas Ludwig positive reviews for his first year as director. Designers and staffers alike are impressed by what a nice guy Mr. Ludwig seems to be. For years the mood in the design department had been somewhat stale, but with Douglas's arrival some life came back into the place. People began to enjoy the new vitality in the department and they found themselves chatting more and complaining less.

Questions

The leadership used by Douglas Ludwig is clearly one of the major types in the style approach.

- What style is it?
- Does it sound as if it is effective within the context of the design department at the furniture company?
- Would you or would you not like to work for Douglas Ludwig?
- Is there a downside to this style of leadership?
- If so, describe it.

Leadership Instrument

Researchers and practitioners alike have used many different instruments to assess the styles of leaders. The two most commonly used measures have been the LBDQ (Stogdill, 1963) and the Leadership Grid (Blake & McCanse, 1991). Both of these measures provide information about the degree to which a leader acts task directed and people directed. The LBDQ was designed primarily for research and has been used extensively since the 1960s. The Leadership Grid was designed primarily for training and development, and it continues to be used today for training managers and supervisors in the leadership process.

To assist you in developing a better understanding of how leadership style is measured and what your own style might be, a leadership style questionnaire is included in this section. This questionnaire is made up of 20 items that assess two factors: *task* and *relationship*. By scoring the style questionnaire, you can obtain a general profile of your leadership behavior.

The score you receive for *task* refers to the degree to which you help others by defining their roles and letting them know what is expected of them. This factor describes your tendencies to be task directed toward others when you are in a leadership position. The score you receive for *relationship* is a measure of the degree to which you try to make subordinates feel comfortable with themselves, each other, and the group itself. It represents a measure of how people oriented you are.

Your results on the style questionnaire give you data about your task orientation and people orientation. What do your scores suggest about your leadership style? Are you more likely to lead with an emphasis on task or with an emphasis on relationship? As you interpret your responses to the style questionnaire, are there ways you could change your style to shift the emphasis you give to tasks and relationships? To gain more information about your style, you may wish to have four or five of your co-workers fill out the questionnaire based on their perceptions of you as a leader. This will give you additional data to compare and contrast to your own scores about yourself.

Style Questionnaire

INSTRUCTIONS: Read each item carefully and think about how often you (or the person you are evaluating) engage in the described behavior. Indicate your response to each item by circling one of the five numbers to the right of each item.

Key: 1 = Never; 2 = Seldom; 3 = Occasionally; 4 = Often; 5 = Always

1. Tells group members what they are supposed to do.	1	2	3	4	⑤	
2. Acts friendly with members of the group.	1	2	③	4	5)	3
3. Sets standards of performance for group members.	1	2	3	4	④	
4. Helps others feel comfortable in the group.	1	2	3	④	5	4
5. Makes suggestions about how to solve problems.	1	2	3	④	5	
6. Responds favorably to suggestions made by others.	1	2	3	④	5	4
7. Makes his/her perspective clear to others.	1	2	3	4	⑤	
8. Treats others fairly.	1	2	3	4	⑤	5
9. Develops a plan of action for the group.	1	2	3	4	⑤	
10. Behaves in a predictable manner toward group members.	1	2	3	4	⑤	5
11. Defines role responsibilities for each group member.	1	2	3	4	⑤	
12. Communicates actively with group members.	1	2	3	4	⑤	5
13. Clarifies his/her own role within the group.	1	2	3	4	⑤	
14. Shows concern for the personal well being of others.	1	2	③	4	5	4
15. Provides a plan for how the work is to be done.	1	2	③	4	5	
16. Shows flexibility in making decisions.	1	2	③	4	5	3
17. Provides criteria for what is expected of the group.	1	2	3	④	5	
18. Discloses thoughts and feelings to group members.	1	②	3	4	5	2
19. Encourages group members to do quality work.	1	2	3	④	5	
20. Helps group members get along.	1	②	3	4	5	2

SCORING: The style questionnaire is designed to measure two major types of leadership behaviors: *task* and *relationship*.

Score the questionnaire by doing the following. First, sum the responses on the odd-numbered items. This is your *task* score. Second, sum the responses on the even-numbered items. This is your *relationship* score.

TOTAL SCORES: Task _____ Relationship _____

Scoring Interpretation

45-50   Very High Range
40-44   High Range
35-39   Moderately High Range
30-34   Moderately Low Range
25-29   Low Range
20-24   Very Low Range

Summary

The style approach is strikingly different from the great-person and trait approaches to leadership because the style approach focuses on *what leaders do* rather than *who leaders are*. It suggests that leaders engage in two primary types of behaviors: task behaviors and relationship behaviors. How leaders combine these two types of behaviors to influence others is the central purpose of the style approach.

The style approach originated from three different lines of research: the Ohio State University studies, the University of Michigan studies, and the work of Blake and Mouton on the Managerial Grid.

Researchers at Ohio State developed a leadership questionnaire called the LBDQ, which identified *initiation of structure* and *consideration* as the core leadership behaviors. The Michigan studies provided similar findings but called the leader behaviors *production orientation* and *employee orientation*.

Using the Ohio State and Michigan studies as a basis, much research has been carried out to find the best way for leaders to combine task and relationship behaviors. The goal has been to find a universal set of leadership behaviors capable of explaining leadership effectiveness in every situation; however, the results from these efforts have not been conclusive. Researchers have had difficulty identifying one best style of leadership.

Blake and Mouton developed a practical model for training managers that described leadership behaviors along a grid with two axes: *concern for production* and *concern for people*. How leaders combine these orientations results in a five major leadership styles: Authority-Compliance (9,1), Country Club Management (1,9), Impoverished

Management (1,1), Middle-of-the-Road Management (5,5), and Team Management (9,9).

The style approach has several strengths and weaknesses. On the positive side, it has broadened the scope of leadership research to include the study of the behaviors of leaders rather than only their personal traits or characteristics. Second, it is a reliable approach because it is supported by a wide range of studies. Third, the style approach is valuable because it underscores the importance of the two core dimensions of leadership behavior: task and relationship. Fourth, it has heuristic value in that it provides us with a broad conceptual map that is useful in gaining an understanding of our own leadership behaviors.

On the negative side, researchers have not been able to associate the behaviors of leaders (task and relationship) with outcomes such as morale, job satisfaction, and productivity. In addition, researchers from the style approach have not been able to identify a universal set of leadership behaviors that would consistently result in effective leadership. Lastly, the style approach implies, but fails to support fully, the idea that the most effective leadership style is a high-high style (i.e., high task and high relationship).

Overall, the style approach is not a refined theory that provides a neatly organized set of prescriptions for effective leadership behavior. Rather, the style approach provides a valuable framework for assessing leadership in a broad way—as assessing behavior with task and relationship dimensions. Finally, the style approach reminds leaders that their impact on others occurs along both dimensions.

Note

1. Scientific Methods, P. O. Box 195, Austin, TX 78767.

References

Blake, R. R., & McCanse, A. A. (1991). *Leadership dilemmas—Grid solutions.* Houston, TX: Gulf Publishing.

Blake, R. R., & Mouton, J. S. (1964). *The managerial grid*. Houston, TX: Gulf Publishing.

Blake, R. R., & Mouton, J. S. (1978). *The new managerial grid*. Houston, TX: Gulf Publishing.

Blake, R. R., & Mouton, J. S. (1985). *The managerial grid III*. Houston, TX: Gulf Publishing.

Bowers, D. G., & Seashore, S. E. (1966). Predicting organizational effectiveness with a four-factor theory of leadership. *Administrative Science Quarterly, 11*, 238-263.

Bryman, A. (1992). *Charisma and leadership in organizations*. London: Sage.

Cartwright, D., & Zander, A. (1960). *Group dynamics research and theory*. Evanston, IL: Row, Peterson.

Fleishman, E. A. (1973). Twenty years of consideration and structure. In E. A. Fleishman & J. G. Hunt (Eds.), *Current developments in the study of leadership*. Carbondale: Southern Illinois University Press.

Hemphill, J. K., & Coons, A. E. (1957). Development of the Leader Behavior Description Questionnaire. In R. M. Stogdill & A. E. Coons (Eds.), *Leader behavior: Its description and measurement*. Columbus: Ohio State University, Bureau of Business Research.

Kahn, R. L. (1956). The prediction of productivity. *Journal of Social Issues, 12*, 41-49.

Katz, D., & Kahn, R. L. (1951). Human organization and worker motivation. In L. R. Tripp (Ed.), *Industrial productivity* (pp. 146-171). Madison, WI: Industrial Relations Research Association.

Likert, R. (1961). *New patterns of management*. New York: McGraw-Hill.

Likert, R. (1967). *The human organization: Its management and value*. New York: McGraw-Hill.

Misumi, J. (1985). *The behavioral science of leadership. An interdisciplinary Japanese research program*. Ann Arbor: University of Michigan Press.

Stogdill, R. M. (1948). Personal factors associated with leadership: A survey of the literature. *Journal of Psychology, 25*, 35-71.

Stogdill, R. M. (1963). *Manual for the Leader Behavior Description Questionnaire—form XII*. Columbus: Ohio State University, Bureau of Business Research.

Stogdill, R. M. (1974). *Handbook of leadership: A survey of theory and research*. New York: Free Press.

Yukl, G. (1994). *Leadership in organizations* (3rd ed.). Englewood Cliffs, NJ: Prentice Hall.

CHAPTER 4

Situational Approach

Description

One of the most widely recognized approaches to leadership is the situational approach, which was developed by Hersey and Blanchard (1969a) based on Reddin's 3-D Management Style Theory (1967). The situational approach has been refined and revised several times since its inception (see Blanchard, Zigarmi, & Nelson, 1993; Blanchard, Zigarmi, & Zigarmi, 1985; Hersey & Blanchard, 1977, 1982, 1988), and it has been used extensively in training and development for organizations throughout the country.

As the name of the approach implies, situational leadership focuses on leadership *in situations*. The basic premise of the theory is that different situations demand different kinds of leadership. From this perspective, to be an effective leader requires that an individual adapt his or her style to the demands of different situations.

Situational leadership stresses that leadership is composed of both a directive and a supportive dimension, and each has to be applied appropriately in a given situation. To determine what is needed in a particular situation, a leader must evaluate her or his employees and assess how competent and committed they are to perform a given task. Based on the assumption that employees' skills and motivation vary over time, situational leadership suggests that leaders should change the degree to which they are directive or supportive to meet the changing needs of subordinates.

In brief, the essence of situational leadership demands that a leader matches his or her style to the competence and commitment of the subordinates. Effective leaders are those who can recognize what employees need and then adapt their own style to meet those needs.

The situational approach is illustrated in the model developed by Blanchard (1985) and Blanchard et al. (1985) called the SLII model (see Figure 4.1). The model is an extension and refinement of the original situational leadership model developed by Hersey and Blanchard (1969a).

The dynamics of situational leadership are best understood by separating the SLII model into two parts: (a) leadership style and (b) development level of subordinates.

Leadership Styles

Leadership style refers to the behavior pattern of an individual who attempts to influence others. It includes both directive (task) behaviors and supportive (relationship) behaviors. *Directive behaviors* assist group members in goal accomplishment through giving directions, establishing goals and methods of evaluation, setting time lines, defining roles, and showing how the goals are to be achieved. Directive behaviors clarify, often with one-way communication, what is to be done, how it is to be done, and who is responsible for doing it. *Supportive behaviors* help group members feel comfortable about themselves, their co-workers, and the situation. Supportive behaviors involve two-way communication and responses that show social and emotional support to others. Examples of supportive behaviors would be asking for input, problem solving, praising, sharing information about self, and listening. Supportive behaviors are mostly job related.

Leadership styles can be classified further into four distinct categories of directive and supportive behaviors (see Figure 4.1). The first style *(S1)* is a *high directive-low supportive* style, which is also referred to as a *"directing"* style. In this approach, the leader focuses communication on goal achievement and spends a smaller amount

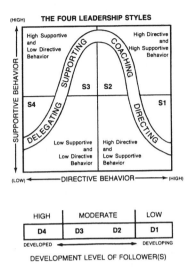

Figure 4.1. Situational Leadership II
SOURCE: K. Blanchard, P. Zigarmi & D. Zigarmi (1985). Used with permission.

of time using supportive behaviors. Using this style, a leader gives instructions about what and how goals are to be achieved by the subordinates and then supervises them carefully.

The second style *(S2)* is called a *"coaching"* approach and is a *high directive-high supportive* style. In this approach the leader focuses communication on both goal achievement and maintenance of subordinates' socioemotional needs. The coaching style requires that the leader involve him- or herself with subordinates through giving encouragement and soliciting subordinate input. However, coaching is an extension of S1 in that it still requires that the leader make the final decision on the what and how of goal accomplishment.

Style 3 *(S3)* is a *"supporting"* approach that requires that the leader take a *high supportive-low directive* style. In this approach the leader does not focus exclusively on goals but uses supportive behaviors that bring out the employees' skills around the task to be accomplished. The supportive style includes listening, praising, asking for input, and giving feedback. A leader using this style gives subordinates control for day-to-day decisions but remains available to facilitate problem solving. An S3 leader is quick to give recognition and social support to subordinates.

Lastly, Style 4 *(S4)* is called the *low supportive-low directive* style, a *"delegating"* approach. In this approach the leader offers less task input and social support, facilitating employees' confidence and motivation in reference to the task. The delegative leader lessens his or her involvement in planning, control of details, and goal clarification. After agreeing on the definition of what they are to do, this style lets subordinates take responsibility for getting the job done the way they see fit. A leader using S4 gives control over to subordinates and also refrains from intervening with unnecessary social support.

The SLII model (see Figure 4.1) illustrates how directive and supportive leadership behaviors combine for each of the four different leadership styles. As shown by the arrows on the bottom and left side of the model, directive behaviors are high in the S1 and S2 quadrants and low in S3 and S4, whereas supportive behaviors are high in S2 and S3 and low in S1 and S4.

Development Levels

A second major part of the situational leadership model is concerned with the development level of subordinates. *Development level* refers to the degree to which subordinates have the *competence* and *commitment* necessary to accomplish a given task or activity (Blanchard et al., 1985). Stated another way, it refers to whether a person has mastered the skills to do a specific task and whether a person has developed a positive attitude regarding the task (Blanchard et al., 1993). Employees are at a high development level if they are interested and confident in their work and they know how to do the task. Employees are at a low development level if they have little skill for the task at hand but feel as if they have the motivation or confidence to get the job done.

The levels of development are illustrated in the lower portion of the diagram in Figure 4.1. The levels describe various combinations of commitment and competence for employees on a given task. They are intended to be task specific and they are not intended to be used for the purpose of labeling employees.

On a particular task, employees can be classified into four categories—D1, D2, D3, and D4, from low development to high development. Specifically, D1 employees are low in competence and high in commitment. They are new to a task and do not know exactly how to do it but they are excited about the challenge of it. D2 employees are described as having some competence but low commitment. They have started to learn a job but they also have lost some of their initial motivation about the job. D3 represents employees who have moderate to high competence but may lack commitment. They have essentially developed the skills for the job but they are uncertain as to whether they can accomplish the task by themselves. Finally, D4 employees are the highest in development, having both a high degree of competence and a high degree of commitment to getting the job done. They have the skills to do the job and the motivation to get it accomplished.

How Does the Situational Approach Work?

The situational approach is constructed around the idea that employees move forward and backward along the developmental continuum—a continuum that represents the relative competence and commitment of subordinates. For leaders to be effective, it is essential that they *diagnose* where subordinates are on the developmental continuum and *adapt* their leadership styles so they directly match their style to the development level of subordinates.

In a given situation, the first task for a leader is to *diagnose* the nature of the situation. Questions such as the following need to be addressed: What is the task that subordinates are being asked to perform? How complicated is the task? Are the subordinates sufficiently skilled to accomplish the task? Do they have the desire to complete the job once they start it? Answers to these questions will help leaders to identify correctly the specific developmental level at which their subordinates are functioning. For example, new employees who are very excited but lack understanding of job requirements would be identified as D1-level employees. Conversely, seasoned workers with proven abilities and great devotion to a company would be identified as functioning at the D4 level.

Having identified the correct development level, the second task for the leader is to *adapt* his or her style to the prescribed leadership style represented in the SLII model. There is a one-to-one relationship between the development level of subordinates (i.e., D1, D2, etc.) and the leader's style (i.e., S1, S2, etc.). For example, if subordinates are at the first level of development, D1, the leader needs to adopt a high directive and low supportive leadership style (S1). If subordinates are more advanced and at the second development level, D2, the leader needs to adopt a selling style (S2). For each level of development there is a specific style of leadership that the leader should adopt.

Because subordinates move back and forth along the development continuum, it is imperative for leaders to be flexible in their leadership behavior. Subordinates may move from one development level to another rather quickly over a short period (e.g., a day or a week), as well as more slowly on tasks that may proceed over much longer periods of time (e.g., a month). Leaders cannot use the same style in all contexts; rather they need to adapt their style to subordinates and their unique situations. Unlike the trait or contingency approaches, which argue a fixed style for leaders, the situational approach demands that leaders demonstrate a strong degree of flexibility.

Strengths

The situational approach to leadership has several strengths, particularly for practitioners. The first strength is that it has stood the test in the marketplace. Situational leadership is one of the most well-known and widely used approaches for training leaders within organizations. It is perceived by corporations as offering a credible model for training individuals to become effective leaders.

A second strength of situational leadership is its practicality. Situational leadership is easy to understand, intuitively sensible, and easily applied in a variety of settings. Whereas some leadership approaches provide complex and sophisticated ways to assess your own leadership behavior (e.g., Vroom and Yetton's, 1973, decision-making approach), situational leadership provides a straightforward approach that is easily utilized. Because it is described at an abstract level that is easily grasped, the ideas behind the approach are quickly acquired. In addition, the principles suggested by situational leadership are easy to apply across a variety of settings, including work, school, and family.

Closely akin to the strength of practicality, is a third strength of situational leadership—its prescriptive value. Although many theories of leadership are descriptive in nature, the situational approach is prescriptive. It tells you what you should and should not do in various contexts. For example, if your subordinates are very low in competence, situational leadership prescribes a *directing* style for you as the leader. If, on the other hand, your employees appear to be competent but lack confidence, the situational approach suggests that you should lead with a *supporting* style. These prescriptions provide leaders with a valuable set of guidelines that can facilitate and enhance leadership.

A final strength of situational leadership is that it emphasizes the concept of leader flexibility (Graef, 1983; Yukl, 1989). Situational leadership stresses that leaders need to find out about their subordinates' needs and then adapt their style accordingly. Leaders cannot lead using a single style; they must be willing to change their style to meet the requirements of the situation. Situational leadership recognizes that employees act differently when doing different tasks and that they may act differently during different stages of the same task. Effective leaders are those who can change their own style based on the task requirements and the subordinates' needs—even in the middle of a project.

Criticisms

Despite its extensive use in leadership training and development, situational leadership does have some limitations. The following criticisms point out several weaknesses in situational leadership and help to provide a more balanced picture of the general utility of this approach in studying and practicing leadership.

The first criticism of situational leadership is that there have been only a few research studies conducted to justify the assumptions and propositions set forth by the approach. Although many doctoral dissertations address dimensions of situational leadership, most of these research studies have not been published. The lack of a strong body of research on situational leadership raises questions concerning the theoretical basis of the approach. Can we be sure it is a valid approach? Is it certain that this approach does indeed improve performance? Does this approach compare favorably in its impact on subordinates to other leadership approaches? It is difficult to give firm answers to these questions when the testing of this approach has not resulted in a significant amount of published research findings.

A second criticism that can be directed at situational leadership concerns the ambiguous conceptualization in the model of subordinates' development levels. The authors of the model do not make clear how "commitment" is combined with "competence" to form four distinct levels of development (Yukl, 1989). In one of the earliest versions of the model, Hersey and Blanchard (1969b) defined the four levels of commitment (maturity) as unwilling and unable (Level 1), willing and unable (Level 2), unwilling and able (Level 3), and willing and able (Level 4). Yet in a more recent version, represented by the SLII model, development level is described as high commitment and low competence in D1, low commitment and some competence in D2, variable commitment and high competence in D3, and high commitment and high competence in D4.

The authors of situational leadership do not explain the theoretical basis for these changes in the composition of each of the development levels. Further, they do not provide an explanation for how competence and commitment are weighted across different development levels. As pointed out by Blanchard et al. (1993), there is a need for further research to establish how competence and commitment are conceptualized for each development level.

Closely related to the general criticism of ambiguity about subordinates' development level is a concern with how commitment itself is conceptualized in the model. Blanchard et al. (1985) suggest that subordinates' commitment is composed of confidence and motivation. According to the SLII model, commitment starts out high in D1, moves down in D2, becomes variable in D3, and then rises again in D4. Intuitively, it would appear more logical to describe subordinate commitment as existing on a continuum moving from low to moderate to high.

The argument provided by Blanchard et al. (1993) for how commitment varies in the SLII model is that subordinates usually start out motivated and eager to learn, then they may become discouraged and disillusioned, next they may begin to lack confidence or motivation, or both, and lastly they become highly confident and motivated. But why is this so? Why do subordinates who learn a task become less committed? Why is there a regression in commitment at development levels 2 and 3? Without research findings to substantiate the way subordinate commitment is conceptualized, this dimension of situational leadership remains unclear.

A fourth criticism of situational leadership has to do with how the model matches leader style with subordinate development level—the prescriptions of the model. To determine the validity of the prescriptions suggested by the Hersey and Blanchard approach, Vecchio (1987) conducted a study of more than 300 high school teachers and their principals. Although he found that the style of leadership suggested by the model was appropriate for relationships between principals and newly hired teachers and those teachers who were relatively inexperienced, he did not find support for the model when it was applied to teachers who were of moderate and high maturity and their respective principals.

Newly hired teachers were more satisfied and performed better under principals who had highly structured leadership styles, but the performance of more experienced and mature teachers was unrelated to the style their principals exhibited. In essence the Vecchio findings suggest that in terms of situational leadership, it is appropriate to match a highly structured S1 style of leadership with immature subordinates but it is not certain whether it is appropriate to match S2, S3, and S4, respectively, with more mature subordinates. Overall these findings point to the need for further research on the basic prescriptions suggested by situational leadership.

Situational leadership can also be criticized from a practical standpoint because it does not fully address the issue of one-to-one versus group leadership in an organizational setting. For example, should a leader with a group of 20 employees lead by matching her or his style to the overall development level of the group or to the development level of individual members of the group? Carew, Parisi-Carew, and Blanchard (1990) suggest that groups go through development stages that are similar to individuals' and therefore leaders should try to match their styles to the group's development level. However, if the leader matches her or his style to the mean development level of a group, how will this affect the individuals whose development levels are quite different from their colleagues? Existing research on situational leadership does not answer this question. More research is needed to explain how leaders can adapt their styles simultaneously to the development levels of individual group members and the group as a whole.

A final criticism of situational leadership can be directed at the leadership questionnaires that accompany the model. Questionnaires on situational leadership typically ask respondents to analyze various work-related situations and select the best leadership style for each situation. The questionnaires are constructed so as to force respondents to describe leadership style in terms of the specific parameters of situational leadership (i.e., Directing, Coaching, Supporting, and Delegating) rather than in terms of other leadership behaviors. Because the best answers available to respondents have been predetermined, the questionnaires are biased in favor of situational leadership (Graef, 1983; Yukl, 1989).

Application

As we discussed earlier in the chapter, situational leadership is widely used in consulting because it is an approach that is easy to conceptualize and also easy to apply. The straightforward nature of situational leadership makes it practical for managers to use.

The principles of this approach can be applied at many different levels in an organization. They can apply to how a CEO of a large corporation works with her or his board of directors, and they can also apply to how a crew chief in an assembly plant leads a small group of production workers. Middle managers can use situational leadership to direct staff meetings, and heads of departments can use this approach in planning structural changes within an organization. There is not a shortage of opportunities for using situational leadership.

Situational leadership applies during the initial stages of a project when idea formation is important, as well as during the various subsequent phases of a project when issues regarding implementation are important. The fluid nature of situational leadership makes it ideal for applying to subordinates as they move forward or go backward (regress) on various projects. Because situational leadership stresses adapting to followers, it is ideal for use with followers whose commitment and competence change over the course of a project.

Given the breadth of the situational approach, it is applicable in virtually any type of organization, at any level, for nearly all types of tasks. It is an encompassing model with a wide range of applications.

Case Studies

To assist in clarifying how situational leadership can be applied in different organizational settings, you may wish to assess case studies 4.1, 4.2, and 4.3. For each of the cases, ask yourself what you would do if you found yourself in a similar situation. At the end of each of these cases there are questions that will assist you in analyzing the context from the perspective of situational leadership.

Case 4.1

Bruce Cannon is the owner of a 5-year-old small plastics company that employs about 20 people. The company is composed of essentially three areas: engineering, sales, and production. For each of these areas there is a single manager.

Jim Day heads up the engineering crew. He is a seasoned engineer who is the oldest employee in the company. Jim was hired because of his engineering ability and because of his experience (he is 55 years old). Prior to joining the company, Jim worked for 20 years as an engineer for Ford Motor Company. He is perceived by his co-workers as very competent, even-tempered, and interested in the company.

Jim has been spending most of his time in recent weeks on developing a long-range plan for the company. His goal is to develop a creative model for making decisions about future expenditures for materials, equipment, plant development, and personnel. Jim feels good about the way upper management has reacted to the first drafts of his plans.

Beth Edwards heads up the sales force, which is the smallest unit in the company. Beth is the most recent hire in the company and has 15 years of sales experience in a different product area. Beth is seen by her peers as highly motivated but not too knowledgeable regarding the nature of the product the company produces. Beth's goal is to increase the company's annual sales by 30%. However, the first-quarter sales figures indicate the rate of growth to be only 2%.

Although Beth has been upbeat since the first day she walked in the door, in recent weeks there have been problems in her department. Her sales staff talk about how little she knows about the plastics industry. In discussions about new products, Beth is often confused. In addition, she has difficulty describing the company's capabilities to outside customers because she does not seem to grasp or understand fully how a plastic company of this type functions.

Steve Lynch is the manager of production and has been with the company since its inception. Steve started out with the company just out of high school, working on the line, and moved up in the company as a result of his hard work. His goal is to streamline production and decrease costs by 10%. He knows production backward and forward but is a bit apprehensive about his new role as production manager. In fact, Steve is afraid he might fail as manager. He does not know if he is ready to have others depend on him when he has always been the one depending on others. The owner, Bruce, has great faith in Steve and has had several meetings with him to clarify his role and reassure him that he can do the work. He is certain that Steve will be an outstanding production manager.

Bruce Cannon meets weekly with each of his managers to talk about how their group is fitting in with the overall company goals. In his forthcoming weekly conference, he wants to discuss with them what new procedures they could implement within their departments to improve their long-term performance. Bruce is wondering how he should approach each of his managers.

Questions

According to the basic assumptions of situational leadership

* Where would you place the three managers in regard to levels of development in the SLII model (see Figure 4.1)?
* If you were Bruce Cannon, would you act the same toward each of the three managers?
* Which conference will be the hardest for you and which will be the easiest?
* Why?

Case 4.2

Jim Anderson is a training specialist in the human resources department of a large pharmaceutical company. In response to a recent companywide survey, Jim specifically designed for the company a 6-week training program on listening and communication skills for effective management. Jim's goals for the seminar are twofold: (a) for participants to learn new communication behaviors, and (b) for participants to enjoy the seminar so they will want to attend future seminars.

The first group to be offered the program was middle-level managers in research and development. This group consisted of about 25 individuals, nearly all of whom had advanced degrees. Most of this group had attended several in-house training programs in the past so they had a sense of how the seminar would be designed and run. Because the outcomes of previous seminars had not always been very productive, many of the managers felt a little disillusioned about coming to the seminar. As one of the managers verbalized, "Here we go again—a fancy in-house training program from which we will gain nothing."

Because Jim recognized that the managers were very experienced, he did not put many restrictions on attendance and participation. He used a variety of presentation methods and he actively solicited involvement from the managers in the seminar. Throughout the first two sessions he went out of his way to be friendly with the group. He gave them frequent coffee breaks during the sessions and during these breaks he promoted socializing and networking.

During the third session Jim became aware of some difficulties with the seminar. Rather than the full complement of 25 managers, attendance had dropped to only about 15 managers. Although the starting time was established at 8:30, attendees had been arriving as late as 10:00. During the afternoon sessions some of the managers were leaving the sessions to return to their offices at the company.

As he approached the fourth session, Jim was apprehensive about why things had been going poorly. He had become quite uncertain about how he should approach the group. Many questions were running through his mind. Had he treated the managers in the wrong way? Had he been too easy regarding attendance at the sessions? Should he have said something about the managers skipping out in the afternoon? Weren't the participants taking the seminar seriously? Jim was certain that the content of the seminars was innovative and substantive, but he just could not figure out what he could change to make the program more successful. He sensed that his style was not working for this group but he didn't have a clue as to how he should change what he was doing to make the sessions better.

Questions

According to the SLII model (see Figure 4.1)

* What style of leadership is Jim Anderson using to run the seminars?
* At what level are the managers?
* From a leadership perspective, what is Jim doing wrong?
* What specific changes could Jim implement to improve the seminars?

Case 4.3

Ann Wilson is the program director of a college campus radio station (WCBA) that is supported by the university. WCBA has a long history and is seen favorably by students, faculty, the board of trustees, and the people in the community.

Ann does not have a problem getting students to work at WCBA. In fact, it is one of the most sought-after university-related activities. The few students who are accepted to work at WCBA are always highly motivated because they value the opportunity to get hands-on media experience. In addition, those who are accepted also tend to be highly confident (sometimes naively so) of their own radio ability. Despite their eagerness, most of them lack a full understanding of the legal responsibilities of being on the air.

One of the biggest problems that confronts Ann every semester is how to train new students to follow the rules and procedures of WCBA when they are doing on-air announcing for news, sports, music, and other radio programs. It seems as if every semester numerous incidents arise in which an announcer violates in no small way the FCC rules for appropriate air-time communication. For example, rumor has it that one year a freshman student disc jockey on the evening shift announced that a new band was playing in town, the cover was five dollars, and everyone should go to hear the group. Making an announcement such as this is a clear violation of FCC rules—it is illegal.

Ann is frustrated with her predicament but cannot seem to figure out why it keeps occurring. She puts a lot of time and effort into helping new DJs, but they just do not seem to get the message that working at WCBA is a serious job and obeying the FCC rules is an absolute necessity. Ann is wondering if her leadership style is missing the mark.

Each semester Ann gives the students a very complete handout on policies and procedures. In addition, she tries to get to know each of the new students personally. Because she wants everybody to be happy at WCBA, she tries very hard to build a relational climate at the station. Repeatedly students say that Ann is the nicest advisor on campus. Because she recognizes the quality of her students, Ann lets them do mostly what they want at the station.

Questions

* What's the problem at WCBA?
* Using SLII as a basis, what would you advise Ann to do differently at the station?
* Based on SL, what creative schemes could she employ to reduce FCC infractions at WCBA?

Leadership Instrument

Although different versions of instruments have been developed to measure situational leadership, nearly all of them are constructed similarly. As a rule, the questionnaires provide a series of 12 to 20 work-related situations and ask respondents to select their preferred style for each situation from four alternatives. The situations and styles are written so as to directly represent the leadership styles of the four quadrants in the model. Questionnaire responses are scored so as to give individuals information about their primary and secondary leadership style, their flexibility, and their leadership effectiveness.

The Brief Questionnaire[1] provided in this section illustrates the way leadership style is measured in questionnaires of situational leadership. For each of the situations on the questionnaire, you have to identify the development level of the employees in the situation and then select one of the four response alternatives that indicate the style of leadership you would employ in that situation.

Expanded versions of the Brief Questionnaire provide respondents an overall profile of their leadership style. By analyzing the alternative choices a respondent makes on the questionnaire, a respondent's primary and secondary leadership styles can be determined. By analyzing the range of choices a respondent makes, leadership flexibility can be determined. Leadership effectiveness and diagnostic ability can be measured by analyzing the number of times the respondent made accurate assessments of a preferred leadership style.

In addition to these self-scored questionnaires, situational leadership also utilizes similar forms to tap the concurrent perceptions that bosses, associates, and followers have of an individual's leadership style. These questionnaires give an individual a wide range of feedback on his or her leadership style as well as the opportunity to compare his or her own view of leadership with the way others view him or her in a leadership role.

Situational Leadership: A Brief Questionnaire

INSTRUCTIONS: Look at the four leadership situations below and indicate what the development level is in each situation, which leadership style each response represents, and which leadership style is needed in the situation—Action **a, b, c,** or **d**?

SITUATION ONE:
Because of budget restrictions imposed on your department, it is necessary to consolidate. You are thinking of asking a highly capable and experienced member of your department to take charge of the consolidation. This person has worked in all areas of your department and has the trust and respect of most of the staff. She is very willing to help with the consolidation.

   a. Assign the project to her and let her determine how to accomplish it.
   b. Assign the task to her, indicate to her precisely what must be done, and supervise her work closely.
   c. Assign the task to her and provide support and encouragement as needed.
   d. Assign the task to her and indicate to her precisely what needs to be done but make sure you incorporate her suggestions.

Development level _____   Action _____

SITUATION TWO:
You have recently been made a department head of the new regional office. In getting to know your departmental staff, you have noticed that one of your inexperienced employees is not following through on assigned tasks. She is enthused about her new job and wants to get ahead in the organization.

   a. Discuss the lack of follow-through with her and explore the alternative ways this problem can be solved.
   b. Specify what she must do to complete the tasks but incorporate any suggestions she may have.

    c. Define the steps necessary to complete the assigned tasks and monitor her performance frequently.

    d. Let her know about the lack of follow-through and give her more time to improve her performance.

Development level _____ Action _____

SITUATION THREE:
Because of a new and very important unit project, for the past 3 months you have made sure that your staff understood their responsibilities and expected level of performance, and you have supervised them closely. Due to some project setbacks recently, your staff has become somewhat discouraged. Their morale has dropped and so has their performance.

    a. Continue to direct and closely supervise their performance.

    b. Give the group more time to overcome the setbacks but occasionally check their progress.

    c. Continue to define group activities, but involve them more in decision making and incorporate their ideas.

    d. Participate in their problem-solving activities and encourage and support their efforts to overcome the project setbacks.

Development level _____ Action _____

SITUATION FOUR:
As a director of the sales department, you have asked a member of your staff to take charge of a new sales campaign. You have worked with this person on other sales campaigns and you know he has the job knowledge and experience to be successful at new assignments. However, he seems a little unsure about his ability to do the job.

    a. Assign the new sales campaign to him and let him function on his own.

    b. Set goals and objectives for this new assignment but consider his suggestions and involve him in decision making.

    c. Listen to his concerns but assure him he can do the job and support his efforts.

    d. Tell him exactly what the new campaign involves, what you expect of him, and supervise his performance closely.

Development level _____ Action _____

SOURCE: Adapted from K. Blanchard, P. Zigarmi, & D. Zigarmi, *Game Plan for Leadership and the One Minute Manager.* Escondido, CA: Blanchard Training and Development, 1992. Figure 4.20, Learning Activity, p. 5. Used with permission.

Scoring Interpretation

A brief discussion of the correct answers to the Brief Questionnaire will help to explain the nature of situational leadership questionnaires.

Situation 1 in the Brief Questionnaire describes a common problem faced by organizations during downsizing: having to consolidate. In this particular situation the leader has identified an individual to direct the downsizing project—an individual who appears to be highly competent, experienced, and motivated. According to the SLII model, this individual is at developmental level 4, which would require a delegative approach. Of the four response alternatives it is the (a) response, "Assign the project to her and let her determine how to accomplish it," that best represents Delegating (S4)—low supportive and low directive leadership.

Situation 2 describes a problem familiar to leaders at all levels in nearly all organizations. It is the problem of lack of follow-through by an enthused employee. In the given example, the described employee would fall in developmental level 1 because she lacks the experience to do the job even though she is highly motivated to succeed. The SLII approach prescribes Directing (S1) leadership for this type of employee. She needs to be told when and how to do her specific job. After being given directions, her performance needs to be closely supervised.

Situation 3 describes a quite different circumstance. In this situation the employees seem to have developed some experience and an understanding of what is required of them, but they have lost some of their motivation to complete the task. Their performance and commitment have stalled because of recent setbacks even though the leader has been directing them closely. According to SLII, the correct response for the leader is to shift to a more supportive Coaching style (S2) of leadership.

Situation 4 describes some of the concerns that arise for a director when attempting to identify the correct person to head up a new sales campaign. The person identified by the director for the position obviously has the skills necessary to do a good job with the new sales campaign but he appears apprehensive about his own abilities. In this context, SLII suggests that the director should employ a Supportive style (S3), which is consistent with leading employees who are competent but lacking a certain degree of confidence.

Now select two employees. Diagnose their current development level on three different tasks and your style of leadership in each situation. Is there a MATCH? If not, what specifically can you do for them as a leader to ensure that they have what they need to succeed?

Summary

Situational leadership is a widely used prescriptive approach to leadership that suggests how leaders can become effective in many different types of organizational settings involving a wide variety of organizational tasks. This approach provides a model that suggests to leaders how they should behave based on the demands of a particular situation.

Situational leadership classifies leadership into four styles: S1 is high directive-low supportive, S2 is high directive-high supportive, S3 is low directive-high supportive, and S4 is low directive-low supportive. The situational model (SLII) describes how each of the four leadership styles applies to subordinates who work at different levels of development, from D1 (low in competence and high in commitment), to D2 (moderately competent and low in commitment), to D3 (moderately competent but lacking commitment), to D4 (great deal of competence and a high degree of commitment).

Effective leadership occurs when the leader can accurately diagnose the development level of subordinates in a task situation and then exhibit the prescribed leadership style that matches that situation.

Leadership is measured in this approach through the use of questionnaires that ask individuals to assess a series of work-related situations. The questionnaires provide information about the leader's diagnostic ability, flexibility, and effectiveness. They are useful in helping leaders to learn about how they can change their leadership style to become more effective across different situations.

There are four major strengths to the situational approach. Foremost, it is an approach to leadership that is recognized throughout the country as a standard for training leaders. Second, it is a practical approach that is easily understood and easily applied. Third, this approach sets forth a clear set of prescriptions for how leaders should act if they want to enhance their leadership effectiveness. Fourth, situational leadership recognizes and stresses that there is not one "best" style of leadership; instead, leaders need to be flexible and adapt their style to the requirements of the situation.

Criticisms of situational leadership suggest it also has limitations. Unlike many other leadership theories, this approach does not have a strong body of research findings to justify and support the theoretical underpinnings on which it stands. As a result, there is ambiguity regarding how the approach conceptualizes certain aspects of the leadership process. It is not clear in explaining how subordinates move from low development levels to high development levels, nor is it clear on how commitment changes over time for subordinates. Without the basic research findings, the validity of the basic prescriptions for matching leader styles to subordinates development levels must also be questioned. Finally, in applying this approach, the model does not provide guidelines for how leaders use this approach in group settings as opposed to one-to-one contexts.

Note

1. Taken from the *Leadership and the One Minute Manager* Game Plan. Used with permission of Blanchard Training and Development, Inc., Escondido, CA, (619) 489-5005.

References

Blanchard, K. H. (1985). *SL II: A situational approach to managing people.* Escondido, CA: Blanchard Training and Development, Inc.

Blanchard, K., Zigarmi, D., & Nelson, R. (1993). Situational leadership after 25 years: A retrospective. *The Journal of Leadership Studies, 1*(1), 22-36.

Blanchard, K., Zigarmi, P., & Zigarmi, D. (1985). *Leadership and the one-minute manager: Increasing effectiveness through situational leadership.* New York: William Morrow.

Carew, P., Parisi-Carew, E., & Blanchard, K. H. (1990). *Group development and situational leadership II.* Escondido, CA: Blanchard Training and Development, Inc.

Graef, C. L. (1983). The situational leadership theory: A critical view. *Academy of Management Review, 8*, 285-291.

Hersey, P., & Blanchard, K. H. (1969a). Life-cycle theory of leadership. *Training and Development Journal, 23*, 26-34.

Hersey, P., & Blanchard, K. H. (1969b). *Management of organizational behavior: Utilizing human resources.* Englewood Cliffs, NJ: Prentice Hall.

Hersey, P., & Blanchard, K. H. (1977). *Management of organizational behavior: Utilizing human resources.* Englewood Cliffs, NJ: Prentice Hall.

Hersey, P., & Blanchard, K. H. (1988). *Management of organizational behavior: Utilizing human resources* (5th ed.). Englewood Cliffs, NJ: Prentice Hall.

Reddin, W. J. (1967). The 3-D management style theory. *Training and Development Journal*, 8-17.

Vecchio, R. P. (1987). Situational leadership theory: An examination of a prescriptive theory. *Journal of Applied Psychology, 72*(3), 444-451.

Vroom, V. H., & Yetton, P. W. (1973). *Leadership and decision-making.* Pittsburgh: University of Pittsburgh Press.

Yukl, G. A. (1989). *Leadership in organizations* (2nd ed.). Englewood Cliffs,
NJ: Prentice Hall.

CHAPTER 5

Contingency Theory

Description

Although several approaches to leadership could be called contingency theories, the most widely recognized is Fiedler's (1964, 1967; Fiedler & Garcia, 1987) contingency theory. Contingency theory is a "leader-match" theory (Fiedler & Chemers, 1974), which means it tries to match leaders to appropriate situations. It is called "contingency" because it suggests that a leader's effectiveness depends on how well the leader's style fits the context. To understand the performance of leaders, it is essential to understand the situations in which they lead. Effective leadership is *contingent* on matching a leader's style to the right setting.

Fiedler developed contingency theory by studying the styles of many different leaders who worked in different contexts, primarily military organizations. He assessed leaders' styles, the situations in which they worked, and whether or not they were effective. After analyzing the styles of hundreds of leaders who were both good and bad, Fiedler and his colleagues were able to make empirically grounded generalizations about which styles of leadership were best and which styles were worst for a given organizational context.

In short, contingency theory is concerned with *styles* and *situations*. It provides the framework for effectively matching the leader and the situation.

Leadership Styles

Within the framework of contingency theory, leadership *styles* are described as task-motivated or relationship-motivated. Task-motivated leaders are concerned primarily with reaching a goal, whereas relationship-motivated leaders are concerned with developing close interpersonal relations. To measure leader styles, Fiedler developed the Least Preferred Co-worker (LPC) Scale (see Leadership Instrument section). Leaders who score high on this scale are described as relationship-motivated and those who score low on the scale are identified as task-motivated.

Situational Variables

Contingency theory suggests that *situations* can be characterized by assessing three factors: (a) leader-member relations, (b) task structure, and (c) position power (see Figure 5.1). *Leader-member relations* refers to the group atmosphere and to the degree of confidence, loyalty, and attraction that followers feel for their leader. If group atmosphere is positive and subordinates trust, like, and get along with their leader, the leader-member relations are defined as good; on the other hand, if the atmosphere is unfriendly and friction exists within the group, the leader-member relations are defined as poor.

The second situational variable, *task structure*, refers to the degree to which the requirements of a task are clear and spelled out. Tasks that are completely structured tend to give more control to the leader, whereas vague and unclear tasks lessen the leader's control and influence. A task is considered structured when (a) the requirements of the task are clearly stated and known by the individuals required to perform them, (b) the path to accomplishing the task has few alternatives, (c) the completion of the task can be clearly demonstrated, and (d) only a limited number of correct solutions to the task exist. An example of a highly structured task would be cleaning the milk shake machine at McDonald's. The rules for doing it are clearly stated to the employees, there is only one way to do it, whether it has been done can be verified, and whether it has been done correctly

Leader-Member Relations	GOOD				POOR			
Task Structure	High Structure		Low Structure		High Structure		Low Structure	
Position Power	Strong Power	Weak Power	Strong Power	Weak Power	Strong Power	Weak Power	Strong Power	Weak Power
Preferred Leadership Style	1	2	3	4	5	6	7	8
	Low LPCs Middle LPCs			High LPCs			Low LPCs	

Figure 5.1. Contingency Model

NOTE: Adapted from F. E. Fiedler, *A Theory of Leadership Effectiveness*, 1967, New York: McGraw-Hill. Used by permission.

can also be easily determined. An example of a highly unstructured task would be the task of running a fund-raiser for a local volunteer organization. Running a fund-raiser would not have any clear set of rules to follow; there would be many alternative ways of doing it; one could not verify the correctness of the way you did it; and no single best way exists to do the fund-raising.

Position power, the third characteristic of situations, refers to the amount of authority a leader has to reward or to punish followers. It includes the legitimate power individuals acquire as a result of the position they hold in an organization. Position power is strong if an individual has the authority to hire and fire or give raises in rank or pay; it is weak if a leader does not have the right to do these things.

Together, these three situational factors determine the "favorable-ness" of various situations in organizations. Situations that are rated "most favorable" are those having good leader-follower relations, defined tasks, and strong leader position power. Situations that are "least favorable" have poor leader-follower relations, unstructured tasks, and weak leader position power.

How Does Contingency Theory Work?

Based on research findings, contingency theory posits that certain styles will be effective in certain situations. Individuals who are task motivated (low LPC score) will be effective in both very favorable and in very unfavorable situations, that is, in situations that are going along very smoothly or when things are out of control. Individuals who are relationship motivated (high LPC score) will be effective in moderately favorable situations, that is, in situations in which there is some degree of certainty but things are neither completely under their control nor out of their control. By measuring a leader's LPC score and the three situational variables, one can predict whether or not a leader is going to be effective in a particular setting.

The relationship between a leader's style and various types of situations is illustrated in Figure 5.1. The figure is best understood by interpreting the rows from top to bottom. For example, a situation that has good leader-member relations, a structured task, and strong position power would fall in Category 1 of preferred leadership style. Or, a situation that has poor leader-member relations, a structured task, and weak position power would fall in Category 6 of leadership style. By assessing the three situational variables, any organizational context can be placed in one of the eight categories represented in Figure 5.1.

Once the nature of the situation is determined, the fit between the leader's style and the situation can be evaluated. The figure indicates that low LPCs (least preferred co-workers) are effective in Categories 1, 2, 3, and 8, while high LPCs are effective in Categories 4, 5, 6, and 7. Middle LPCs are effective in Categories 1, 2, and 3. If an individual's style matches the appropriate category in the model, the leader will be effective; if the individual's style does not match the category, that leader will not be effective.

At this point it is important to point out that contingency theory stresses that leaders will not be effective in all situations. If your style is a good match for the situation in which you work, you will be good at the job; if your style does not match the situation, you will most likely fail.

Strengths

Contingency theory has several major strengths. First, it is a theory that is supported by a great deal of empirical research (see Peters,

Hartke, & Pohlman, 1985; Strube & Garcia, 1981). In an era in which popular newsstand accounts of "How to Be a Successful Leader" abound, contingency theory offers an approach to leadership that has a long tradition. Many researchers have tested it and have found it to be a valid and reliable approach to explaining how effective leadership can be achieved. Contingency theory is grounded in research.

Second, contingency theory has broadened our understanding of leadership by forcing us to consider the impact of situations on leaders. Before contingency theory was developed, leadership theories focused on whether there was a single best type of leadership (e.g., trait approach). Contingency theory, however, emphasized the importance of focusing on the relationship between the leader's style and the demands of various situations. In essence, contingency theory shifted the emphasis to leadership contexts, particularly the link between the leader and situations.

Third, contingency theory is predictive and therefore provides useful information regarding the type of leadership that will most likely be effective in certain contexts. From the data provided by the LPC and the descriptions of three aspects of a situation (i.e., leader-member relations, task structure, and position power), it is possible to determine the probability of success for a given individual in a given situation. This gives contingency theory predictive power that other leadership theories do not have.

Fourth, this theory is advantageous because it does not require that people be effective in all situations. So often leaders in organizations feel the need to be all things to all people, which may be asking too much of leaders. Contingency theory argues that leaders should not expect to be able to lead in every situation. Companies should try to place leaders in optimal situations, in situations that are ideal for their leadership style. When it is obvious that leaders are in the wrong situation, efforts should be made to change the work variables or move the leader to another context. Contingency theory matches the leader *and* the situation but does not demand that the leader fit every situation.

Fifth, contingency theory provides data on leaders' styles that could be useful to organizations in developing leadership profiles. The LPC score is one piece of information that could be used, along with other assessments in human resource planning, to develop profiles on individuals to determine how and where they would best serve an organization.

Criticisms

Although many studies underscore the validity of contingency theory, it has also received much criticism in the research literature. A brief discussion of these criticisms will help to clarify the overall value of contingency theory as a leadership theory.

First, contingency theory has been criticized because it fails to explain fully why individuals with certain leadership styles are more effective in some situations than in others. Fiedler (1993) calls this a "black box" problem because a level of mystery remains about why task-motivated leaders are good in extreme settings and relationship-motivated leaders are good in moderately favorable settings.

The answer provided by the theory for why individuals with low LPC scores are effective in extremes is that these individuals feel more certain in contexts where they have a lot of control and they feel comfortable strongly exerting themselves. On the other hand, high LPCs are not effective in extreme situations because when they have a lot of control they overreact; in situations in which they have little control, they tend to focus so much on relationships that they fail to do the task. In moderate situations, high LPCs are effective because they are allowed to focus on relationship issues, whereas low LPCs feel frustrated because of the lack of certainty. Because critics find these explanations somewhat inadequate, contingency theory is often challenged.

A second major criticism of this theory concerns the LPC scale. The LPC scale has been questioned because it does not seem valid on the surface, it does not correlate well with other standard leadership measures (Fiedler, 1993), and it is not easy to complete correctly.

The LPC scale measures a person's leadership style by asking the person to characterize another person's behavior. Because projection is involved in the measure, it is difficult for respondents to understand how their descriptions of another individual on the scale are a reflection of their own leadership style. It does not make sense on the surface to measure your style through your evaluations of another person's style.

Although it may not be adequate for many people, the answer to this criticism is that the LPC scale is a measure of an individual's motivational hierarchy. Those individuals who are highly task motivated see their least preferred co-worker in a very negative light because that person gets in the way of their own accomplishment of a task. The primary need for these people is to get the job done, and only their secondary needs shift toward people issues. On the other hand, individuals who are relationship motivated see their LPC in more positive terms because their primary need motivation is to get along with people, and only their secondary needs revolve around tasks. In short, the LPC scale measures a respondent's style by assessing the degree to which the respondent sees another person getting in the way of his or her own goal accomplishment.

Although it takes only a few minutes to complete, the instructions on the LPC scale are not clear; they do not fully explain how the respondent is to select his or her least preferred co-worker. Some respondents may get confused between an individual who is their least liked co-worker and their least preferred co-worker. Because their final LPC score is predicated on who they choose as a least preferred co-worker, the lack of clear directions on who to choose as a least preferred co-worker makes the LPC measure problematic.

Although Fiedler and his colleagues have research to back up the test-retest reliability of the LPC scale (Fiedler & Garcia, 1987), the scale remains suspect for many practitioners because it lacks face validity.

Another criticism of contingency theory is that it is cumbersome to use in real-world settings. It is cumbersome because it requires assessing the leader's style as well as three relatively complex situational variables (leader-member relations, task structure, and position power), each of which requires a different instrument. Administering a battery of questionnaires in ongoing organizations can be difficult because it breaks up the normal flow of organizational communication and operations.

A final criticism of contingency theory is that it fails to explain adequately what organizations should do when there is a mismatch between the leader and the situation in the workplace. Because it is a personality theory, contingency theory does not advocate teaching leaders how to adapt their styles to various situations as a means to improve leadership in an organization. Rather, this approach advocates that leaders engage in "situational engineering," which means in essence changing situations to fit the leader. Although Fiedler and his colleagues argue that most situations can be changed in one respect or another to fit the leader's style, the prescriptions for how one engages in situational engineering are not clearly set forth in the theory.

In fact, situations are not always easily changed to match the leader's style. For example, if a leader's style does not match an unstructured, low-power situation, it may be impossible to make the task more structured and increase the position power to fit the leader's style. Similarly, progression up the management ladder in organizations may mean that a leader moves into a new situation in which her or his style does not fit. For example, a manager with a high LPC (relationship-motivated) score might receive a promotion that places her in a context that has good leader-member relations, task structure, and position power, thus rendering her ineffective according to contingency theory. Certainly it would be questionable for a company to change this situation—which otherwise would be labeled nearly ideal in most ways. Overall, changing the situations can result in positive outcomes, but this does present significant workability problems for organizations.

Application

Contingency theory has many applications in the organizational world—it can be used to answer a host of questions about the leadership of individuals within various types of organizations. For example, it can be used to explain why an individual is ineffective in a particular position even though the person is a conscientious, loyal, and hard-working manager. Also, the theory can be used to predict whether an individual who has worked well in one position within an organization will be equally effective if moved into another quite different position within the same company. Furthermore, contingency theory can point to changes that upper management might like to make in a lower-level position in order to guarantee a good fit between an existing manager and a particular work context. These are just a few of the ways that this theory could be applied in organizational settings.

Case Studies

The following three case studies (Cases 5.1, 5.2, and 5.3) provide leadership situations that can be analyzed and evaluated from the perspective of contingency theory. As you read the cases, try to diagnose them using the principles of contingency theory. It will be helpful to try to categorize each case using information provided in Figure 5.1. At the end of each case there is a series of questions that will assist your analysis of the case.

Case 5.1

Lisa Jones has been elected president of the student council at the local college she attends. She likes the other council members and they seem to like her. Her first job as president of the council is to develop a new policy for student computer fees. Because this is the first year that computer fees are being assessed, there are no specific guidelines for what should be included in this policy. Because the council members are elected by the student body, Lisa has no control over how they work. She has no way of rewarding or punishing them. In a leadership course Lisa took, she filled out the LPC questionnaire and her score was 98.

Questions

- How will Lisa Jones do as president of the student council?
- According to her LPC score, what are her primary needs?
- How will these needs affect her ability to develop the new policy for computer fees?
- How can Lisa Jones change the situation to match her management style?

Case 5.2

Bill Smith has been the high school band teacher for 15 years. Every year he is in charge of planning and conducting a different type of concert for the holidays. This year his plan is to present a special jazz program in conjunction with the senior choir. For some reason, the band and choir members have it in for Bill and are constantly giving him trouble. Band and choir are extracurricular activities in which students volunteer to partici- pate. While taking a management class at a local university, Bill took the LPC scale and his score was 44.

Questions

According to Figure 5.1

* What category does this situation fall into?
* Will Bill be successful in his efforts to run the holiday program?
* Should the school administration make any changes regarding Bill's position?

Case 5.3

Universal Drugs is a family-owned pharmaceutical company that manu- factures generic drugs such as aspirin and vitamin pills. The owners of the company have expressed a strong interest in making the management of the company, which traditionally has been very authoritarian, more team- work oriented.

To design and implement the new management structure the owners have decided to create a new position. The person in this position would report directly to the owners and have complete freedom to conduct performance reviews of all managers directly involved in the new system.

Two applicants from within the company have applied for the new position.

Mrs. Lee has been with Universal for 15 years and has been voted by her peers "most outstanding manager" three different times. She is friendly, honest, and extremely conscientious about reaching short-term and long- term goals. When given the LPC scale by the personnel department, Mrs. Lee received a score of 52.

Mr. Washington came to Universal 5 years ago with an advanced degree in organizational development. He is presently director of training, where all of his subordinates say he is the most caring manager they have ever had. While at Universal, Mr. Washington has built a reputation for being a real "people person." Reflecting his reputation is his score on the LPC scale, a 89.

Questions

According to contingency theory

- Which of the two applicants should the new owner choose to head up the new management structure?
- Why?
- Could the owner define the new position, according to contingency theory, in such a way that it would qualify one of the applicants better than the other?
- Will Universal Drugs benefit by using contingency theory in their decision making regarding their new management structure?

Leadership Instrument

The LPC scale is used in contingency theory to measure a person's leadership style. For example, it measures your style by having you describe a co-worker with whom you had difficulty completing a job. This does not need to be a co-worker you disliked a great deal, but rather someone with whom you least like to work. After you have selected this individual, the LPC instrument asks you to describe your co-worker on 18 sets of adjectives.

Low LPCs are task motivated. They are individuals whose primary needs are to accomplish tasks and whose secondary needs are focused on getting along with people. In a work setting, they are concerned with achieving success on assigned tasks, even if at the cost of having poor interpersonal relationships with co-workers. Low LPCs gain self-esteem through achieving their goals. They attend to interpersonal relationships, but only after they first have directed themselves toward the tasks of the group.

Middle LPCs are socio-independent leaders. In the context of work, they are self-directed and not overly concerned with the task or with how others view them. They are more removed from the situation and act more independent than low or high LPCs.

High LPCs are motivated by relationships. These individuals derive their major satisfaction in an organization from getting along with people—interpersonal relationships. A high LPC sees positive qualities even in the co-worker she or he least prefers, even though the high LPC does not work well with that person. In an organizational setting, the high LPC attends to tasks, but only after she or he is certain that the relationships between people are in good shape.

Least Preferred Co-Worker (LPC) Measure

INSTRUCTIONS: Think of the person with whom you can work least well. He or she may be someone you work with now or he or she may be someone you knew in the past. He or she does not have to be the person you like least well, but should be the person with whom you had the most difficulty in getting a job done. Describe this person as he or she appears to you.

Scoring

Pleasant	8	7	6	5	4	3	2	1	Unpleasant	6
Friendly	8	7	6	5	4	3	2	1	Unfriendly	4
Rejecting	1	2	3	4	5	6	7	8	Accepting	1
Tense	1	2	3	4	5	6	7	8	Relaxed	6
Distant	1	2	3	4	5	6	7	8	Close	4
Cold	1	2	3	4	5	6	7	8	Warm	2
Supportive	8	7	6	5	4	3	2	1	Hostile	1
Boring	1	2	3	4	5	6	7	8	Interesting	1
Quarrelsome	1	2	3	4	5	6	7	8	Harmonious	7
Gloomy	1	2	3	4	5	6	7	8	Cheerful	1
Open	8	7	6	5	4	3	2	1	Closed	1
Backbiting	1	2	3	4	5	6	7	8	Loyal	1
Untrustworthy	1	2	3	4	5	6	7	8	Trustworthy	1
Considerate	8	7	6	5	4	3	2	1	Inconsiderate	1
Nasty	1	2	3	4	5	6	7	8	Nice	1
Agreeable	8	7	6	5	4	3	2	1	Disagreeable	1
Insincere	1	2	3	4	5	6	7	8	Sincere	1
Kind	8	7	6	5	4	3	2	1	Unkind	1
									Total:	25

SOURCE: Adapted from F. E. Fiedler & M. M. Chemers (1984). *Improving Leadership Effectiveness: The Leader Match Concept* (2nd ed.). New York: John Wiley & Sons, Inc. Used by permission.

Scoring Interpretation

Your final LPC score is determined by adding up the numbers you circled on all of the 18 scales.

If your score is 57 or below, you are a low LPC, which suggests that you are task motivated. If your score is within the range of 58 to 63, you are a middle LPC, which means you are independent. Individuals who score 64 or above are called high LPCs and they are thought to be more relationship motivated.

Because the LPC is a personality measure, the score you get on the LPC scale is believed to be quite stable over time and not easily changed. Low LPCs tend to remain low, moderates tend to remain moderate, and high LPCs tend to remain high. As was pointed out earlier in the chapter, research shows that the test-retest reliability of the LPC is very strong (Fiedler & Garcia, 1987).

Summary

Contingency theory represents a shift in leadership research from focusing on only the leader to looking at the leader in conjunction with the situation in which the leader works. It is a leader-match theory that emphasizes the importance of matching a leader's *style* with the demands of a *situation*.

To measure leadership style, a personality-like measure called the Least Preferred Co-worker (LPC) Scale is used. It delineates individuals who are highly task motivated (low LPCs), those who are socio-independent (middle LPCs), and those who are relationship motivated (high LPCs).

To measure situations, three variables are assessed: leader-member relations, task structure, and position power. Taken together these variables point to the style of leadership that has the best chance of being successful. In general, contingency theory suggests that low LPCs are effective in extremes, and that high LPCs are effective in moderately favorable situations.

The strengths of contingency theory include that it is backed by a considerable amount of research, it is the first leadership theory to emphasize the impact of situations on leaders, it is predictive of leadership effectiveness, it allows leaders not to be effective in all situations, and it can provide useful leadership profile data.

On the negative side, contingency theory can be criticized because it has not adequately explained the link between styles and situations, and it relies heavily on the LPC Scale, which has been questioned for its face validity and workability. Contingency theory is not easily used in ongoing organizations. Lastly, it does not fully explain how organizations can use the results of this theory in situational engineering. Regardless of these criticisms, contingency theory has made a substantial contribution to our understanding of the leadership process.

References

Fiedler, F. E. (1964). A contingency model of leadership effectiveness. In L. Berkowitz (Ed.), *Advances in experimental social psychology* (Vol. I, pp. 149-190). New York: Academic Press.

Fiedler, F. E. (1967). *A theory of leadership effectiveness.* New York: McGraw-Hill.

Fiedler, F. E. (1993). The leadership situation and the black box in contingency theories. In M. M. Chemers & R. Ayman (Eds.), *Leadership, theory, and research: Perspectives and directions* (pp. 1-28). New York: Academic Press.

Fiedler, F. E., & Chemers, M. M. (1974). *Leadership and effective management.* Glenview, IL: Scott, Foresman.]

Fiedler, F. E. & Chemers, M. M. (1984). *Improving leadership effectiveness: The leader match concept* (2nd. ed.). New York: John Wiley.

Fiedler, F. E., & Garcia, J. E. (1987). *New approaches to leadership: Cognitive resources and organizational performance.* New York: John Wiley.

House, R. J. (1976). A 1976 theory of charismatic leadership. In J. G. Hunt & L. L. Larson (Eds.), *Leadership: The cutting edge* (pp. 189-207). Carbondale: Southern Illinois University Press.

Peters, L. H., Hartke, D. D., & Pohlman, J. T. (1985). Fiedler's contingency theory of leadership: An application of the meta-analysis procedures of Schmidt and Hunter. *Psychological Bulletin, 97,* 274-285.

Strube, M. J., & Garcia, J. E. (1981). A meta-analytic investigation of Fiedler's contingency model of leadership effectiveness. *Psychological Bulletin, 90,* 307-321.

| # Path-Goal Theory

Description

Path-goal theory is about how leaders motivate subordinates to accomplish designated goals. Drawing heavily from research on what motivates employees, path-goal theory first appeared in the leadership literature in the early 1970s in the works of Evans (1970), House (1971), House and Dessler (1974), and House and Mitchell (1974). The stated goal of this leadership theory is to enhance employee performance and employee satisfaction by focusing on employee motivation.

In contrast to the situational approach, which suggests that a leader must adapt to the development level of subordinates (see Chapter 4), and unlike contingency theory, which emphasizes the match between the leader's style and specific situational variables (see Chapter 5), the path-goal theory emphasizes the relationship between the leader's style and the characteristics of the subordinates and the work setting. The underlying assumption of path-goal theory is derived from expectancy theory, which suggests that subordinates will be motivated if they think they are capable of performing their work, if they believe their efforts will result in a certain outcome, and if they believe that the payoffs for doing their work are worthwhile.

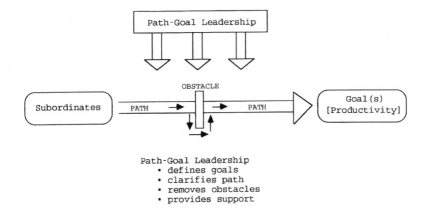

Path-Goal Leadership
- defines goals
- clarifies path
- removes obstacles
- provides support

Figure 6.1. Representation of the Basic Idea Behind Path-Goal Theory

For the leader, the challenge is to use a leadership style that best meets subordinates' motivational needs. This is done by choosing behaviors that complement or supplement what is missing in the work setting. Leaders try to enhance subordinates' goal attainment by providing information or rewards in the work environment (Indvik, 1986); leaders provide subordinates with the elements they think that their subordinates need to reach their goals.

According to House and Mitchell (1974), leadership generates motivation when it increases the number and kinds of payoffs that subordinates receive from their work. Leadership also motivates when it makes the path to the goal clear and easy to travel through coaching and direction, when it removes obstacles and roadblocks to attaining the goal, and when it makes the work itself more personally satisfying (see Figure 6.1).

In brief, path-goal theory is designed to explain how leaders can help subordinates along the path to their goals by selecting specific behaviors that are best suited to subordinates' needs and to the situation in which subordinates are working. By choosing the appropriate style, leaders increase subordinates' expectations for success and satisfaction.

Conceptually, the path-goal theory is relatively complex; it is therefore useful to break it down into smaller units so that we can better understand the complexities of this approach.

Figure 6.2 illustrates the different components of path-goal theory including leader behaviors, subordinate characteristics, task char-

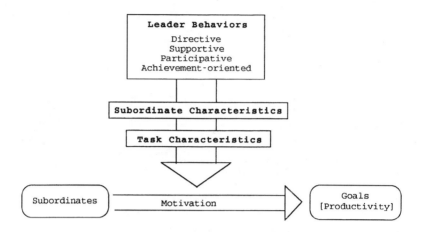

Figure 6.2. Major Components of Path-Goal Theory

acteristics, and motivation. Path-goal theory suggests that each type of leader behavior has a different kind of impact on subordinates' motivation. Whether or not a particular leader behavior is motivating to subordinates is contingent upon the subordinates' characteristics and the characteristics of the task.

Leader Behaviors

Although many different leadership behaviors could have been se-lected to be a part of path-goal theory, this approach has so far exam-ined directive, supportive, participative, and achievement-oriented leadership behaviors (House & Mitchell, 1974, p. 83). Path-goal the-ory is explicitly left open to the inclusion of other variables.

Directive Leadership

Directive leadership is similar to the "initiating structure" concept described in the Ohio State studies (Halpin & Winer, 1957) and the "telling" style described in situational leadership. It characterizes a leader who gives subordinates instructions about their task, includ-ing what is expected of them, how it is to be done, and the time line for when it should be completed. A directive leader sets clear standards of performance and makes the rules and regulations clear to subordinates.

Supportive Leadership

Supportive leadership resembles the "consideration behavior" construct that was identified by the Ohio State studies. Supportive leadership refers to being friendly and approachable as a leader and includes attending to the well-being and human needs of subordinates. Leaders using supportive behaviors go out of their way to make work pleasant for subordinates. In addition, supportive leaders treat subordinates as equals and give them respect for their status.

Participative Leadership

Participative leadership refers to leaders who invite subordinates to share in the decision making. A participative leader consults with subordinates, obtains their ideas and opinions, and integrates their suggestions into the decisions regarding how the group or organization will proceed.

Achievement-Oriented Leadership

Achievement-oriented leadership is characterized by a leader who challenges subordinates to perform work at the highest level possible. This leader establishes a high standard of excellence for subordinates and seeks continuous improvement. In addition to expecting a lot from subordinates, achievement-oriented leaders show a high degree of confidence that subordinates are capable of establishing and accomplishing challenging goals.

House and Mitchell (1974) suggest that leaders may exhibit any or all of these four styles with various subordinates and in different situations. Path-goal theory is not a trait approach that locks leaders into only one kind of leadership; leaders should adapt their styles to the situation or to the motivational needs of their subordinates. For example, if subordinates need participative leadership at one point in a task and directive leadership at another, the leader can change her or his style as needed. Different situations may call for different types of leadership behavior. Furthermore, there may be instances when it is appropriate for a leader to use a blend of leadership styles that incorporates more than one style at the same time.

In addition to leader behaviors, Figure 6.2 illustrates two other major components of path-goal theory: subordinate characteristics and task characteristics. Each of these two sets of characteristics influences the way leaders' behaviors affect subordinate motivation. In other words, the impact of leadership is *contingent* on the characteristics of both subordinates and their task.

Subordinate Characteristics

Subordinate characteristics determine how a leader's behavior will be interpreted by subordinates in a given work context. Researchers have focused on subordinates' needs for affiliation, preferences for structure, desires for control, and self-perceived level of task ability. These characteristics, as well as many others, determine the degree to which subordinates find the behavior of a leader an immediate source of satisfaction or instrumental to some future satisfaction.

Path-goal theory predicts that subordinates who have strong needs for affiliation prefer supportive leadership because friendly and concerned leadership is a source of satisfaction. For subordinates who are dogmatic and authoritarian and have to work in uncertain situations, path-goal theory suggests directive leadership because that provides psychological structure and task clarity. Directive leadership helps these subordinates by clarifying the path to the goal and making it less ambiguous. The authoritarian type of individual feels more comfortable when the leader provides a greater sense of certainty in the work setting.

Subordinates' desires for control have received special attention in path-goal research through studies of a personality construct locus of control that can be subdivided into internal and external dimensions. Subordinates with internal locus of control believe that they are in charge of the things that occur in their life, while individuals with external locus of control believe that chance, fate, or outside forces are the determinants of life events. Path-goal theory suggests that for subordinates with internal locus of control, participative leadership is most satisfying because it allows subordinates to feel in charge of their work and to be an integral part of the decision-making process. For subordinates with external locus of control, the path-goal theory suggests that directive leadership is best because it parallels subordinates' feelings that outside forces control their circumstances.

Another way that leadership affects subordinates' motivation is the subordinates' perception of their own ability to perform a specific task. As subordinates' perception of their own abilities and competence goes up, the need for directive leadership goes down. In effect, directive leadership becomes redundant and perhaps excessively controlling in situations where subordinates feel competent to complete their own work.

Task Characteristics

In addition to subordinate characteristics, *task characteristics* also have a major impact on the way a leader's behavior influences the motivation of subordinates (see Figure 6.2). Task characteristics include the design of the subordinate's task, the formal authority system of the organization, and the primary work group of subordinates. Collectively, these characteristics in and of themselves can provide motivation for subordinates. When a situation provides a clearly structured task, strong group norms, and an established authority system, then subordinates will find the paths to desired goals apparent and will not have a need for a leader to clarify goals or to coach subordinates in how to reach these goals. Subordinates will feel as if they can accomplish their work and that their work is of value. Leadership in these types of contexts could be seen as unnecessary, unempathic, and excessively controlling.

In some situations, however, the task characteristics may call for leadership involvement. Tasks that are unclear and ambiguous call for leadership input that provides structure. Also, tasks that are highly repetitive require leadership that gives support in order to maintain subordinates' motivation. In work settings where the formal authority system is weak, leadership becomes a tool that helps subordinates by making the rules and work requirements clear. In contexts where the group norms are weak or nonsupportive, leadership assists in building cohesiveness and role responsibility.

A special focus of path-goal theory is on helping subordinates to overcome obstacles. Obstacles could be just about anything in the work setting that gets in the way of subordinates. Specifically, obstacles create excessive uncertainties, frustrations, or threats for subordinates. In these settings, path-goal theory suggests that it is the leader's responsibility to help subordinates by removing these obstacles or helping them around them. Assisting subordinates around these obstacles will increase subordinates' expectations to complete the task and increase their sense of job satisfaction.

How Does Path-Goal Theory Work?

Path-goal theory is an approach to leadership that is theoretically complex but also pragmatic. In theory, it provides a set of assumptions about how various leadership styles will interact with characteristics of subordinates and the work setting to affect the motivation of subordinates. In practice, the theory provides direction about how leaders can help subordinates to accomplish their work in a satisfactory manner.

Theoretically, the path-goal approach suggests that leaders need to choose a leadership style that best fits the needs of subordinates and the work they are doing. The theory predicts that a directive style of leadership is best in situations in which subordinates are dogmatic and authoritarian, the task demands are ambiguous, and the organizational rules and procedures are unclear. In these situations, directive leadership complements the work by providing guidance and psychological structure for subordinates (House & Mitchell, 1974, p. 90).

For work that is structured, unsatisfying, or frustrating, path-goal theory suggests that leaders should use a supportive style. The supportive style provides what is missing by giving nurturance to subordinates when they are engaged in tasks that are repetitive and unchallenging. Supportive leadership offers a sense of "human touch" for subordinates engaged in mundane mechanized activity.

Participative leadership is considered best when a task is ambiguous because participation gives greater clarity to how certain paths lead to certain goals—it helps subordinates to learn what leads to what (House & Mitchell, 1974, p. 92). In addition, participative leadership has a positive impact when subordinates are autonomous and have a strong need for control, because this kind of subordinate responds favorably to being involved in decision making and in the structuring of work.

Furthermore, the path-goal theory predicts that achievement-oriented leadership is most effective in settings in which subordinates are required to perform ambiguous tasks. In settings such as these, leaders who challenge and set high standards for subordinates raise subordinates' confidence that they have the ability to reach their goals. In effect, achievement-oriented leadership helps subordinates feel that their efforts will result in effective performance. In settings where the task is more structured and less ambiguous, however, achievement-oriented leadership appears to be unrelated to subordinates' expectations about their work efforts.

Pragmatically, path-goal theory is straightforward. An effective leader has to attend to the needs of subordinates. The leader should help subordinates to define their goals and the paths they wish to take in reaching those goals. When obstacles arise, the leader needs to help subordinates confront them. This may mean helping the subordinate around the obstacle or it may mean removing the obstacle. The leader's job is to help subordinates reach their goals by directing, guiding, and coaching them along the way.

Strengths

Path-goal theory is an approach to leadership that has several positive features. First, path-goal theory provides a useful theoretical framework for understanding how various leadership behaviors (e.g., directive, supportive, achievement-oriented, and participative) affect the satisfaction and goal-directed activity of subordinates in differing work contexts. It was one of the first situational/contingency theories of leadership to explain how task and subordinate characteristics affect the impact of leadership on subordinate performance. The framework provided in path-goal theory informs leaders about how to choose an appropriate leadership style based on the various demands of the task and the type of subordinates being asked to do the task.

A second positive feature of path-goal theory is that it attempts to integrate the motivation principles of expectancy theory into a theory of leadership. This makes path-goal theory unique because no other leadership approach deals directly with motivation in this way. Path-goal theory forces us continually to ask questions about subordinate motivation such as: How can I motivate subordinates to feel that they have the ability to do the work? How can I help them feel that if they successfully do their work, they will be rewarded? What can I do to improve the payoffs that subordinates expect from their work? Path-goal theory is designed to keep these kinds of questions, which address issues of motivation, in the forefront of the leader's mind.

A third strength, and perhaps its greatest, is that path-goal theory provides a model that in certain ways is very practical. The representation of the model (see Figure 6.1) underscores and highlights the important ways leaders help subordinates. It shouts out, in essence, for leaders to clarify the paths to the goals and remove or help subordinates around the obstacles to the goals. In its simplest form, the theory reminds leaders that the overarching purpose of leadership is to guide and coach subordinates as they move along the path to achieve a goal.

Criticisms

Although path-goal theory has various strengths, it also has several identifiable weaknesses. First, path-goal theory is so complex and incorporates so many different aspects of leadership that interpreting the meaning of the theory can be confusing. For example, path-goal theory makes predictions about which of four different leadership styles is appropriate for tasks with different degrees of structure, for goals with different levels of clarity, for workers at different levels of ability, and for organizations with different degrees of formal authority. To say the least, it is a daunting task to incorporate all of these factors simultaneously into one's selection of a preferred leadership style. Because the scope of path-goal theory is so broad and encompasses so many different interrelated sets of assumptions, it is difficult to utilize this theory fully in trying to improve the leadership process in a given organizational context.

A second limitation of path-goal theory is that it has received only partial support from the many empirical research studies that have been conducted to test its validity (House & Mitchell, 1974; Indvik, 1986; Schriesheim & Kerr, 1977; Schriesheim & Schriesheim, 1980;

Stinson & Johnson, 1975; Wofford & Liska, 1993). For example, some research supports the prediction that leader directiveness is positively related to worker satisfaction when tasks are ambiguous, but other research has failed to confirm this relationship. Furthermore, not all aspects of the theory have been given equal attention. There has been a great deal of research designed to study directive and supportive leadership and only a limited number of studies that address participative and achievement leadership. The claims of path-goal theory remain tentative because the research findings to date do not provide a full and consistent picture of the basic assumptions and corollaries of path-goal theory.

Another criticism of path-goal theory is that it fails to explain adequately the relationship between leadership behavior and worker motivation. Path-goal theory is unique because it incorporates the tenets of expectancy theory; however, it must be criticized because it does not go far enough in explicating how leadership is related to these tenets. The principles of expectancy theory suggest that subordinates will be motivated if they feel competent and trust that their efforts will get results; but path-goal theory does not describe how a leader could employ various styles directly to assist subordinates to feel competent or assured of success. For example, path-goal theory does not explain how directive leadership during ambiguous tasks increases subordinate motivation. Similarly, it does not explain how supportive leadership during tedious work relates to subordinate motivation. The result is that the practitioner is left with an inadequate understanding of how her or his leadership will affect subordinates' expectations about their work.

A final criticism that can be made of path-goal theory concerns a practical outcome of the theory. Path-goal theory suggests that it is important for leaders to provide coaching, guidance, and direction for subordinates; to help subordinates to define and clarify goals; and to help subordinates around obstacles as they attempt to reach their goals. In effect, this approach treats leadership as a one-way event— the leader affects the subordinate. The potential difficulty in this type of "helping" leadership is that subordinates may easily become dependent on the leader to accomplish their work. Path-goal theory places a great deal of responsibility on leaders and much less on subordinates. Over time this kind of leadership could be counterproductive because it promotes dependency and fails to recognize the full abilities of subordinates.

Application

Path-goal theory is not an approach to leadership for which many management training programs have been developed. Nor will you find many seminars with titles such as "Improving Your Path-Goal Leadership" or "Assessing Your Skills in Path-Goal Leadership." Nevertheless, path-goal theory does offer significant insights that can be applied in ongoing settings to improve one's leadership.

Path-goal theory provides a set of general recommendations based on the characteristics of subordinates and tasks for how leaders should act in various situations if they want to be effective. It informs us about when to be directive, supportive, participative, or achievement oriented. For instance, the theory suggests that leaders should be directive when tasks are complex, and when tasks are dull the leader should give support. Similarly, it suggests that leaders be participative when subordinates need control, and leaders should be achievement oriented when subordinates have needs to excel. In a general way, path-goal theory offers leaders a road map that gives directions about ways to improve subordinate satisfaction and performance.

The principles of path-goal theory can be employed by leaders at all levels within the organization as well as for all types of tasks. To apply path-goal theory, a leader must carefully assess his or her subordinates and their tasks and then choose an appropriate leadership style to match those characteristics. If subordinates are feeling insecure about doing a task, the leader needs to adopt a style that builds subordinate confidence. If subordinates are uncertain if their efforts will result in reaching their goals, the leader needs to prove to them that their efforts will be rewarded. As discussed earlier in the chapter, path-goal theory is useful because it continually reminds leaders that their central purpose as a leader is to help subordinates define their goals and then to help subordinates reach their goals in the most efficient manner.

Case Studies

The following cases provide descriptions of various situations in which a leader is attempting to apply path-goal theory. Two of the cases, Cases 6.1 and 6.2, are from traditional business contexts; the third, Case 6.3, is from an informal social organization. As you read the cases, try to apply the principles of path-goal theory to determine the degree to which you think the leaders in the cases have done a good job of using this theory.

Case 6.1

Brako is a small manufacturing company that produces parts for the automobile industry. The company has several patents on parts that fit in the brake assembly of nearly all domestic and foreign cars. Each year the company produces three million parts that it ships to assembly plants throughout the world. To produce the parts, Brako runs three shifts with about 40 workers on each shift.

The supervisors for the three shifts (Art, Tom, and Carol) are experienced employees, each of whom has been with the company for more than 20 years. The supervisors appear satisfied with their work and have reported no major difficulty in supervising employees at Brako.

Art supervises the first shift. Employees describe him as being a very hands-on type of leader. He gets very involved in the day-to-day operations of the facility. Workers joke that Art knows to the milligram the amount of raw materials the company has on hand at any given time. Art can frequently be found walking through the plant and reminding people of the correct procedures to follow in doing their work. Even for those working on the production line, Art always has some directions and reminders.

Workers on the first shift have relatively few negative comments to make about Art's leadership. However, they are negative about many other aspects of their work. Most of the work on this shift is very straightforward and repetitive and as a result is monotonous. The rules for working on the production line or in the packaging area are all clearly spelled out and require no independent decision making on the part of workers. Workers simply need to show up and go through the motions. On lunch breaks, workers are often heard complaining about how bored they are doing the same old thing over and over. Workers do not criticize Art, but they do not think he really understands their situation.

Tom supervises the second shift. He really enjoys working at Brako and wants all the workers on the afternoon shift to enjoy their work as well. Tom is a people-oriented supervisor whom workers describe as very genuine and caring. Hardly a day goes by that Tom does not post a message about someone's birthday or someone's personal accomplishment. Tom works hard at creating comradery, including sponsoring a company softball team, taking people out to lunch, and having people over to his house for social events.

Despite Tom's personableness, absenteeism and turnover are highest on the second shift. The second shift is responsible for setting up the machines and equipment when changes are made from making one part to making another. In addition, the second shift is responsible for the complex computer programs that monitor the machines. Workers on the second shift take a lot of heat from others at Brako for not doing a good job. Workers on the second shift feel pressure because it is not always easy to figure out how to do their tasks. Each setup is different and requires different procedures. Although the computer is extremely helpful when it is calibrated appropriately to the task, it can be extremely problematic when the software it uses is off the mark. Workers have complained to Tom and upper management many times about the difficulty of their jobs.

Carol supervises the third shift. Her style is different than others at Brako. Carol routinely has meetings, which she labels troubleshooting sessions, for the purpose of identifying problems workers may be experiencing. Any time there is a glitch on the production line, Carol wants to know about it so she can help workers find a solution. If workers cannot do a particular job, she shows them how. For those who are uncertain of their competencies, Carol gives reassurance. Carol tries to spend time with each worker and help the workers focus on their personal goals. In addition, she stresses company goals and the rewards that are available if workers are able to make the grade.

Individuals on the third shift like to work for Carol. They find she is good at helping them do their job. They say she has a wonderful knack for making everything fall into place. When there are problems, she addresses them. When workers feel down, she builds them up. Carol was described by one worker as an interesting mixture of part parent, part coach, and part manufacturing expert. Upper management at Brako is pleased with Carol's leadership, but they have experienced problems repeatedly when workers from Carol's shift have been rotated to other shifts at Brako.

Questions

Based on the principles of path-goal theory

- Describe why Art and Tom appear to be less effective than Carol.
- How does the leadership of each of the three supervisors affect the motivation of their respective subordinates?
- If you were consulting with Brako about leadership, what changes and recommendations would you make regarding the supervision of Art, Tom, and Carol?

Case 6.2

Daniel Shivitz is the manager of a small business called The Copy Center, which is located near a large university. The Copy Center employs about 18 people, most of whom work part-time while going to school full-time. The store caters to the university community by specializing in coursepacks, but it also provides desktop publishing and standard copying services. It has three large state-of-the-art copy machines and several computer work stations.

There are two other national chain copy stores in the immediate vicinity of The Copy Center, yet this store does more business than both of the other stores combined. A major factor contributing to the success of this store is Daniel Shivitz's leadership style.

One of the things that stands out about Daniel is the way he works with his part-time staff. Most of these people are students who have to schedule their work hours around their class schedules, and Daniel has a reputation of being really helpful with working out schedule conflicts. No conflict is too small for Daniel, who is always willing to juggle schedules to meet the needs of everyone. Students talk about how much they feel included and like the spirit at The Copy Center. It is as if Daniel makes the store like a second family for them.

Work at The Copy Center divides itself into primarily two areas: duplicating services and desktop publishing. In both areas, Daniel Shivitz's leadership is effective.

Duplicating is a rather straightforward operation that simply requires taking a customer's originals and making copies of them. Because this job is tedious, Daniel goes out of his way to help the staff make it tolerable. He promotes a friendly work atmosphere by doing such things as letting the staff wear casual attire, letting them choose their own tapes for background music, and letting them be a bit wild on the job. Daniel spends a lot of time each day conversing informally with each employee; he also welcomes staff talking with each other. Daniel has a knack for making each worker feel significant even when the work is insignificant. He promotes comradery among his staff and he is not afraid to become involved in their activities.

The desktop publishing area is more complex than duplicating. It involves creating business forms, advertising pieces, and résumés for customers. Working in desktop publishing requires skills in writing, editing, design, and layout. It is challenging work because it is not always easy to satisfy these customers' needs. Most of the employees in this area are full-time workers.

Through the years, Daniel Shivitz has found that employees who work best in desktop publishing are a unique type of individual, very different from those who work in duplicating. They are usually quite independent, self-assured, and self-motivated. In supervising them, Daniel gives them a lot of space, is available when they need help, but otherwise leaves them alone.

Daniel likes the role of being the resource person for these employees. For example, if an employee is having difficulty on a customer's project, he willingly joins the employee in troubleshooting the problem. Similarly, if one of the staff is having problems with a software program, Daniel is quick to offer his technical expertise. Because the employees in desktop publishing are self-directed, Daniel spends far less time with them than with those who work in duplicating.

Overall, Daniel feels successful with his leadership at The Copy Center. Profits for the store continue to grow each year and its reputation for quality service is widespread.

Questions

According to path-goal theory

* Why is Daniel an effective leader?
* How does his leadership style affect the motivation of employees at The Copy Center?
* How do characteristics of the task and the subordinates influence Daniel's leadership?
* One of the principles of path-goal theory is to make the end goal valuable to workers. What could Daniel do to improve subordinate motivation in this area?

Case 6.3

David Smith is the newly elected president of the Metrocity Striders Track Club (MSTC). As president of the track club, one of his duties is to serve as the coach for runners who hope to complete the New York City Marathon. Because David has run many marathons and ultramarathons successfully, he feels quite comfortable assuming the role and responsibilities of acting as coach for the marathon runners.

The training period for runners intending to run New York is 16 weeks. During the first couple of weeks of training, David was pleased with the progress of the runners and had little difficulty in his role as coach. However, when the runners reached week eight, the halfway mark, some things began to occur that raised some questions in David's mind regarding how best to help his runners. The issues of concern for runners seemed quite different from those that David had expected to hear from runners in a marathon training program. All in all, the runners and their concerns could be divided into three different groups.

One group of runners, most of whom had never run a marathon, peppered the coach with all kinds of questions. They were very concerned about how to do the marathon and whether they had the ability to complete such a challenging event successfully. They asked questions about how far to run in training, what to eat, how much to drink, and what kind of shoes to wear. One runner wanted to know what to eat the night before the marathon, and another wanted to know if it was likely that he would pass out when he crossed the finish line. For David the questions were never-ending and rather basic in nature.

Another set of individuals seemed most concerned about the effects of training on their running. For example, they wanted to know precisely how their per-week running mileage related to their possible marathon finishing time. Would running long practice runs help them through "the wall" at the 20-mile mark in the marathon? Would "carbo-loading" improve their overall performance during the marathon? Would taking a rest day during training actually help their overall conditioning? Basically, all the runners in this group seemed to want assurances from David that they were training in the "right" way for New York.

A third group of runners were seasoned runners, most of whom had run several marathons and many of whom had finished in the top 10 of their respective age divisions. Regardless of their experience, these runners still seemed to be having troubles. They complained of feeling flat and acted a bit moody and down about training. Even though they had confidence in their ability to compete and finish well, they lacked excitement about running in the New York event. The occasional questions they raised usually concerned such things as whether their overall training strategy was appropriate or whether their training would help them in other races besides the New York City Marathon.

Questions

Based on the principles described in path-goal theory

- What kind of leadership should David exhibit with each of the three running groups?
- What is it that David has to do to help the runners accomplish their goals?
- Are there obstacles that David can remove or help runners to confront?
- In general, how can David motivate each of the three groups?

Leadership Instrument

Because the path-goal theory was developed as a complex set of theoretical assumptions to direct researchers in developing new leadership theory, it has utilized many different instruments to measure the leadership process. The Path-Goal Leadership Questionnaire illustrates one of the questionnaires that has been useful in measuring and learning about important aspects of path-goal leadership (Indvik, 1985, 1988).

This questionnaire provides information for respondents about four different leadership styles: directive, supportive, participative, and achievement oriented. The way respondents score on each of the different styles provides them with information on their strong and weak styles, as well as the relative importance they place on each of the styles.

To understand the path-goal questionnaire better, it may be useful to analyze a hypothetical set of scores. For example, hypothesize that your scores on the questionnaire were 29 for directive, which is high; 22 for supportive, which is low; 21 for participative, which is average; and 25 for achievement, which is high. These scores suggest that you are a leader who is typically more directive and achievement oriented than most other leaders, less supportive than other leaders, and quite similar to other leaders in the degree to which you act participatively.

6+6+ 5 +6+
5+3 +3+7+

PATH-GOAL THEORY

6 +6+ 2 + 6+ 5

Path-Goal Leadership Questionnaire
7+ 5+ 6+ 5 +5 -d

INSTRUCTIONS: This questionnaire contains questions about different styles of path-goal leadership. Indicate how often each statement is true of your own behavior.

KEY: 1 = never; 2 = hardly ever; 3 = seldom; 4 = occasionally; 5 = often; 6 = usually; 7 = always

__6__ 1. I let subordinates know what is expected of them.

__5__ 2. I maintain a friendly working relationship with subordinates.

__6__ 3. I consult with subordinates when facing a problem.

__6__ 4. I listen receptively to subordinates' ideas and suggestions.

__6__ 5. I inform subordinates about what needs to be done and how it needs to be done.

__7__ 6. I let subordinates know that I expect them to perform at their highest level.

__2__ 7. I act without consulting my subordinates.

__3__ 8. I do little things to make it pleasant to be a member of the group.

__5__ 9. I ask subordinates to follow standard rules and regulations.

__5__ 10. I set goals for subordinates' performance that are quite challenging.

__3__ 11. I say things that hurt subordinates' personal feelings.

__6__ 12. I ask for suggestions from subordinates concerning how to carry out assignments.

__6__ 13. I encourage continual improvement in subordinates' performance.

__6__ 14. I explain the level of performance that is expected of subordinates.

__7__ 15. I help subordinates overcome problems that stop them from carrying out their tasks.

__3__ 16. I show that I have doubts about their ability to meet most objectives.

__5__ 17. I ask subordinates for suggestions on what assignments should be made.

__2__ 18. I give vague explanations of what is expected of subordinates on the job.

__5__ 19. I consistently set challenging goals for subordinates to attain.

__6__ 20. I behave in a manner that is thoughtful of subordinates' personal needs.

SOURCE: Adapted from *A Path-Goal Theory Investigation of Superior Subordinate Relationships,* by J. Indvik, unpublished doctoral dissertation, University of Wisconsin, Madison, 1985, and Indvik (1988). Based on the work of House and Dessler (1974) and House (1976) cited in Fulk and Wendler (1982). Used by permission.

SCORING:

1. Reverse the scores for items 7, 11, 16, and 18.
2. Directive Style: Sum of scores on items 1, 5, 9, 14, and 18.
3. Supportive Style: Sum of scores on items 2, 8, 11, 15, and 20.
4. Participative Style: Sum of scores on items 3, 4, 7, 12, and 17.
5. Achievement-oriented: Sum of scores on items 6, 10, 13, 16, and 19.

Scoring Interpretation

- *Directive style,* a common score is 23; scores above 28 are considered high and scores below 18 are considered low.

- *Supportive style,* a common score is 28; scores above 33 are considered high and scores below 23 are considered low.

- *Participative style,* a common score is 21; scores above 26 are considered high and scores below 16 are considered low.

- *Achievement-oriented style,* a common score is 19; scores above 24 are considered high and scores below 14 are considered low.

The scores you received on the path-goal questionnaire provide information about which style of leadership you use most often and which you use less frequently. In addition, these scores can be used to assess your use of each style relative to your use of the other styles.

According to the principles of path-goal theory, if your scores matched these hypothetical scores, you would be effective in situations where the tasks and procedures are unclear and your subordinates have a need for certainty. You would be less effective in work settings that are structured and unchallenging. In addition, you would be moderately effective in ambiguous situations with subordinates who want control. Lastly, you would do very well in uncertain situations where you could set high standards, challenge subordinates to meet these standards, and help them feel confident in their abilities.

In addition to the Path-Goal Leadership Questionnaire, leadership researchers have commonly used multiple instruments to study the path-goal theory, including measures of task structure, locus of control, employee expectancies, employee satisfaction, and others. Although the primary use of these instruments has been for theory building, many of the instruments offer valuable information related to practical leadership issues.

Summary

Path-goal theory was developed to explain how leaders motivate sub-ordinates to be productive and satisfied with their work. It is a contingency approach to leadership because effectiveness depends on the "fit" between the leader's behavior and the characteristics of sub-ordinates and the task.

The basic principles of path-goal theory are derived from expectancy theory, which suggests that employees will be motivated if they feel competent, if they think their efforts will be rewarded, and if they find the payoff for their work is valuable. A leader can help subordinates by selecting a style of leadership (directive, supportive, participative, or achievement oriented) that provides "what is missing" for subordinates in a particular work setting. In simple terms, it is the leader's responsibility to help subordinates to reach their goals by directing, guiding, and coaching them along the way.

Path-goal theory offers a large set of predictions for how a leader's style interacts with subordinates' needs and the nature of the task. Among other things, it predicts that directive leadership is effective with ambiguous tasks, that supportive leadership is effective for repetitive tasks, that participative leadership is effective when tasks are unclear and subordinates are autonomous, and that achievement-oriented leadership is effective for challenging tasks.

Path-goal theory has three major strengths. First, it provides a theoretical framework that is useful for understanding how directive, supportive, participative, and achievement-oriented styles of leadership affect the productivity and satisfaction of subordinates. Second, path-goal theory is unique in that it integrates the motivation principles of expectancy theory into a theory of leadership. Third, it provides a practical model that underscores the important ways that leaders help subordinates.

On the negative side, four criticisms can be leveled at path-goal theory. Foremost, the scope of path-goal theory encompasses so many interrelated sets of assumptions that it is hard to use this theory in a given organizational setting. Second, research findings to date do not support a full and consistent picture of the claims of the theory. Furthermore, path-goal theory does not show in a clear way how leader behaviors directly affect subordinate motivation levels. Lastly, path-goal theory is very leader oriented and fails to recognize the transactional nature of leadership. It does not promote subordinate involvement in the leadership process.

References

Evans, M. G. (1970). The effects of supervisory behavior on the path-goal relationship. *Organizational Behavior and Human Performance, 5,* 277-298.

Fulk, J., & Wendler, E. R. (1982). Dimensionality of leader-subordinate interactions: A path-goal investigation. *Organizational Behavior and Human Performance, 30,* 241-264.

Halpin, A. W., & Winer, B. J. (1957). A factorial study of the leader behavior descriptions. In R. M. Stogdill & A. E. Coons (Eds.), *Leader behavior: Its description and measurement.* Columbus: Ohio State University, Bureau of Business Research.

House, R. J. (1971). A path-goal theory of leader effectiveness. *Administrative Science Quarterly, 16,* 321-328.

House, R. J., & Dessler, G. (1974). The path-goal theory of leadership: Some post hoc and a priori tests. In J. Hunt & L. Larson (Eds.), *Contingency approaches in leadership* (pp. 29-55). Carbondale: Southern Illinois University Press.

House, R. J., & Mitchell, R. R. (1974). Path-goal theory of leadership. *Journal of Contemporary Business, 3,* 81-97.

Indvik, J. (1986). Path-goal theory of leadership: A meta-analysis. *Proceeding of the Academy of Management Meeting,* 189-192.

Indvik, J. (1988). *A more complete testing of path-goal theory.* Paper presented at Academy of Management, Anaheim, California.

Schriesheim, C. A., & Kerr, S. (1977). Theories and measures of leadership: A critical appraisal. In J. G. Hunt & L. L. Larson (Eds.), *Leadership: The cutting edge* (pp. 9-45). Carbondale: Southern Illinois University Press.

Schriesheim, J. R., & Schriesheim, C. A. (1980). A test of the path-goal theory of leadership and some suggested directions for future research. *Personnel Psychology, 33,* 349-370.

Stinson, J. E., & Johnson, R. W. (1975). The path-goal theory of leadership: A partial test and suggested refinement. *Academy of Management Journal, 18,* 242-252.

Wofford, J. C., & Liska, L. Z. (1993). Path-goal theories of leadership: A meta-analysis. *Journal of Management, 19*(4), 857-876.

| # Leader-Member Exchange Theory

Description

Most of the leadership theories discussed thus far in the book have emphasized leadership from the point of view of the leader (e.g., trait approach and style approach) or the follower and the context (e.g., situational leadership, contingency theory, and path-goal theory). The Leader-member exchange (LMX) theory takes still another approach and conceptualizes leadership as a process that is centered in the interactions between leaders and followers. As Figure 7.1 illustrates, LMX theory makes the *dyadic relationship* between leaders and followers the focal point of the leadership process.

LMX theory was first described 25 years ago in the works of Dansereau, Graen, and Haga (1975), Graen and Cashman (1975), and Graen (1976). Since it first appeared it has undergone several revisions, and it continues to be of interest to researchers who study the leadership process.

Prior to LMX theory, researchers treated leadership as something leaders did toward all of their followers. This assumption implied

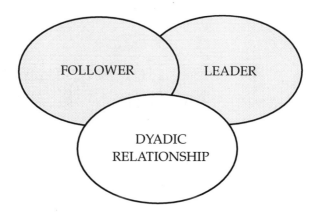

Figure 7.1. Dimensions of Leadership
SOURCE: Adapted from "Relationship-Based Approach to Leadership: Development of Leader-Member Exchange (LMX) Theory of Leadership Over 25 Years: Applying a Multi-Level, Multi-Domain Perspective," by G. B. Graen & M. Uhl-Bien, *Leadership Quarterly, 6*(2), 219-247, 1995.

that leaders treated followers in a collective way, as a group, using an average leadership style. The LMX theory challenged this assumption and directed researchers' attention to the differences that might exist between the leader and each of her or his followers.

Early Studies

In the first studies of exchange theory, which was then called vertical dyad linkage (VDL) Theory, researchers focused on the nature of the *vertical linkages* leaders formed with each of their followers (see Figure 7.2). A leader's relationship to the work unit as a whole was viewed as a series of vertical dyads (see Figure 7.3). In assessing the characteristics of these vertical dyads, researchers found two general types of linkages (or relationships): those that were based on expanded and negotiated role responsibilities (extra-roles), which were called the *in-group*, and a second set that were based on the formal employment contract (defined roles), which were called the *out-group* (see Figure 7.4).

Within an organizational work unit, subordinates become a part of the in-group or the out-group based on how well they work with the leader and how well the leader works with them. Personality and other personal characteristics are related to this process (Dansereau

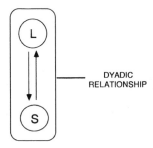

Figure 7.2. The Vertical Dyad. The leader forms an individualized working relationship with each of his or her subordinates. The exchanges (both content and process) between the leader and subordinate define their dyadic relationship.

et al., 1975). In addition, becoming part of one group or the other is based on how subordinates involve themselves in expanding their role responsibilities with the leader (Graen, 1976). Subordinates who are interested in negotiating with the leader what they are willing to do for the group can become a part of the in-group. These negotiations involve exchanges in which subordinates do certain activities that go beyond their formal job descriptions, and the leader, in turn, does more for these subordinates. If subordinates are not interested in taking on new and different job responsibilities, they become a part of the out-group.

Subordinates in the in-group receive more information, influence, confidence, and concern from their leaders than do out-group subordinates (Dansereau et al., 1975). In addition, they are more de-

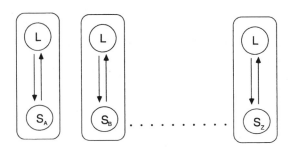

Figure 7.3. Vertical Dyads. The leader forms special relationships with all of his or her subordinates. Each of these relationships is special and has its own unique characteristics.

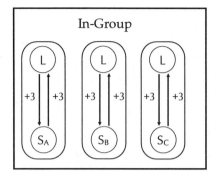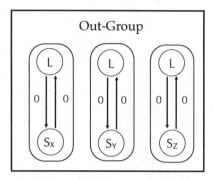

Figure 7.4. In-Groups and Out-Groups. A leader and his or her subordinate form unique relationships. Relationships within the in-group are marked by mutual trust, respect, liking, and reciprocal influence. Relationships within the out-group are marked by formal communication based on job descriptions. Plus 3 is a high-quality relationship and zero is a stranger.

pendable, more highly involved, and more communicative than out-group subordinates (Dansereau et al., 1975). Whereas in-group members do extra things for the leader and the leader does the same for them, subordinates in the out-group are less compatible with the leader and usually just come to work, do their job, and go home.

Later Studies

After the first set of studies there was a shift in the focus of LMX theory. Whereas the initial studies of this theory primarily addressed the nature of the differences between in-groups and out-groups, a subsequent line of research addressed how LMX theory was related to organizational effectiveness. Specifically, these studies focused on how the quality of leader-member exchanges was related to positive outcomes for leaders, followers, groups, and the organization in general (Graen & Uhl-Bien, 1995). Researchers found that high-quality leader-member exchanges produced less employee turnover, more positive performance evaluations, higher frequency of promotions, greater organizational commitment, more desirable work assignments, better job attitudes, more attention and support from the leader, greater participation, and faster career progress over 25 years (Graen & Uhl-Bien, 1995; Liden, Wayne, & Stilwell, 1993).

In essence, the above findings clearly illustrate that organizations stand to gain much from having leaders who can create good working relationships. When leaders and followers have good exchanges, they feel better, accomplish more, and the organization prospers.

Leadership Making

The findings from the later studies were the impetus for the most current research on LMX theory, which focuses on how exchanges between leaders and subordinates can be used for "leadership making" (Graen & Uhl-Bien, 1991). Leadership making is a prescriptive approach to leadership that emphasizes that a leader should develop high-quality exchanges with all of her or his subordinates, rather than just a few. It attempts to make every subordinate feel as if he or she is a part of the in-group and, by so doing, avoids the inequities and negative implications of being in an out-group. In general, leadership making promotes building partnerships in which the leader tries to build effective dyads with all employees in the work unit (Graen & Uhl-Bien, 1995). In addition, leadership making suggests that leaders can create networks of partnerships throughout the organization, which will benefit the organization's goals as well as their own career progress.

Graen and Uhl-Bien (1991) suggest that leadership making develops progressively over time in three phases: (a) the stranger phase, (b) the acquaintance phase, and (c) the mature partnership phase (see Figure 7.5). During Phase 1, the stranger phase, the interactions within the leader-subordinate dyad are generally rule bound, relying heavily on contractual relationships. Leaders and subordinates relate to each other within prescribed organizational roles. They have lower quality exchanges, similar to those of out-group members that we discussed earlier in the chapter. The subordinate complies with the formal leader, who has hierarchical status for the purpose of achieving the economic rewards the leader controls. The motives of the subordinate during the stranger phase are directed toward self-interest rather than the good of the group (Graen & Uhl-Bien, 1995).

Phase 2, the acquaintance phase, begins with an "offer" by the leader or the subordinate for improved career-oriented social exchanges, which involve sharing more resources and personal or work-

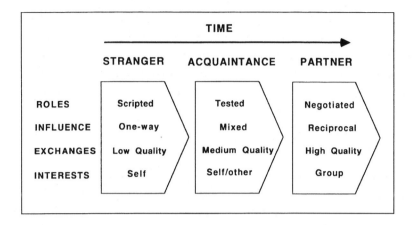

Figure 7.5. Phases in Leadership Making
SOURCE: Adapted from the Life Cycle of Leadership Making in "Relationship-Based Approach to Leadership: Development of Leader-Member Exchange (LMX) Theory of Leadership Over 25 Years: Applying a Multi-Level Multi-Domain Perspective," by G. B. Graen & M. Uhl-Bien, *Leadership Quarterly, 6*(2), p. 231, 1995.

related information. It is a testing period for both the leader and the subordinate to assess whether the subordinate is interested in taking on more roles and responsibilities, and to assess whether the leader is willing to provide new challenges for subordinates. During this time, dyads shift away from interactions that are strictly governed by job descriptions and defined roles and move toward new ways of relating. As measured by LMX theory, it could be said that the quality of their exchanges has improved. Successful dyads in the acquaintance phase begin to develop greater trust and respect for each other. They also tend to focus less on their own self-interests and more on the purposes and goals of the group.

Phase three, mature partnership, is marked by high-quality leader-member exchanges. Individuals who have progressed to this stage in their relationships experience a high degree of mutual trust, respect, and obligation toward each other. They have tested their relationship and found that they can depend on each other. In mature partnerships, there is a high degree of reciprocity between leaders and subordinates; each affects and is affected by the other. In addition, members may depend on each other for favors and special assistance. Leaders, for example, may rely on subordinates to do extra assignments, and subordinates may rely on leaders for needed support or encouragement. The point is that leaders and subordinates are tied together in productive ways that go well beyond a traditional hierarchically defined work relationship. They have developed an extremely effective way of relating that produces positive outcomes for both themselves and the organization. In effect, partnerships are transformational in that they assist leaders and followers in moving beyond their own self-interests to accomplish the greater good of the team and organization (see Chapter 8).

To evaluate leader-member exchanges, researchers have typically used a brief questionnaire that asks leaders and followers to report on the effectiveness of their working relationships. The questionnaire assesses the degree to which respondents express respect, trust, and obligation in their exchanges with others. At the end of this chapter, a version of the LMX questionnaire is provided for you to take for the purpose of analyzing some of your own leader-member relationships.

How Does LMX Theory Work?

LMX theory works in two ways: It describes leadership and it prescribes leadership. In both instances, the central concept is the dyadic relationship that a leader forms with each of her or his subordinates. Descriptively, LMX theory suggests it is important to recognize the existence of in-groups and out-groups within a group or organization.

The differences in how goals are accomplished using in-groups as compared to out-groups are substantial. Working with an in-group allows a leader to accomplish more work in a more effective manner than working without one. In-group members are willing to do more than is required in their job description and look for innovative ways to advance the group's goals. In response to their extra effort and devotion, leaders give them more responsibilities and more opportunities. Leaders also give in-group members more of their time and support.

Out-group members act quite differently from in-group members. Rather than trying to do extra work, out-group members operate strictly within their prescribed organizational roles. They do what is required of them, but nothing more. Leaders treat out-group members fairly and according to the formal contract but they do not give them special attention. For their efforts, out-group members receive the standard benefits as described by the job description.

Prescriptively, LMX theory is best understood within the Leadership Making Model of Graen and Uhl-Bien (1991). The authors advocate that leaders should create a special relationship with all subordinates, similar to those relationships described as in-group relationships. Leaders should offer each subordinate the opportunity to take on new roles and responsibilities. Furthermore, leaders should nurture high-quality exchanges with their subordinates. Rather than focusing on the differences between in-group and out-group members, the leadership making model suggests that leaders should look for ways to build trust and respect with all of their subordinates, thus making the entire work unit an in-group. In addition, leaders should look beyond their own work unit and create quality partnerships with individuals throughout the organization.

Whether descriptive or prescriptive, LMX theory works by focusing our attention on the special, unique relationship that leaders can create with others. When these relationships are of high quality, the goals of the leader, the followers, and the organization are all advanced.

Strengths

LMX theory makes several positive contributions to our understanding of the leadership process. First, it is a strong descriptive theory. Intuitively it makes sense to describe work units in terms of those who contribute more and those who contribute less or the bare minimum to the organization. Anyone who has ever worked in an organization has felt the presence of in-groups and out-groups. Despite the potential harm of out-groups, we all know that leaders have special relationships with certain people who do more and get more. We may not like this because it seems unfair, but it is a reality and the LMX theory has accurately described this situation. LMX theory validates our experience of how people within organizations relate to each other and the leader. Some contribute more and receive more; others contribute less and get less.

Second, LMX theory is unique because it is the only leadership approach that makes the concept of the dyadic relationship the centerpiece of the leadership process. Other approaches emphasize the characteristics of leaders, followers, contexts, or a combination of these, but none of them addresses the specific relationships between the leader and each subordinate. LMX theory underscores that effective leadership is contingent on effective leader-member exchanges.

Third, LMX theory is noteworthy because it directs our attention to the importance of communication in leadership. The high-quality exchanges advocated in LMX theory are inextricably bound to effective communication. Communication is the vehicle through which leaders and subordinates create, nurture, and sustain useful exchanges. Effective leadership occurs when the communication of leaders and subordinates is characterized by mutual trust, respect, and commitment.

Fourth, there is a large body of research that substantiates how the practice of LMX theory is related to positive organizational outcomes. In a review of this research, Graen and Uhl-Bien (1995) point out that it is related to performance, organizational commitment, job climate, innovation, organizational citizenship behavior, empowerment, procedural and distributive justice, career progress, and many other important organizational variables. By linking the use of LMX theory to real outcomes, researchers have been able to validate the theory and increase its practical value.

Criticisms

The most obvious criticism that can be made of LMX theory is that on the surface it runs counter to the basic human value of fairness. Throughout our lives, beginning when we were very young, we have been taught to try to get along with everyone and to treat everyone equally. We have been taught that it is wrong to form in-groups or cliques because they are harmful to those who cannot be a part of them. Because LMX theory divides the work unit into two groups and one group receives special attention, it gives the appearance of discrimination against the out-group.

Our culture is replete with examples of people of different genders, ages, cultures, and abilities who have been discriminated against. Although LMX theory was not designed to do so, it supports the development of privileged groups in the workplace. In so doing, it appears unfair and discriminatory. Furthermore, as reported by McClane (1991), the existence of in-groups and out-groups may have undesirable effects on the group as a whole. Whether LMX theory actually creates inequalities is questionable. If a leader does not intentionally keep out-group members "out," and if they are free to become members of the in-group, then LMX theory may not create inequalities. However, the theory does not elaborate on strategies for how one gains access to the in-group if one chooses.

A second criticism of LMX theory is that the basic ideas of the theory are not fully developed. For example, it fails to explain fully the way high-quality leader-member exchanges are created. In the early studies it was implied that they were formed because a leader found certain subordinates more compatible in regard to personality, interpersonal skills, or job competencies, but these studies never described the relative importance of these factors or how this process worked (Yukl, 1994). In more recent research, it is suggested that leaders should work to create high-quality exchanges with all subordinates, but the guidelines for how this is done are not clearly spelled out. For example, the model on leadership making highlights the importance of role making, incremental influence, and type of reciprocity (see Figure 7.5), but it does not explain how these concepts function to build mature partnerships. Similarly, the model strongly promotes building trust, respect, and obligation in leader-subordinate relationships, but it does not describe the means through which these factors are developed in relationships.

Third, there have been questions raised regarding the measurement of leader-member exchanges in LMX theory (Graen & Uhl-Bien, 1995). In past years, the measurement of exchanges was done with different versions of a leader-member exchange scale so the results were not always directly comparable. In addition, there have been questions regarding whether the standard scale used to measure exchanges is unidimensional or multidimensional (Graen & Uhl-Bien, 1995).

Application

Although LMX theory has not been packaged in a way to be used in standard management training and development programs, it offers many insights that managers could use to improve their own leadership behavior. Foremost, LMX theory directs managers to assess their leadership from a relationship perspective. This assessment will sensitize managers to how in-groups and out-groups develop within their own work unit. In addition, LMX theory suggests ways that managers can improve their work unit by building strong leader-member exchanges with all of their subordinates.

The ideas set forth in LMX theory can be used by managers at all levels within an organization. For example, LMX theory could be used to explain the way CEOs develop special relationships with select individuals in upper management to develop new strategic and tactical corporate goals. So, too, it could be used to explain how line managers in a plant use a select few workers to accomplish the production quotas of their work unit. The point is that the ideas presented in LMX theory have application throughout organizations.

In addition, the ideas of LMX theory can be used to explain how individuals create leadership networks throughout an organization to help them accomplish work more effectively (Graen & Scandura, 1987). A person with a network of high-quality partnerships can call on many people to help solve problems and advance the goals of the organization.

LMX theory can also be applied in different types of organizations. It applies in volunteer settings as well as traditional business, education, and government settings. Imagine a community leader who heads up a volunteer program to assist the elderly. To run the program effectively, the leader depends on a few of the volunteers who are more dependable and committed than the rest of the volunteers. This process of working closely with a small cadre of trusted volunteers is explained by the principles of LMX theory. Similarly, a manager of a traditional business setting might utilize certain individuals to achieve a major change in the company's policies and procedures. The way the manager goes about this process is explicated in LMX theory.

In summary, LMX theory tells us to be aware of how we relate to our subordinates. It tells us to be sensitive to whether some subordinates receive special attention and some subordinates do not. In addition, it tells us to be fair to all employees and allow each of them to become as much involved in the work of the unit as they want to be. LMX theory tells us to be respectful and to build trusting relationships with all of our subordinates, recognizing that each employee is unique and wants to relate to us in a special way.

Case Studies

In the following section, three case studies (Cases 7.1, 7.2, and 7.3) are presented to clarify how LMX theory can be applied to various group settings. The first case is about the creative director at an advertising agency, the second is about a production manager at a mortgage company, and the third describes the leadership of the manager of a district office of the Social Security Administration. Following each of the case studies, there are questions that will help you to analyze the case, using the ideas from LMX theory.

Case 7.1

Carly Peters directs the creative department of the advertising agency of Mills, Smith, & Peters. The agency has about 100 employees, 20 of whom work for Carly in the creative department. Typically, the agency maintains 10 major accounts as well as a number of smaller accounts. It has a reputation for being one of the best advertising and public relations agencies in the country.

In the creative department, there are four major account teams. Each is led by an associate creative director who reports directly to Carly. In addition, each team has a copywriter, an art director, and a production artist. At Mills, Smith, & Peters, the account teams are headed up by Jack, Terri, Julie, and Sarah.

Jack and his team get along really well with Carly and they have done excellent work for their clients at the agency. Of all the teams, Jack's team is the most creative and talented, and the most willing to go the extra mile for Carly. As a result, when Carly has to showcase accounts to upper management, she often uses the work of Jack's team. Jack and his team members are comfortable confiding with Carly and she with them. Carly is not afraid to allocate extra resources to Jack's team or to give them free rein on their accounts because they always come through for her.

Terri's team also performs well for the agency, but Terri is unhappy with how her team is treated by Carly. She feels that Carly is not fair because she favors Jack's team. For example, Terri's team was counseled out of pursuing an ad campaign because the campaign was too risky, whereas Jack's group was praised for developing a very provocative campaign. Terri feels that Jack's team is Carly's pet—they get the best assignments, accounts, and budgets. Terri finds it hard to hold back the animosity she feels toward Carly.

Like Terri, Julie is also concerned that her team is not in the inner circle, close to Carly. She has noticed repeatedly that Carly favors the other teams. For example, whenever additional people are assigned to team projects, it is always the other teams who get the best writers and art directors. Julie is mystified as to why Carly doesn't notice her team or try to help them with their work. She feels Carly undervalues her team because Julie knows the quality of her team's work is indisputable.

Although Sarah agrees with some of Terri's and Julie's observations about Carly, she does not feel any antagonism about Carly's leadership. Sarah has worked for the agency for nearly 10 years and nothing seems to bother her. Her account teams have never been "earth-shaking," but they have never been problematic either. Sarah views her team and its work more like a "nuts-and-bolts" operation in which the team is given an assignment and they carry it out. Being in Carly's inner circle would require putting in extra time in the evening or on weekends, and would create more headaches for Sarah. Hence, Sarah is happy with her role as it is, and she has little interest in trying to change the way the department works.

Questions

Based on the principles in LMX theory

- What observations would you make about Carly's leadership at Mills, Smith, & Peters?
- Is there an in-group and out-group and, if so, who are they?
- In what way is Carly's relationship with the four groups productive or counterproductive to the overall goals of the agency?
- Do you think Carly should change her approach toward the associate directors?
- If so, what should she do differently?

Case 7.2

City Mortgage is a medium-sized mortgage company that employs about 25 people. Jenny House, who has been with the company for 10 years, is the production manager who oversees its day-to-day operations. Reporting to Jenny are loan originators (sales people), closing officers, mortgage underwriters, and processing and shipping personnel. Jenny is proud of the company and feels as if she has contributed substantially to its steady growth and expansion.

The climate at City Mortgage is very positive. People like to come to work because the office environment is comfortable. They respect each other at the company and show tolerance for those who are different from themselves. Whereas at many mortgage companies it is common for resentments to build between individuals who earn different incomes, this is not the case at City Mortgage.

Jenny House's leadership has been instrumental in shaping the success of City Mortgage. Her philosophy stresses listening to employees and then determining how they can best contribute to the mission of the company. She makes a point of helping each individual explore her or his own talents and challenges each one to try new things.

At the annual holiday party, Jenny devised an interesting event that symbolizes her leadership style. She bought a large piece of colorful glass and had it cut into 25 pieces and handed out one piece to each person. Then she asked each employee to come forward with the piece of glass and briefly state what he or she liked about City Mortgage and how he or she felt he or she had contributed to the company in the past year. After the statements were made, the pieces of glass were formed into a cut glass window that hangs in the front lobby of the office. The glass is a reminder of how each individual contributes his or her uniqueness to the overall purpose of the company.

Another characteristic of Jenny's style is her fairness. She does not want to give anyone the impression that certain people have the "inside track," and she goes to great lengths to prevent this from happening. For example, she avoids social lunches because she thinks they foster the perception of favoritism. Similarly, even though her best friend is one of the loan originators, she is seldom seen talking with her, and if she is, it is always about business matters.

Ms. House also applies her fairness principle to how information is shared in the office. She does not want anyone to feel as if they are "out of the loop," so she tries very hard to keep everyone informed on all the matters that could affect them. Much of this she does through her open-door office policy. Jenny does not have a special group of employees with whom she confides her concerns; rather, she shares openly with each of them.

Jenny House is very committed to her work at City Mortgage. She works long hours and carries a beeper on the weekend. At this point in her career, her only concern is that she could be burning out.

Questions

Based on the LMX model, which was presented in Figure 7.5

- How would you describe Jenny House's leadership?
- How do you think the employees at City Mortgage respond to Jenny?
- If you were asked to follow in the footsteps of Ms. House, do you think you could or would want to manage City Mortgage with a similar style?

Case 7.3

Jim Madison is manager of a district office for the Social Security Administration. The office serves a community of 200,000 people and has a staff of 30 employees, most of whom work as claims representatives. The primary work of the office is to provide the public with information about social security benefits, and to process retirement, survivor, disability, and Medicare claims.

Mr. Madison has been the manager of the office for 6 years, and during that time has made a considerable number of improvements in the overall operations of the office. People in the community have a favorable view of the office and have few complaints about the services it provides. On the annual survey of community service organizations, the district office receives consistently high marks for overall effectiveness and customer satisfaction.

Almost all of the employees who work for Jim have been employed at the district office for 6 years or more, one employee having been there for 22 years. Although Jim takes pride in knowing all of them personally, he calls on a few of them more frequently to help him accomplish his goals.

When it comes to training staff members about new laws affecting claims procedures, Mr. Madison relies heavily on two particular claims representatives, Shirley and Patti, both of whom are very knowledgeable and competent. Shirley and Patti view the additional training responsibilities as a challenge. This helps Jim because he does not need to do the job himself nor supervise them closely because they are highly respected people within the office and they have a history of being mature and conscientious about their work. Shirley and Patti like the additional responsibilities because it gives them greater recognition as well as increased benefits from receiving positive job appraisals.

To showcase the office's services to the community, Mr. Madison calls on two other employees, Ted and Jana. Ted and Jana serve as field representatives for the office and give presentations to community organizations about the nature of social security and how it serves the citizens of the district. In addition, they speak on local radio stations, answering call-in questions about the various complexities of social security benefits.

Although many of the claims people in the office could act as field representatives, Mr. Madison typically calls on Ted and Jana because of their willingness to take on the public relations challenge and because of their special capabilities in this area. This is advantageous for Jim for two reasons: One, these individuals do an outstanding job in representing the office to the public, and two, Jim is a reticent person and he finds it quite threatening to be in the public's eye. Ted and Jana like to take on this additional role because it gives them added prestige and greater freedom. Being a field representative has its perks because field staff can actually function as their own bosses when they are not in the office—they can set their own schedules and come and go as they please.

A third area in which Mr. Madison calls on a few representatives for added effort is in helping him supervise the slower claims representatives who seem to be continually behind in writing up the case reports of their clients. When even a few staff get behind with their work, it affects the entire office operation. To ameliorate this problem, Jim calls on Glenda and Annie, who are both highly talented, to help the slower staff complete their case reports. Although it means taking on more work themselves, Glenda and Annie do it to be kind and to help the office run smoother. Other than personal satisfaction, no additional benefits accrue to these individuals for taking on the additional responsibilities.

Overall, the people who work under Mr. Madison's leadership are satisfied with his supervision. There are some who feel that he caters too much to a few special representatives, but most of the staff think Jim is fair and impartial. Even though he depends more on these few, Jim tries very hard to attend to the wants and needs of his entire staff.

Questions

From an LMX theory point of view

- How would you describe Jim Madison's leadership at the district social security office?
- Can you identify an in-group and an out-group?

- Do you think the trust and respect Jim places in some of his staff is productive or counterproductive?
- Why?

Leadership Instrument

Many different questionnaires have been used by researchers to study LMX theory. All of them have been designed to measure the quality of the working relationship between leaders and followers. We have selected to include in this chapter the LMX 7, a 7-item questionnaire that provides a reliable and valid measure of the quality of leader-member exchanges (Graen & Uhl-Bien, 1995).

The LMX 7 is designed to measure three dimensions of leader-member relationships: respect, trust, and obligation. It assesses the degree to which leaders and followers have mutual respect for each other's capabilities, feel a deepening sense of reciprocal trust, and have a strong sense of obligation to one another. Taken together, these dimensions are the ingredients necessary to create strong partnerships.

By completing the LMX 7, you can gain a fuller understanding of how LMX theory works. The score you obtain on the questionnaire is reflective of the quality of your leader-member relationship(s), and it indicates the degree to which your relationships are characteristic of partnerships, as described in the LMX model.

You can complete the questionnaire both as a leader and as a subordinate. In the leader role, you can complete the questionnaire multiple times, making an assessment of the quality of the relationships you have with each one of your subordinates. In the subordinate role, you would complete the questionnaire based on the leader(s) to whom you report.

Although the LMX 7 is most commonly used by researchers to explore theoretical questions, it can also be used to analyze your own leadership. The scores you obtain on the LMX 7 can be interpreted using the following guidelines: very high = 30-35, high = 25-29, moderate = 20-24, low = 15-19, and very low = 7-14. Scores in the upper range are indicative of stronger, higher-quality leader-member exchanges (e.g., in-group members), whereas scores in the lower ranges are indicative of exchanges of lesser quality (e.g., out-group members).

LMX 7 Questionnaire

INSTRUCTIONS: This questionnaire contains items that ask you to describe your relationship with either your leader or one of your subordinates. For each of the items, indicate the degree to which you think the item is true for you by circling one of the responses that appear below the item.

1. Do you know where you stand with your leader (follower) . . . do you usually know how satisfied your leader (follower) is with what you do?

Rarely	Occasionally	Sometimes	Fairly often	Very often
1	2	(3)	4	5

2. How well does your leader (follower) understand your job problems and needs?

Not a bit	A little	A fair amount	Quite a bit	A great deal
1	(2)	3	4	5

3. How well does your leader (follower) recognize your potential?

Not at all	A little	Moderately	Mostly	Fully
1	(2)	3	4	5

4. Regardless of how much formal authority he or she has built into his or her position, what are the chances that your leader (follower) would use his or her power to help you solve problems in your work?

None	Small	Moderate	High	Very high
1	2	(3)	4	5

5. Again, regardless of the amount of formal authority your leader (follower) has, what are the chances that he or she would "bail you out" at his or her expense?

None	Small	Moderate	High	Very high
(1)	2	3	4	5

6. I have enough confidence in my leader (follower) that I would defend and justify his or her decision if he or she were not present to do so.

Strongly disagree	Disagree	Neutral	Agree	Strongly agree
(1)	2	3	4	5

7. How would you characterize your working relationship with your leader (follower)?

Extremely ineffective	Worse than average	Average	Better than average	Extremely effective
(1)	2	3	4	5

SOURCE: Based on an version of the LMX 7 that appears in an article by G. B. Graen & M. Uhl-Bien in *Leadership Quarterly*, 6(2), p. 237, 1995. Used by permission of JAI Press, Inc.

Summary

Since it first appeared 25 years ago, under the title "vertical dyad linkage theory," LMX theory has been and continues to be a much-studied approach to leadership. LMX theory addresses leadership as a process centered in the interactions between leaders and followers. It makes the leader-member relationship the pivotal concept in the leadership process.

In the early studies of LMX theory, a leader's relationship to the overall work unit was viewed as a series of vertical dyads, categorized as being of two different types. Leader-member dyads based on expanded role relationships were called the leader's in-group, and those based on formal job descriptions were called the out-group. It is believed that subordinates become in-group members based on how well they get along with the leader and whether they are willing to expand their role responsibilities. Subordinates who maintain only formal hierarchical relationships with their leader become out-group members. While in-group members receive extra influence, opportunities, and rewards, out-group members receive standard job benefits.

Subsequent studies of LMX theory were directed toward how leader-member exchanges affected organizational performance. Researchers found that high-quality exchanges between leaders and followers produced multiple positive outcomes (e.g., less employee turnover, greater organizational commitment, and more promotions). In general, researchers determined that good leader-member exchanges resulted in followers feeling better, accomplishing more, and helping the organization prosper.

The most recent emphasis in LMX research has been on leadership making, which emphasizes that leaders should try to develop high-quality exchanges with all of their subordinates. Leadership making develops over time and includes a stranger phase, acquaintance phase, and partner phase. By taking on and fulfilling new role responsibilities, followers move through these three phases to develop mature partnerships with their leaders. These partnerships, which are marked by a high degree of mutual trust, respect, and obligation toward one another, have positive payoffs for the individuals themselves and they also help the organization run more effectively.

There are several positive features to LMX theory. First, LMX theory is a strong descriptive approach that explains how leaders utilize some subordinates (in-group members) more than others (out-group members) to accomplish organizational goals effectively. Second, LMX theory is unique in that, unlike other approaches, it makes the leader-member relationship the focal point of the leadership process. Related to this focus, LMX theory is noteworthy because it directs our attention to the importance of effective communication in leader-member relationships. Lastly, LMX theory is supported by a multitude of studies that link high-quality leader-member exchanges to positive organizational outcomes.

There are also negative features in LMX theory. Foremost, LMX theory runs counter to our principles of fairness and justice in the workplace by suggesting that some members of the work unit receive special attention and others do not. The perceived inequalities created by the use of in-groups can have a devastating impact on the feelings, attitudes, and behavior of out-group members. Second, LMX theory emphasizes the importance of leader-member exchanges, but fails to explain the intricacies of how one goes about creating high-quality exchanges. Although the model promotes building trust, respect, and commitment in relationships, it does not fully explicate how this takes place. Finally, there are questions regarding whether the principal measure of LMX theory is sufficiently refined to measure the complexities of leadership.

References

Dansereau, F., Graen, G. G., & Haga, W. (1975). A vertical dyad linkage approach to leadership in formal organizations. *Organizational Behavior and Human Performance, 13*, 46-78.

Graen, G. B. (1976). Role-making processes within complex organizations. In M. D. Dunnette (Ed.), *Handbook of industrial and organizational psychology* (pp. 1202-1245). Chicago: Rand McNally.

Graen, G. B., & Cashman, J. (1975). A role-making model of leadership in formal organizations: A developmental approach. In J. G. Hunt & L. L. Larson (Eds.), *Leadership frontiers* (pp. 143-166). Kent, OH: Kent State University Press.

Graen, G. B., & Scandura, T. A. (1987). Toward a psychology of dyadic organizing. In B. Staw & L. L. Cumming (Eds.), *Research in organizational behavior* (Vol. 9, pp. 175-208). Greenwich, CT: JAI.

Graen, G. B., & Uhl-Bien, M. (1991). The transformation of professionals into self-managing and partially self-designing contributions: Toward a theory of leader-making. *Journal of Management Systems, 3*(3), 33-48.

Graen, G. B., & Uhl-Bien, M. (1995). Relationship-based approach to leadership: Development of leader-member exchange (LMX) theory of leadership over 25 years: Applying a multi-level multi-domain perspective. *Leadership Quarterly, 6*(2), 219-247.

Liden, R. C., Wayne, S. J., & Stilwell, D. (1993). A longitudinal study on the early development of leader-member exchange. *Journal of Applied Psychology, 78,* 662-674.

McClane, W. E. (1991). Implications of member role differentiation: Analysis of a key concept in the LMX model of leadership. *Group & Organization Studies, 16*(1), 102-113.

Yukl, G. (1994). *Leadership in organizations* (3rd ed.). Englewood Cliffs, NJ: Prentice Hall.

CHAPTER 8

Transformational Leadership

Description

One of the current approaches to leadership that has been the focus of much research since the early 1980s is the transformational approach. It is part of "the New Leadership" paradigm (Bryman, 1992). As its name implies, transformational leadership is a process that changes and transforms individuals. It is concerned with values, ethics, standards, and long-term goals. Transformational leadership involves assessing followers' motives, satisfying their needs, and treating them as full human beings. It is a process that subsumes charismatic and visionary leadership.

Transformational leadership is an encompassing approach that can be used to describe a wide range of leadership, from very specific attempts to influence followers on a one-to-one level, to very broad attempts to influence whole organizations and even entire cultures. Although the transformational leader plays a pivotal role in precipitating change, followers and leaders are inextricably bound together in the transformation process.

Transformational Leadership Defined

The term *transformational leadership* was first coined by Downton (1973); however, its emergence as an important approach to leadership began with a classic work by the political sociologist James MacGregor Burns titled *Leadership* (1978). In his work, Burns attempts to link the roles of leadership and followership. He writes of leaders as those individuals who tap the motives of followers in order to better reach the goals of leaders and followers (p. 18). For Burns, leadership is quite different from wielding power because it is inseparable from followers' needs.

Burns distinguishes between two types of leadership: transactional and transformational. *Transactional leadership* refers to the bulk of leadership models, which focus on the exchanges that occur between leaders and their followers. Politicians who win votes by promising no new taxes are demonstrating transactional leadership. Similarly, managers who offer promotions to employees who surpass their goals are exhibiting transactional leadership. In the classroom, teachers are being transactional when they give students a grade for work completed. The exchange dimension of transactional leadership is very common and can be observed at many levels throughout all types of organizations.

In contrast to transactional leadership, *transformational leadership* refers to the process whereby an individual engages with others and creates a connection that raises the level of motivation and morality in both the leader and the follower. This type of leader is attentive to the needs and motives of followers and tries to help followers reach their fullest potential. Burns points to Mahatma Gandhi as a classic example of transformational leadership. Gandhi raised the hopes and demands of millions of his people and in the process was changed himself. A more recent example of transformational leadership can be observed in the life of Ryan White. Ryan White raised the American people's awareness about AIDS and in the process became a spokesperson for increasing government support of AIDS research. In the organizational world, an example of transformational leadership would be a manager who attempts to change his or her company's corporate values to reflect a more human standard of fairness and justice. In the process, both the manager and followers may emerge with a stronger and higher set of moral values.

Transformational Leadership and Charisma

At about the same time Burns's book was published, House (1976) published a theory of charismatic leadership. Since its publication, charismatic leadership has received a great deal of attention by researchers. It is often described in ways that make it similar, to if not synonymous with, transformational leadership.

The concept "charisma" was first used to describe a special gift that select individuals possess that gives them the capacity to do extraordinary things. Weber (1947) provided the most well-known definition of charisma as a special personality characteristic that gives a person superhuman or exceptional powers and is reserved for a few, is of divine origin, and results in the person being treated as a leader. Despite Weber's emphasis on charisma as a personality characteristic, he also recognized the important role played by followers in validating charisma in these leaders (Bryman, 1992; House, 1976).

In his theory of charismatic leadership, House suggested that charismatic leaders act in unique ways that have specific charismatic effects on their followers (see Figure 8.1). For House, the personal characteristics of a charismatic leader include being dominant, having a strong desire to influence others, being self-confident, and having a strong sense of one's own moral values.

In addition to displaying certain personality characteristics, charismatic leaders also demonstrate specific types of behaviors. First, they are strong role models for the beliefs and values they want their followers to adopt. For example, Gandhi advocated nonviolence and was an exemplary role model of civil disobedience. Second, charismatic leaders appear competent to followers. Third, they articulate ideological goals that have moral overtones. Martin Luther King Jr.'s famous "I Have a Dream" speech is an example of this type of charismatic behavior.

Fourth, charismatic leaders communicate high expectations for followers, and they exhibit confidence in followers' abilities to meet these expectations. The impact of this behavior is to increase followers' sense of competence and self-efficacy (Avolio & Gibbons, 1988), which in turn increases their performance. Fifth, charismatic leaders arouse task-relevant motives in followers that may include affiliation, power, or esteem. For example, John F. Kennedy appealed to the human values of the American people when he stated, "Ask not what your country can do for you; ask what you can do for your country."

Personality Characteristics	Behaviors	Effects on Followers
Dominant	Sets strong role model	Trust in leader's ideology
Desire to influence	Shows competence	Belief similarity between leader and follower
Confident	Articulates goals	Unquestioning acceptance
Strong values	Communicates high expectations	Affection toward leader
	Expresses confidence	Obedience
	Arouses motives	Identification with leader
		Emotional involvement
		Heightened goals
		Increased confidence

Figure 8.1. Personality Characteristics, Behaviors, and Effects on Followers of Charismatic Leadership

According to House's charismatic theory, there are several effects that are the direct result of charismatic leadership. They include follower trust in the leader's ideology, similarity between the follower's beliefs and the leader's beliefs, unquestioning acceptance of the leader, expression of warmth toward the leader, follower obedience, identification with the leader, emotional involvement in the leader's goals, heightened goals for followers, and follower confidence in goal achievement. Consistent with Weber, House contends that these charismatic effects are more likely to occur in contexts in which followers feel distress, because in stressful situations followers look to leaders to deliver them from their difficulties.

A Model of Transformational Leadership

In the mid-1980s, Bass (1985) provided a more expanded and refined version of transformational leadership that was based on, but not fully consistent with, the prior works of Burns (1978) and House (1976). In his approach, Bass extended Burns's work by giving more attention to followers' rather than leaders' needs, by suggesting that transformational leadership could apply to situations in which the outcomes were not positive, and by describing transactional and transformational leadership as a single continuum (see Figure 8.2) rather than mutually independent continua (Yammarino, 1993). Bass extended House's work

Figure 8.2. Leadership as a Single Continuum From Transformational to Laissez-Faire Leadership

by giving more attention to the emotional elements and origins of charisma, and by suggesting that charisma is a necessary but not sufficient condition for transformational leadership (Yammarino, 1993).

Bass (1985) argues that transformational leadership motivates followers to do more than the expected by doing the following: (a) raising followers' levels of consciousness about the importance and value of specified and idealized goals, (b) getting followers to transcend their own self-interest for the sake of the team or organization, and (c) moving followers to address higher-level needs (p. 20). An elaboration of the dynamics of the transformation process is provided in his Model of Transformational and Transactional Leadership (Bass, 1985, 1990; Bass & Avolio, 1993, 1994). As can be seen in Figure 8.3, the model of transformational and transactional leadership incorporates seven different factors. These factors are also illustrated in the Full Range of Leadership Model, which is provided in Figure 8.4. A discussion of each of these seven factors will help to clarify Bass's model. This discussion will be divided into three parts: transformational factors (4), transactional factors (3), and the nonleadership/nontransactional factor (1).

Transformational Leadership Factors

Transformational leadership is concerned with the performance of followers and also with developing followers to their fullest potential (Bass & Avolio, 1990a). Individuals who exhibit transformational leadership often have a strong set of internal values and ideals, and they are effective at motivating followers to act in ways that support the greater good rather than their own self-interests (Kuhnert, 1994).

Idealized Influence

Factor 1 is called *charisma* or *idealized influence*. It describes leaders who act as strong role models for followers; followers identify

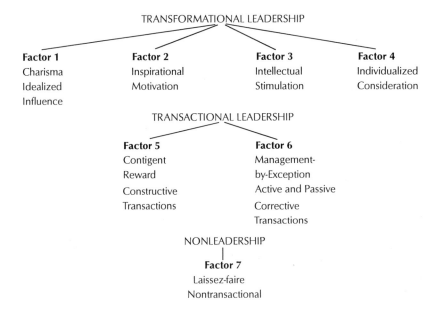

Figure 8.3. A Model of Transformational and Transactional Leadership: Leadership Factors From Nonleadership to Transformational Leadership

with these leaders and want very much to emulate them. These leaders usually have very high standards of moral and ethical conduct and can be counted on to do the right thing. They are deeply respected by followers, who usually place a great deal of trust in them. They provide followers with a vision and a sense of mission.

In essence, the charisma factor describes individuals who are special and who make others want to follow the vision they put forward. A person whose leadership exemplifies the charisma factor is Nelson Mandela, the first nonwhite president of South Africa. Mandela is viewed as a leader with high moral standards and a vision for South Africa that resulted in monumental change in how the people of South Africa would be governed. His charismatic qualities and the people's response to them transformed an entire nation.

Inspirational Motivation

Factor 2 is labeled *inspiration* or *inspirational motivation*. This factor is descriptive of leaders who communicate high expectations

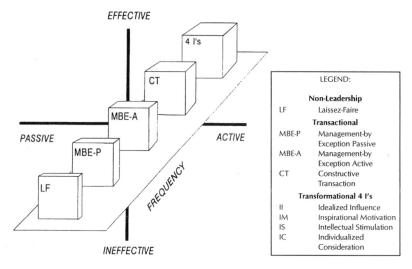

Figure 8.4. Full Range of Leadership Model
SOURCE: B. M. Bass & B. J. Avolio (1994). Used with permission of the author.

to followers, inspiring them through motivation to become committed to and a part of the shared vision in the organization. In practice, leaders use symbols and emotional appeals to focus group members' efforts to achieve more than they would in their own self-interest. Team spirit is enhanced by this type of leadership. An example of this factor would be a sales manager who motivates his or her sales force to excel in their work through encouraging words and pep talks that clearly communicate the integral role they play in the future growth of the company.

Intellectual Stimulation

Factor 3 refers to *intellectual stimulation.* It includes leadership that stimulates followers to be creative and innovative, and to challenge their own beliefs and values as well as those of the leader and the organization. This type of leadership supports followers as they try new approaches and develop innovative ways of dealing with organizational issues. It promotes followers thinking things out on their own and engaging in careful problem solving. An example of this type of leadership is a plant manager who promotes workers' individual efforts to develop unique ways to solve problems that have caused slowdowns in production.

Individualized Consideration

Factor 4 of the transformational factors is called *individualized consideration*. This factor is representative of leaders who provide a supportive climate in which they listen carefully to the individual needs of followers. Leaders act as coaches and advisors while trying to assist individuals in becoming fully actualized. These leaders may use delegation as a means to help followers grow through personal challenges. An example of this type of leadership is a manager who spends time treating each employee in a caring and unique way. For some employees the leader may give strong affiliation, while for others the leader may give specific directives with a high degree of structure.

In essence, transformational leadership produces greater effects than transactional leadership (see Figure 8.5). While transactional leadership results in expected outcomes, transformational leadership results in performance that goes well beyond what is expected. Transformational leadership helps followers to transcend their own self-interests for the good of the group or organization (Bass & Avolio, 1990a).

Transactional Leadership Factors

Transactional leadership diverges from transformational leadership in that the transactional leader does not individualize the needs of subordinates nor focus on their personal development. Transactional leaders exchange things of value with subordinates to advance their own as well as their subordinates' agenda (Kuhnert, 1994). Transactional leaders are influential because it is in the best interest of subordinates to do what the leader wants (Kuhnert & Lewis, 1987).

Contingent Reward

Factor 5, labeled *contingent reward*, is the first of two transactional leadership factors (see Figure 8.3). It refers to an exchange process between leaders and followers in which effort by followers is exchanged for specified rewards. With this kind of leadership, the leader tries to obtain agreement from followers on what needs to be done and what the payoffs will be for the people doing it. An example of this type of transaction is a parent who negotiates with a child how much television she or he can watch after practicing on the piano.

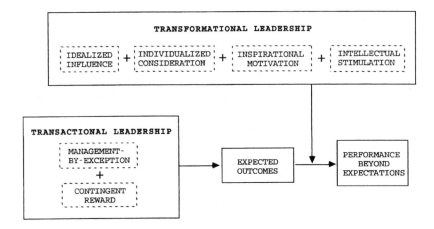

Figure 8.5. The Additive Effect of Transformational Leadership
SOURCE: Adapted from B. M. Bass & B. J. Avolio, "The Implications of Transactional and Transformational Leadership for Individual, Team, and Organizational Development," 1990, *Research in Organizational Change and Development, 4,* 231-272.

Another example often occurs in the academic setting—a dean negotiates with a college professor about the number and quality of publications he or she needs in order to receive tenure and promotion.

Management-by-Exception

Factor 6 is labeled in the model as *management-by-exception* and refers to leadership that involves corrective criticism, negative feedback, and negative reinforcement. Management-by-exception takes two forms: active and passive. A leader using the active form of management-by-exception watches followers closely for mistakes or rule violations and then takes corrective action. An example of active management-by-exception can be illustrated in the leadership of a sales supervisor who daily monitors how employees approach customers; she quickly corrects those sales people who are slow to approach customers in the prescribed manner. A leader using the passive form intervenes only after standards have not been met or problems have arisen. An example of passive management-by-exception is illustrated in the leadership of a supervisor who gives an employee a poor performance evaluation without ever talking with the employee about her or his prior work performance. In essence, both the active and passive management types use more negative reinforcement patterns than the positive reinforcement pattern described in Factor 5 under contingent reward.

Nonleadership Factor

In the model, the nonleadership factor diverges further from transactional leadership and represents behaviors that are nontransactional.

Laissez-Faire

Factor 7 describes leadership that falls at the far right side of the transactional-transformational leadership continuum (see Figure 8.2). This factor represents the absence of leadership. As the French phrase implies, the laissez-faire leader takes a "hands-off—let-things-ride" approach. This leader abdicates responsibility, delays decisions, gives no feedback, and makes little effort to help followers satisfy their needs. There is no exchange with followers or any attempt to help them grow. An example of a laissez-faire leader is the president of a small manufacturing firm who calls no meetings with plant supervisors, has no long-range plan for her or his company, and makes little contact with employees within the organization.

Other Transformational Perspectives

In addition to Bass's work, two other lines of research have contributed in unique ways to our understanding of the nature of transformational leadership. They are the research of Bennis and Nanus (1985) and the work of Tichy and DeVanna (1986, 1990). The methods used by these researchers to collect data were quite similar. They simply identified a number of CEOs or leaders at large corporations and then interviewed them, using a relatively unstructured open-ended question-and-answer format.

Bennis and Nanus

Bennis and Nanus asked 90 leaders basic questions such as: What are your strengths and weaknesses? What past events most influenced your leadership approach? What were the critical points in your career? From the answers leaders provided to these questions, Bennis and Nanus identified four common strategies utilized by leaders in transforming organizations.

First, transforming leaders had a clear *vision* of the future state of their organizations. It was an image of an attractive, realistic, and believable future (Bennis & Nanus, 1985, p. 89). The vision was usually simple, understandable, beneficial, and energy creating. The compelling nature of the vision touched the experiences of followers and pulled them into supporting the organization. When an organization has a clear vision it is easier for individuals within the organization to learn how they fit in with the overall direction of the organization and even the society in general. It empowers them because they feel they are a significant dimension of a worthwhile enterprise (pp. 90-91). Bennis and Nanus found that in order to be successful, the vision needed to grow out of the needs of the entire organization and be claimed by those within it. Although leaders play a large role in articulating the vision, the emergence of the vision originates from both the leaders and the followers within the organization.

Second, transforming leaders were *social architects* for their organizations. This means they created a shape or form for the shared meanings individuals maintained within their organizations. These leaders communicated a direction that transformed their organization's values and norms. In many cases these leaders were able to mobilize people to accept a new group identity or a new philosophy for their organizations.

Third, transforming leaders *created trust* in their organizations by making their own positions clearly known and then standing by them. Trust has to do with being predictable or reliable, even in situations that are uncertain. For organizations, leaders built trust by articulating a direction and then consistently implementing the direction even though the vision may have involved a high degree of uncertainty. Bennis and Nanus (1985) found that when leaders established trust in an organization it gave the organization a sense of integrity analogous to a healthy identity (p. 48).

Fourth, transforming leaders used *creative deployment of self through positive self-regard*. Leaders knew their strengths and weaknesses and they emphasized their strengths rather than dwelling on their weaknesses. Based on an awareness of their own competence, effective leaders were able to immerse themselves in their tasks and the overarching goals of their organizations. They were able to fuse a sense of self with the work at hand. Bennis and Nanus also found that positive self-regard in leaders had a reciprocal impact on followers, creating in them feelings of confidence and high expectations. In addition, leaders in the study were committed to learning and relearning, so in their organizations there was consistent emphasis on education.

Tichy and DeVanna

Similar to Bennis and Nanus, Tichy and DeVanna studied the transformational leadership of 12 CEOs at mostly large corporations. Tichy and DeVanna were interested in how organizations change— how they are transformed. In particular, they were concerned with how leaders carried out the change process.

Tichy and DeVanna wanted to find out how leaders worked under the challenging conditions brought about by rapid technological change, social and cultural changes, increased competition, and increased interdependence with economies of other nations. The data from their interviews suggested that leaders manage change in organizations through a *three-act process.*

Act 1 of this transformation process involves recognizing the need for change. There is a tendency for organizations and individuals within organizations to be comfortable with the status quo and to resist change. People want to sustain the present system. As a result, the need for change may go unrecognized. Transformational leaders are change agents. They have the responsibility of pointing out to the organization how change in the environment could positively or negatively affect how the organization operates.

Tichy and DeVanna suggest several techniques that can assist organizations in increasing their openness to change. First, encourage dissent and allow people to disagree. Next, encourage objective assessment of how well the organization is meeting its goals. Third, encourage members of the organization to visit other organizations within and outside the organization to obtain alternative viewpoints of how other organizations work and solve problems. Last, encourage organizations to assess their performance based on a wide range of economic and noneconomic indicators relative to other companies on these same indicators.

Act 2 in the change process requires the creation of a vision. The vision acts as a conceptual road map for where the organization is headed in the future and what it will look like (Tichy & DeVanna, 1990, p. 128). For Tichy and DeVanna, a vision is constructed not by a single leader but as a result of bringing together the differing viewpoints within an organization. A central aspect of creating a vision is developing a mission statement that describes the vision and the values implied by it.

Act 3 in transforming organizations involves institutionalizing changes. To do this, leaders need to break down old structures and establish new ones. They need to find appropriate followers to implement new ideas. The breaking down of old structures may require that the leader creates new coalitions of employees who will be compatible with the new vision. In the process, individuals will need to be helped to find new roles in the organization as different structures are designed so as to enhance the new directions for the organization.

How Does the Transformational Approach Work?

The transformational approach to leadership is a broad-based perspective that encompasses many facets and dimensions of the leadership process. In general, it describes how leaders can initiate, develop, and carry out significant changes in organizations. Although not definitive, the steps followed by transformational leaders usually take the following form.

Transformational leaders set out to empower followers and nurture them in change. They attempt to raise the consciousness in individuals and to get them to transcend their own self-interests for the sake of others.

To create change, transformational leaders become strong role models for their followers. They have a highly developed set of moral values and a self-determined sense of identity (Avolio & Gibbons, 1988). They are confident, competent, and articulate, and they express strong ideals. They listen to followers and they are not intolerant of opposing viewpoints. A spirit of cooperation often develops between these leaders and their followers. Followers want to emulate transformational leaders because they learn to trust them and believe in the ideas for which they stand.

It is common for transformational leaders to create a vision. The vision emerges from the collective interests of various individuals and units within an organization. The vision is a focal point for transformational leadership. It gives the leader and the organization a conceptual map for where the organization is headed; it gives meaning and clarifies the organization's identity. Furthermore, the vision gives followers a sense of identity within the organization and also a sense of self-efficacy (Shamir, House, & Arthur, 1993).

Transformational leaders also act as change agents who initiate and implement new directions within organizations. They listen to opposing viewpoints within the organization as well as threats to the organization that may arise from outside the organization. Sometimes leaders generate instability themselves through nurturing the expression of discordant viewpoints or issues. Out of the uncertainty, transformational leaders create change.

The transformational approach also requires that leaders become social architects. This means they make clear the emerging values and norms of the organization. They involve themselves in the culture of the organization and help shape its meaning. People need to know their roles and understand how they are contributors to the greater purposes of the organization. Transformational leaders are out front in interpreting and shaping for organizations the shared meanings that exist within them.

Strengths

In its present stage of development, the transformational approach has several strengths. First, transformational leadership has been widely researched from many different perspectives including a series of qualitative studies of prominent leaders and CEOs in large, well-known organizations, and has also been the focal point for a large body of leadership research since its introduction in the 1970s. For example, a special issue of *Leadership Quarterly* (1993, issue #3) was devoted entirely to charisma, a central aspect of transformational leadership. In addition, there have been well over 200 theses, dissertations, and research projects conducted using this approach.

Second, transformational leadership has intuitive appeal. The transformational perspective describes how the leader is "out front" advocating change for others and this concept is consistent with society's popular notion of what leadership means. People are attracted to transformational leadership because it makes sense to them. It is appealing that a leader will provide a vision for the future.

Third, transformational leadership treats leadership as a process that occurs between followers and leaders. Because this process incorporates both the followers' and the leader's needs, leadership is not the sole responsibility of a leader but rather emerges from the interplay between leaders and followers. The needs of others are central to the transformational leader. As a result, followers gain a more prominent position in the leadership process because the attributions of followers are instrumental in the evolving transformational process (Bryman, 1992, p. 176).

Fourth, the transformational approach provides a broader view of leadership that augments other leadership models. Many leadership models focus primarily on how leaders exchange rewards for achieved goals—the transactional process. The transformational approach provides an expanded picture of leadership that includes not only the exchange of rewards but also leaders' attention to the needs and growth of followers (Bass, 1985).

Finally, transformational leadership places a strong emphasis on followers' needs, values, and morals. Burns (1978) suggests that transformational leadership involves attempts by leaders to move individuals to higher standards of moral responsibility. It includes motivating followers to transcend their own self-interests for the good of the team, organization, or community (Howell & Avolio, 1992; Shamir et al., 1993). This emphasis sets the transformational approach apart from all other approaches to leadership because it suggests that leadership has a moral dimension. By emphasizing this aspect, the coercive uses of power by individuals such as Hitler, Jim Jones, and David Koresch can be disregarded as models of leadership.

Criticisms

Transformational leadership also has several weaknesses. One criticism is that it lacks conceptual clarity. Because it covers such a wide range, including creating a vision, motivating, being a change agent, building trust, giving nurturance, and acting as a social architect, to name a few, it is difficult to define clearly the parameters of transformational leadership. Furthermore, the parameters of transformational leadership often overlap with other similar conceptualizations of leadership. For example, Bryman (1992) points out that transformational and charismatic leadership are often treated synonymously even though in some models of leadership (e.g., Bass, 1985) charisma is only one component of transformational leadership.

Another difficulty with transformational leadership is that it is often interpreted too simplistically as an "either-or" approach and not as a matter of degree. There is a tendency to fail to see transformational leadership as occurring along a continuum that incorporates several components of leadership.

A third criticism some have made is that transformational leadership treats leadership as a personality trait or personal predisposition rather than a behavior in which people can be instructed (Bryman, 1992, pp. 100-102). If it is a trait, training people in this approach becomes more problematic because it is difficult to teach people how to change their traits. Even though many scholars, including Weber, House, and Bass, emphasize that transformational leadership is concerned with leader behaviors, such as how leaders involve themselves with followers, there is an inclination to see this approach from a trait perspective. Perhaps this problem is exacerbated because the word *transformational* creates images of one person being the most active component in the leadership process. For example, even though "creating a vision" involves follower input, there is a tendency to see transformational leaders as visionaries. There is also a tendency to see transformational leaders as individuals who have special qualities that *transform* others. These images accentuate a trait characterization of transformational leadership.

A fourth criticism some have made is that transformational leadership is elitist and antidemocratic (Bass & Avolio, 1993). Transformational leaders often play a direct role in creating changes, establishing a vision, and advocating new directions. This gives the strong impression that the leader is acting independently of followers or putting himself or herself above the followers' needs. Although this criticism of elitism has been refuted by Bass and Avolio (1993), who contend that transformational leaders can be directive and participative as well as democratic and authoritarian, the substance of the criticism raises valid questions about transformational leadership.

Another criticism is that transformational leadership is based primarily on qualitative data collected from leaders who were very visible serving in positions that were at the top of their organizations (Bryman, 1992). As Bryman points out (p. 157), the data apply to leadership *of* organizations but not necessarily leadership *in* organizations. For example, can transformational leadership be applied equally to plant managers and CEOs? Can supervisors and department heads learn about leadership from a model that was constructed from interviews with senior corporate leaders? Bass and his associates have begun to report findings from quantitative studies of leaders at all levels that substantiate the assumptions of transformational leadership. But until more data are available, the questions remain of how transformational leadership applies to lower-level leaders.

A final criticism of transformational leadership is that it has the potential to be abused. Transformational leadership is concerned with changing people's values and moving them to a new vision. But who is to determine if the new directions are good and more affirming? Who decides that a new vision is a better vision? If the values to which the leader is moving his or her followers are not better, and if the set of human values is not more redeeming, then the leadership must be challenged. The charismatic nature of transformational leadership presents significant risks for organizations because it can be used for destructive purposes (Howell & Avolio, 1992). History is full of examples of charismatic individuals who used coercive power to lead people to evil ends. For this reason, transformational leadership puts a burden on individuals and organizations to be aware of how they are being influenced and in what directions they are being asked to go.

Application

Rather than being a model that tells leaders what to do, transformational leadership provides a broad set of generalizations of what is typical of leaders who are transforming or who work in transforming contexts. Unlike other leadership approaches, such as contingency theory and situational leadership, transformational leadership does not provide a clearly defined set of assumptions about how leaders should act in a particular situation in order to be successful. Rather, it provides a general way of thinking about leadership that emphasizes ideals, inspiration, innovations, and individual concerns. Transformational leadership requires that leaders be aware of how their own behavior relates to the needs of their subordinates and the changing dynamics within their organizations.

Bass and Avolio (1990a) suggest that transformational leadership can be taught to individuals at all levels within an organization and that it can positively affect a firm's performance. It can be used in recruitment, selection and promotion, and training and development. It can also be used in improving team development, decision-making groups, quality initiatives, and reorganizations (Bass & Avolio, 1994).

Programs designed to develop transformational leadership usually require that individuals or their associates take the Multifactor Leadership Questionnaire (MLQ; Bass & Avolio, 1990b) or a similar questionnaire to determine the leader's particular strengths and weaknesses in transformational leadership. Taking the MLQ assists leaders in pinpointing areas in which they could improve their leadership. For example, leaders might learn that it would be beneficial if they were more confident in expressing their goals, or that they needed to spend more time nurturing followers, or that they needed to be more tolerant of opposing viewpoints within the organization. The MLQ is the springboard to helping leaders improve a whole series of their leadership attributes.

One particular aspect of transformational leadership that has been given special emphasis in training programs is the process of building a vision. For example, it has become quite common for training programs to have leaders write elaborate statements that describe their own 5-year career plans as well as their perceptions of the future directions for their organizations. Working with leaders on vision statements is one way to help them enhance their transformational leadership behavior.

Overall, transformational leadership provides leaders with information about a full range of their behaviors, from nontransactional, to transactional, to transformational. In the next section we provide some actual leadership examples to which an application can be made of the principles of transformational leadership.

Case Studies

In the following section three brief case studies (Cases 8.1, 8.2, and 8.3) from very different contexts are provided. Each case describes a situation in which transformational leadership is present to some degree. The questions at the end of each case point to some of the unique issues surrounding the use of transformational leadership in ongoing organizations.

Case 8.1

High Tech Engineering (HTE) is a 50-year-old family-owned manufacturing company with 250 employees that produces small parts for the aircraft industry. The president of HTE is Mr. B, who came to the company from a smaller business with strong credentials as a leader in advanced aircraft technology. Prior to Mr. B, the only president of HTE was the founder and owner of the company. The organizational structure at HTE was very traditional, and it was supported by a very rich organizational culture.

As the new president, Mr. B sincerely wanted to transform HTE. He wanted to prove that new technologies and advanced management techniques could make HTE one of the best manufacturing companies in the country. To that end, Mr. B created a vision statement that was displayed throughout the company. The two-page statement, which had a strong democratic tone, described the overall purposes, directions, and values of the company.

During the first 3 years of Mr. B's tenure as president, several major reorganizations took place at the company. These were designed by Mr. B and a select few of his senior managers. The intention of each reorganization was to implement advanced organizational structures in order to bolster the declared HTE vision.

Yet the major outcome of each of the changes was to dilute the leadership and create a feeling of instability among the employees. Most of the changes were made from the top down, with little input from lower or middle management. Some of the changes gave employees more control in circumstances where they needed less, whereas other changes limited employee input in contexts where employees should have been given more input. There were some situations in which individual workers reported to three different bosses and other situations where one manager had far too many workers to oversee. Rather than feeling comfortable in their various roles within HTE, employees began to feel uncertain about their responsibilities and how they contributed to stated goals of the company. The overall effect of the reorganizations was a precipitous drop in worker morale and production.

In the midst of all the changes, the vision that Mr. B had for the company became lost. The instability that employees felt made it difficult for them to support the company's vision. People at HTE complained that although mission statements were displayed throughout the company, no one understood in which direction they were going.

To the employees at HTE, Mr. B was an enigma. HTE was an American company that produced U.S. products, but Mr. B drove a foreign car. Mr. B claimed to be democratic in his style of leadership, but he was arbitrary in how he treated people; he acted in a nondirective style toward some people and he showed arbitrary control toward others. He wanted to be seen as a "hands-on" manager but he delegated operational control of the company to others while he focused on external customer relations and board of director matters.

At times Mr. B appeared to be insensitive to employees' concerns. He wanted HTE to be an environment in which everyone could feel empowered, but he often failed to listen closely to what employees were saying. He seldom engaged in open, two-way communication. HTE had a long rich history with many unique stories, but the employees felt that Mr. B either misunderstood or did not care about that history.

Four years after arriving at HTE, Mr. B stepped down as president after his operations officer ran the company into a large debt and cash flow crisis. His dream of building HTE into a world-class manufacturing company was never realized.

Questions

If you were consulting with the board of directors at HTE

- What would you advise them regarding Mr. B's leadership from a transformational perspective?
- Did Mr. B have a clear vision for HTE and was he able to implement it?
- How effective was Mr. B as a change agent and a social architect for HTE?
- What would you tell Mr. B to do differently if he had the chance to return as president of HTE?

Case 8.2

Every year, Dr. Cook, a college professor, leads a group of 25 college students to the Mideast on an archaeological dig that usually lasts about 8 weeks. The participants, who come from big and small colleges throughout the country, usually have little knowledge or background in what takes place during an excavation. Dr. Cook enjoys leading these expeditions because he likes teaching students about archaeology and because the outcomes of the digs actually advance his own scholarly work.

While planning for his annual summer excavation, Dr. Cook told the following story:

This summer will be interesting because I have 10 people returning from last year. Last year was quite a dig. During the first couple of weeks everything was very disjointed. Team members seemed lost, unmotivated, and tired. In fact, there was one time early on when it seemed as if nearly half the students were either physically ill or mentally exhausted. Students seemed lost and uncertain about the meaning of the entire project.

For example, it is our tradition to get up every morning at 4:30 A.M. in order to depart for the excavation site at 5:00 A.M. However, during the first weeks of the dig, few people were ever ready at 5:00, even after several reminders.

Every year it takes some time for people to learn where they fit with each other and with the purposes of the dig. The students all come from such different backgrounds. Some are from small, private, religious schools and others are from large state universities. Each comes with a different agenda, with different skills, and with different work habits. One person may be a good photographer, another a good drawer, and another a good surveyor. It is my job to complete the excavation with the resources available to us.

At the end of Week Two, I called a meeting to assess how things were going. We talked about a lot of things including personal things, how our work was progressing, and what we needed to change. The students seemed to appreciate the chance to talk at this meeting. Each of them described their special circumstances and their hopes for the summer.

I told the students several stories about past digs; some were humorous and others highlighted accomplishments. I shared my particular interests in this project and how I thought we as a group could accomplish the work that needed to be done at this important historical site. In particular, I stressed two points: (a) that they shared the responsibility for the successful outcome of the venture, and (b) that they had independent authority to design, schedule, and carry out the details of their respective assignments, with the director and other senior staff available at all times as advisors and resource persons. In regard to the departure time issue, I told the participants that the standard departure time on digs was 5:00 A.M.

Well, shortly after our meeting I observed a real shift in the group attitude and atmosphere. People seemed to become more involved in the work, there was less sickness, and there was more camradery. All assignments were completed without constant prodding and in a spirit of mutual support. Each morning at 5:00 A.M. everyone was ready to go.

I find that each year my groups are different. It's almost as if each of them has a unique personality. Perhaps that is why I find it so challenging. I try to listen to the students and utilize their particular strengths. It really is quite amazing how these students can develop in 8 weeks. They really become good at archaeology and they accomplish a great deal.

This coming year will again be different because of the 10 returning "veterans."

Questions

- How is this an example of transformational leadership?
- Where are Dr. Cook's strengths on the full range of leadership model (see Figure 8.4)?
- What is the vision Dr. Cook has for the archaeology excavations?

Case 8.3

Ms. Adams began as a researcher at a large pharmaceutical company. After several years of observing the way clinical drug studies were conducted, she realized that there was a need and opportunity for a research center not connected with a specific pharmaceutical company. In collaboration with other researchers, she launched a new company that was the first of its kind in the country. Within 5 years, Ms. Adams became president and CEO of Independent Center for Clinical Research (ICCR). Under Ms. Adams's leadership, ICCR grew over a 10-year period to become a company with revenues of $6 million and profits of $1 million. ICCR employed 100 full-time employees, most of whom were women.

Ms. Adams wants ICCR to continue its pattern of formidable growth. Her vision for the company is to make it a model research center that will blend credible science with efficient and cost-effective clinical trials. To that end, the company, which is situated in a large urban setting, maintains strong links to academia, industry, and the community.

Ms. Adams and her style have a great deal to do with the success of ICCR. She is a free thinker who is always open to new ideas, opportunities, and approaches. She is a positive person who enjoys the nuances of life, and she is not afraid to take risks. Her optimistic approach has had a significant influence on the company's achievements and its organizational climate. People employed at ICCR claim they have never worked at a place that is so progressive and so positive in how it treats its employees and customers. The women employees at ICCR feel particularly strongly about Ms. Adams's leadership, and many of them use Ms. Adams as a role model. It is not by accident that the majority (85%) of the people who work at ICCR are women. Her support for women's concerns is evident in the type of drug studies the company selects to conduct and in her service to national committees on women's health and research issues. Within ICCR, Ms. Adams has designed an on-site day care program, flex-time scheduling for mothers with young children, and a benefits package that gives full health coverage to part-time employees. At a time when most companies are searching for ways to include more women in decision making, ICCR has women in established leadership positions at all levels.

Although Ms. Adams has been extremely effective at ICCR, the success of the company has resulted in many changes that have affected Ms. Adams's leadership at the company.

Rapid growth of ICCR has required that Ms. Adams spend a great deal of time traveling throughout the country. Due to her excessive travel, Ms. Adams has begun to feel distant from the day-to-day operations of ICCR. She has begun to feel as if she is losing her handle on what makes the company "tick." For example, though she used to give weekly pep talks to supervisors, she finds that she now gives two formal presentations a year. Ms. Adams also complains of feeling estranged from employees at the company. At a recent directors meeting she expressed frustration that people no longer called her by her first name and others did not even know who she was.

Growth at ICCR has also demanded that more planning and decision making be delegated to department heads. This has been problematic for Ms. Adams, particularly in the area of strategic planning. Ms. Adams finds the department heads are beginning to shift the focus of ICCR in a direction that contradicts her ideal model of what the company should be and what it is best at doing. Ms. Adams built the company on the idea that ICCR be a strong blend of credible science and cost-effective clinical trials and she does not want to give up that model. The directors, on the other hand, would like to see ICCR become similar to a standard pharmaceutical company dedicated primarily to the research and development of new drugs.

Questions

- What is it about Ms. Adams's leadership that clearly suggests that she is engaged in transformational leadership?
- In what ways has the growth of ICCR had an impact on the leadership of Ms. Adams?
- Given the problems Ms. Adams is confronting as a result of the growth of the company, what should she do to reestablish herself as a transformational leader at ICCR?

Leadership Instrument

The most widely used measure of transformational leadership is the Multifactor Leadership Questionnaire (MLQ). An earlier version of the MLQ was originally developed by Bass (1985), based on a series of interviews he and his associates conducted with 70 senior executives in South Africa. These executives were asked to recall leaders within their experiences who had raised their awareness to broader goals, moved them to higher motives, or inspired them to put others' interests ahead of their own. The executives were then asked to describe how these leaders behaved—what they did to affect change. From these descriptions and from numerous other interviews with both junior and senior executives, Bass constructed the questions that make up the MLQ. Since it was first designed, the MLQ has gone through many revisions, and it continues to be refined to strengthen its reliability and validity (Bass & Avolio, 1993).

The MLQ is made up of questions that measure followers' perceptions of a leader's behavior for each of the seven factors in the transformational and transactional leadership model (see Figure 8.3), and it also has items that measure extra effort, effectiveness, and satisfaction.

Based on a summary analysis of a series of studies that used the MLQ to predict how transformational leadership relates to outcomes such as effectiveness, Bryman (1992) and Bass and Avolio (1994) have suggested that the charisma and motivation factors on the MLQ are the most likely to be related to positive effects. Individualized consideration, intellectual stimulation, and contingent reward are the next most important factors. Management-by-exception in its passive form has been found to be somewhat related to outcomes, and in its active form it has been found to be negatively related to outcomes. Generally, laissez-faire leadership has been found to be negatively related to outcomes such as effectiveness and satisfaction in organizations.

Bass and Avolio (1992) have developed an abbreviated version of the MLQ, called the MLQ-6S. We present it in this section so that you can assess your own transformational, transactional, and non-transactional leadership style. At the end of the questionnaire we provide information you can use to interpret your scores.

As you assess your own scores, you may wish to divide the seven factors into three groups. The first group would be your scores on Factors 1 through 4, which represent items that directly assess the degree to which your leadership is transformational. Higher scores on these factors indicate more frequently displayed transformational leadership. The second group would be your totals for Factors 5 and 6. These factors represent the transactional dimensions of your leadership. Higher scores on these factors suggest you tend to use reward systems and/or corrective structures in your leadership style. The last factor, laissez-faire leadership, assesses the degree to which you employ "hands-off" leadership or nonleadership. On this factor, higher scores indicate that you tend to provide little structure or guidance to subordinates.

As you can see, the MLQ-6S covers a number of dimensions of leadership or what Bass and Avolio (1994) have called a full range of leadership styles. This questionnaire should give you a clearer picture of your own style as well as the complexity of transformational leadership itself.

Multifactor Leadership Questionnaire
Form 6S

INSTRUCTIONS: This questionnaire provides a description of your leadership style. Twenty-one descriptive statements are listed below. Judge how frequently each statement fits you. The word *others* may mean your followers, clients, or group members.

KEY: 0 = not at all; 1 = once in a while; 2 = sometimes; 3 = fairly often; 4 = frequently, if not always

1. I make others feel good to be around me.	1	2 ③ 4
2. I express with a few simple words what we could and should do.	1	2 3 ④
3. I enable others to think about old problems in new ways.	1	2 3 ④
4. I help others develop themselves.	1	2 3 ④
5. I tell others what to do if they want to be rewarded for their work.	1	2 ③ 4
6. I am satisfied when others meet agreed-upon standards.	1	2 3 4
7. I am content to let others continue working in the same way as always.	1	2 3 4
8. Others have complete faith in me.	1	2 ③ 4
9. I provide appealing images about what we can do.	1	2 3 4
10. I provide others with new ways of looking at puzzling things.	1	2 ③ 4
11. I let others know how I think they are doing.	1	2 3 ④
12. I provide recognition/rewards when others reach their goals.	1	2 ③ 4
13. As long as things are working, I do not try to change anything.	1	2 3 4
14. Whatever others want to do is O.K. with me.	1	2 3 4
15. Others are proud to be associated with me.	1	2 ③ 4
16. I help others find meaning in their work.	1	2 ③ 4
17. I get others to rethink ideas that they had never questioned before.	1	2 3 ④
18. I give personal attention to others who seem rejected.	1	2 ③ 4
19. I call attention to what others can get for what they accomplish.	1	2 ③ 4
20. I tell others the standards they have to know to carry out their work.	1	2 ③ 4
21. I ask no more of others than what is absolutely essential.	1	2 3 4

SOURCE: Copyright © 1992 B. M. Bass and B. J. Avolio. Adapted with permission. MLQ Form 5x can be obtained from Mind Garden, P.O. Box 60669, Palo Alto, CA 94306; (415) 424-8493.

SCORING: The MLQ-6S measures your leadership on seven factors related to transformational leadership. Your score for each factor is determined by summing three specified items on the questionnaire. For example, to determine your score for Factor 1, *Idealized Influence*, sum your responses for items #1, #8, and #15. Complete this procedure for all seven factors.

Total

Idealized Influence (items 1, 8, & 15)	_9_ Factor 1
Inspirational Motivation (items 2, 9, & 16)	_7_ Factor 2 M
Intellectual Stimulation (items 3, 10, & 17)	_14_ Factor 3
Individualized Consideration (items 4, 11, & 18)	_11_ Factor 4
Contingent Reward (items 5, 12, & 19)	_9_ Factor 5
Management-by-exception (items 6, 13, & 20)	_3_ Factor 6
Laissez-faire Leadership (items 7, 14, & 21)	_0_ Factor 7

Score Range: High = 9-12, Moderate = 5-8, Low = 0-4

Score Interpretation

Factor 1. *Idealized influence* indicates whether you hold subordinates' trust, maintain their faith and respect, show dedication
to them, appeal to their hopes and dreams, and act as their
role model.

Factor 2. *Inspirational motivation* measures the degree to which you
provide a vision, use appropriate symbols and images to
help others focus on their work, and try to make others feel
their work is significant.

Factor 3. *Intellectual stimulation* shows the degree to which you encourage others to be creative in looking at old problems in new
ways, create an environment that is tolerant of seemingly extreme positions, and nurture people to question their own values and beliefs and those of the organization.

Factor 4. *Individualized consideration* indicates the degree to which
you show interest in others' well-being, assign projects individually, and pay attention to those who seem less involved
in the group.

Factor 5. *Contingent reward* shows the degree to which you tell others what to do in order to be rewarded, emphasize what you
expect from them, and recognize their accomplishments.

Factor 6. *Management-by-exception* assesses whether you tell others
the job requirements, are content with standard performance, and are a believer in "if it ain't broke, don't fix it."

Factor 7. *Laissez-faire* measures whether you require little of others, are
content to let things ride, and let others do their own thing.

Summary

One of the newest and most encompassing approaches to leadership,
transformational leadership, is concerned with the process of how cer-

tain leaders are able to inspire followers to accomplish great things. This approach stresses that leaders need to understand and adapt to the needs and motives of followers. Transformational leaders are recognized as change agents who are good role models, who can create and articulate a clear vision for an organization, who empower followers to achieve at higher standards, who act in ways that make others want to trust them, and who give meaning to organizational life.

Transformational leadership emerged from and is rooted in the writings of scholars such as Burns (1978), Bass (1985), Bennis and Nanus (1985), and Tichy and DeVanna (1986).

Transformational leadership can be assessed through use of the Multifactor Leadership Questionnaire (MLQ), which measures a leader's behavior in seven areas: individualized consideration (charisma), inspirational motivation, intellectual stimulation, idealized influence, contingent reward, management-by-exception, and laissez-faire behavior. High scores on individualized consideration and motivation factors are most indicative of strong transformational leadership.

There are several positive features of the transformational approach, including that it is a current model that has received a lot of attention by researchers, it has strong intuitive appeal, it emphasizes the importance of followers in the leadership process, it goes beyond traditional transactional models and broadens leadership to include the growth of followers, and it places strong emphasis on morals and values.

Balancing off the positive features of transformational leadership are several weaknesses. These include that the approach lacks conceptual clarity, it is often interpreted too simplistically as an "either-or" approach, it creates a framework that implies that transformational leadership has a trait-like quality, it is sometimes seen as elitist and undemocratic, it is derived from and supported by data that focus heavily on senior-level leaders, and it has the potential to be used counterproductively in negative ways by leaders. Despite the weaknesses, transformational leadership appears to be a valuable and widely used approach.

References

Avolio, B. J., & Gibbons, T. C. (1988). Developing transformational leaders: A life span approach. In J. A. Conger, R. N. Kanungo, & Associates (Eds.), *Charismatic leadership: The elusive factor in organizational effectiveness* (pp. 276-308). San Francisco: Jossey-Bass.

Bass, B. M. (1985). *Leadership and performance beyond expectations.* New York: Free Press.

Bass, B. M. (1990). From transactional to transformational leadership: Learning to share the vision. *Organizational Dynamics, 18,* 19-31.

Bass, B. M., & Avolio, B. J. (1990a). The implications of transactional and transformational leadership for individual, team, and organizational development. *Research in Organizational Change and Development, 4,* 231-272.

Bass, B. M., & Avolio, B. J. (1990b). *Multifactor leadership questionnaire.* Palo Alto, CA: Consulting Psychologist Press.

Bass, B. M., & Avolio, B. J. (1992). *Multifactor leadership questionnaire—Short Form 6S.* Binghamton, NY: Center for Leadership Studies.

Bass, B. M., & Avolio, B. J. (1993). Transformational leadership: A response to critiques. In M. M. Chemers & R. Ayman (Eds.), *Leadership theory and research: Perspectives and directions* (pp. 49-80). San Diego, CA: Academic Press.

Bass, B. M., & Avolio, B. J. (1994). *Improving organizational effectiveness through transformational leadership.* Thousand Oaks, CA: Sage.

Bennis, W. G., & Nanus, B. (1985). *Leaders: The strategies for taking charge.* New York: Harper & Row.

Bryman, A. (1992). *Charisma and leadership in organizations.* London: Sage.

Burns, J. M. (1978). *Leadership.* New York: Harper & Row.

Downton, J. V. (1973). *Rebel leadership: Commitment and charisma in a revolutionary process.* New York: Free Press.

House, R. J. (1976). A 1976 theory of charismatic leadership. In J. G. Hunt & L. L. Larson (Eds.), *Leadership: The cutting edge* (pp. 189-207). Carbondale: Southern Illinois University Press.

Howell, J. M., & Avolio, B. J. (1992). The ethics of charismatic leadership: Submission or liberation? *Academy of Management Executive, 6*(2), 43-54.

Kuhnert, K. W. (1994). Transforming leadership: Developing people through delegation. In B. M. Bass & B. J. Avolio (Eds.), *Improving organizational effectiveness through transformational leadership* (pp. 10-25). Thousand Oaks, CA: Sage.

Kuhnert, K. W., & Lewis, P. (1987). Transactional and transformational leadership: A constructive/developmental analysis. *Academy of Management Review, 12*(4), 648-657.

Shamir, B., House, R. J., & Arthur, M. B. (1993). The motivational effects of charismatic leadership: A self-concept based theory. *Organization Science, 4*(4), 577-594.

Tichy, N. M., & DeVanna, M. A. (1986). *The transformational leader.* New York: John Wiley.

Tichy, N. M., & DeVanna, M. A. (1990). *The transformational leader* (2nd ed.). New York: John Wiley.

Weber, M. (1947). *The theory of social and economic organizations* (T. Parsons, Trans.). New York: Free Press.

Yammarino, F. J. (1993). Transforming leadership studies: Bernard Bass' leadership and performance beyond expectations. *Leadership Quarterly, 4*(3), 379-382.

CHAPTER 9

Team Leadership Theory

SUSAN E. KOGLER HILL

Description

Leadership in organizational groups or work teams has become one of the most popular and rapidly growing areas of leadership theory and research. Teams are organizational groups composed of members who are interdependent, who share common goals, and who must coordinate their activities to accomplish these goals. Examples of such groups might include project management teams, task forces, work units, standing committees, quality teams, and improvement teams.

Some of the earliest group research conducted in the 1940s and 1950s focused on developing social science theory with little emphasis on practical problems of real-life groups and the leadership within them. These early studies were typically conducted on temporary, laboratory-type groups that did not have permanence or collective goals. Such research, although valuable to increasing our understanding of groups, provided little practical information that was helpful to real-life work groups or teams. Current research focuses on the practical problems of ongoing work teams and how to make them more effective (Ilgen, Major, Hollenbeck, & Sego, 1993).

Some of the reasons for this increased interest in work teams stems from the rapidly changing conditions facing today's organizations, such as organizational restructuring, global economic competition, increasing diversity within the workforce, and expanding technology. Within this rapidly changing environment the use of organizational teams has been found to lead to greater productivity, more effective use of resources, better decisions and problem solving, better quality products and services, and increased innovation and creativity (Parker, 1990). The failures of teams have also been very dramatic and visible, however, making the need for information about and understanding of team effectiveness and team leadership essential for today's organizations (Ilgen et al., 1993).

Organizational restructuring in the American workplace has in essence shifted the decision-making powers of the organization downward from the traditional hierarchy to more self-managed teams, empowering them in new ways. These "new" teams still might have a team leader in the traditional sense, or the leader's role might be rotated among the team members. The formal team leader's role might be limited to serving as a liaison with those external to the group, serving mainly as a process facilitator within the group (Wellins, Byham, & Wilson, 1991), or both. Leadership within this new framework, though still necessary, is complex and presents a significant challenge to researchers (Ilgen et al., 1993).

With the increase in organizational work teams and their expanding role in the complex and rapidly changing organizational structures, it is essential to understand the role of leadership within these teams to ensure team success and to avoid team failure. The practical necessity of understanding the nature of organizational teams and the leadership within them is forcing theory and research into new directions that offer great promise for understanding team leadership.

Many theories and models exist for understanding groups, teams, and leadership. Most models, however, do not clearly show the complex relationship between team leadership and team effectiveness. The Leadership and Group Effectiveness Approach (Hackman, 1990; Hackman & Walton, 1986; Hughes, Ginnett, & Curphey, 1993) provides the most useful framework for understanding the current theories of work teams and team leadership. This approach is practical in that it is built around and focuses on group outcomes and productivity, that is, effectiveness. Also, the approach is theoretical in that it takes into account the complexity of teamwork by focusing on the many structural, individual, contextual, and process factors that contribute to team effectiveness. And most notably, the approach demonstrates the role of leadership in designing and coaching teams to achieve effectiveness. The leadership and group effectiveness approach presents a very useful tool for understanding the very complex phenomenon of team leadership with its critical functions, its complexity, and its focus on outcomes of excellence.

Critical Functions of Team Leadership

In the 1960s, McGrath originally formulated the critical leadership functions necessary for group effectiveness. The critical leadership functions cross two dimensions of behavior, (a) monitoring versus taking action and (b) focusing on internal group issues versus external group issues, which result in the following four types of group leadership functions:

1. Diagnosing group deficiencies (monitoring/internal)
2. Taking remedial action to correct deficiencies (executive action/internal)
3. Forecasting impending environmental changes (monitoring/external)
4. Taking preventive action in response to environmental changes (executive action/external). (Hackman & Walton, 1986, p. 76)

The functional perspective attempts to focus on the notion of critical functions specific to the organizational work group to ensure that productivity meets standards, to maintain the group, and to contribute to individual growth (Hackman, 1990). These functions need not be carried out by the leader. A mature group with experienced members might well take on these behaviors itself. As long as the team's critical needs have been met, the leadership, whether by an individual or the group, has been effective.

The functional perspective was designed to be practical and to answer the question: What functions does a leader have to perform to help a group be more effective? From the functional perspective, the leader is seen as the one who designs, builds, and maintains effective groups (Hackman & Walton, 1986). The leader possesses special responsibility for functioning in a manner that will help the group achieve effectiveness. Within this perspective, leadership behavior would be seen as team-based problem solving in which the leader attempts to achieve team goals by cognitively analyzing the complex social context and then selecting and implementing the appropriate behaviors to ensure team effectiveness (Fleishman et al., 1991).

The functional team leadership perspective was designed to help both the leader and the organization. Leaders would be able to know how to help teams in task or interpersonal trouble. Organizations would be able to know how to select and train leaders across situational demands. The key "assertion" of the functional perspective is that the leader is to do whatever is necessary to take care of unmet needs of the group.

Complexity of Team Leadership

In determining the appropriate functions of leadership at any particular point in time it becomes readily apparent that team leadership is a very complex process. Fisher (1985) describes the leader metaphorically as the "medium" or the one who processes and acts upon information. A good leader has a wide and loosely connected system of beliefs and makes judgments based on information present in the situation or context and not merely based on personal beliefs. A good leader also has a wide repertoire of actions or functions when performing leadership and can correctly match these actions to situations.

When the leader's behavior matches the complexity in the situation, the leader is behaving with "requisite variety," or the required set of behaviors necessary to meet the group's needs (Drecksel, 1991). Because every team is different and possesses a different amount of ambiguous information that needs to be understood, leadership then is the process by which that information is interpreted and acted upon. The major role of leadership is to "mediate" among the environment of the group, the group's actions, and performance outcomes. Leadership occurs when actions are taken to adjust the group to overcome various obstacles in the environment, interpersonal relationships, or group procedures (Drecksel, 1991).

In this framework, leadership is not a role but an ongoing process to continually reduce equivocality, provide structure, and overcome barriers. All members of the group can engage in this process and collectively help the group adapt to changing conditions. In fact, the official leader of the group might be so busy processing information from the environment that his or her actual participation might be low while gathering the needed information to select the most appropriate action for the good of the group. Good leaders need to be very good receivers of information, focused outward on the environment and not focused on self (Barge, 1989). In addition to being effective decoders, good leaders also need to learn to encode by effectively conveying messages and taking the most appropriate actions to overcome problems (Barge, 1994). The complex nature of team leadership demonstrates that there are no simple recipes for team success. Team leaders must learn to be open and objective in understanding and diagnosing team problems and skillful in selecting the most appropriate actions to help achieve team goals.

Outcomes of Team Leadership

In addition to being functional and complex, team leadership also needs to be practical and to focus on team needs and outcomes. Organizational work groups or teams are judged on their performance outcomes and their achievements. Team leadership theory must focus on what makes teams effective or what constitutes team excellence. Leaders cannot cognitively analyze and then appropriately function to improve groups without a clear focus on team goals or outcomes. Just what makes an excellent team? What do excellent teams have in common? What type of leadership exists in excellent teams?

Hackman and Walton (1986) suggested the components necessary for effectiveness of task-performing teams in organizations:

1. Clear, engaging direction
2. An enabling performance situation
   - A group structure that fosters competent task work
   - An organizational context that supports and reinforces excellence
   - Available, expert coaching and process assistance
3. Adequate material resources. (Hackman & Walton, 1986, p. 87)

Conditions of Group Effectiveness (Hackman & Walton, 1986)	Characteristics of Team Excellence (Larson & LaFasto, 1989)
Clear, engaging direction	Clear, elevation goal
Enabling structure	Results-driven structure
	Competent team members
	Unified commitment
	Collaborative climate
Enabling context	Standards of excellence
Expert coaching	Principled leadership
Adequate material resources	External support

Figure 9.1. Comparison of Theory and Research Criteria

Researchers have begun systematically to study organizational work teams to understand better what makes them effective or ineffective (Hackman, 1990; Hughes, Ginnett, & Curphey, 1993; Larson & LaFasto, 1989). These studies of real-life teams have provided a research base for the development of criteria or standards of team excellence. These criteria can then be used by leaders in a normative fashion to diagnose the health of any specific team and to take correspondingly appropriate action.

Larson and LaFasto (1989) report on a grounded approach to understanding team excellence. Rather than developing a set of characteristics a priori regarding effective team functioning, a theoretical sampling of excellent teams was interviewed to gain "insight into what characterizes effectively functioning teams" (Larson & LaFasto, 1989, p. 20). Their findings demonstrated that regardless of type of team, there were eight characteristics regularly associated with team excellence. These characteristics are quite consistent with the theoretical components suggested by Hackman and Walton (1986) above, providing grounded research support for the group effectiveness approach (see Figure 9.1).

It is important to understand just how these various criteria or characteristics actually impact group effectiveness and just how understanding them relates to team leadership theory.

Clear, Elevating Goal

Team goals need to be very clear so that one can tell if the performance objective has been realized. Groups often fail because they are given a vague task and then asked to work out the details (Hackman, 1990). In addition, the goal needs to be involving or motivating so that the members believe it to be worthwhile and important. Teams often fail because they let something else replace their goal, such as personal agendas or power issues (Larson & LaFasto, 1989).

Results-Driven Structure

Teams need to find the best structure to accomplish their goals. Teams or work groups have different work content with which they deal. Top management teams typically deal with power and influence, task forces deal with ideas and plans, customer service teams deal with clients, and production teams deal with technology (Hackman, 1990). These can be classified into three general types of teams: problem-resolution teams, creative teams, and tactical teams. Problem-resolution teams such as task forces need to have a structure that emphasizes trust so that all will be willing and able to contribute. Creative teams such as advertising teams need to emphasize autonomy so that all will be willing to take risks and be free from undue censorship. Tactical teams such as emergency room teams need to emphasize clarity so that everyone knows what to do and when. In addition, all teams need to have clear roles for group members, a good communication system, methods to diagnose individual performance, and an emphasis on fact-based judgments (Larson & LaFasto, 1989). Groups with appropriate structures can meet the needs of the group as well as accomplish team goals.

Competent Team Members

Groups should be composed of the right number and mix of members to accomplish all the tasks of the group. In addition, members need to be provided with sufficient information, education, and training to become or to remain competent team members (Hackman & Walton, 1986). As a total group, the members need to possess the requisite technical competence to accomplish the team's goals. Members also need to be personally competent in interpersonal skills or teamwork. A common mistake in forming teams is to assume that people who have all the technical skills necessary to solve a problem also have the interpersonal skills necessary to work together effectively (Hackman, 1990). In addition to their technical competence, team members need to know how to engage in collaborative work and how to communicate effectively with one another (Larson & LaFasto, 1989).

Unified Commitment

A mistake commonly made is to call a work group a "team" but treat it as a collection of individuals (Hackman, 1990). Teams do not just happen, they need to be carefully designed and developed. Excellent teams have developed a sense of unity or identification. Such team spirit can frequently be developed by involving members in all aspects of the process (Larson & LaFasto, 1989).

Collaborative Climate

Trust based on honesty, openness, consistency, and respect seems to be essential for building a collaborative climate in which members can stay problem-focused, be open with one another, listen to each other, feel free to take risks, and be willing to compensate for each other (Larson & LaFasto, 1989).

Standards of Excellence

Effective group norms are important for group functioning. Team members' performance needs to be regulated so that actions can be coordinated and tasks can be completed (Hackman & Walton, 1986). It is especially important that the organizational context or the team itself sets up normative standards of excellence so that members will feel a pressure to perform at their highest levels. The standards need to be clear and concrete, and all team members need to be required to perform to standard (Larson & LaFasto, 1989). If such standards are not in place, members might become "lazy" and not bother to perform at their highest levels.

External Support and Recognition

Another frequent mistake is to give organizational teams challenging assignments but give them no organizational support to accomplish these assignments (Hackman, 1990). The best goals, team members, and commitment will not mean much without money, equipment, or supplies to accomplish that goal. Also, organizations frequently ask employees to work on a difficult team assignment but then do not reward them in terms of raises or bonuses for that performance. Teams that are supported by external sources by being given the resources needed to do their jobs, by being recognized for team accomplishments, and by tying rewards collectively to team member performance rather than individual achievement can achieve excellence (Larson & LaFasto, 1989).

Principled Leadership

Effective team leaders serve as coaches to help the team members work interdependently. They can help with team effort by assisting in building unified commitment, by motivating team members, and by reducing the problems of coordination. Leaders can help the team's knowledge and skills by avoiding the focus on individual efforts and can assist in developing shared expertise. Leaders can help with performance quality by helping members avoid inappropriate plans and developing new ones (Hackman, 1990). Effective team leaders possess a personal commitment to the team's goal and give members autonomy to unleash their talents when possible. Leaders can reduce the effectiveness of their team when they are unwilling to confront inadequate performance, dilute the team's ability to perform by having too many priorities, and by overestimating the positive aspects of team performance, that is, by being too easy (Larson & LaFasto, 1989).

Leadership and Group Effectiveness Model

Hughes et al. (1993) have suggested a model that integrates the critical functions of team leadership, the complexity involved in the process, and the focus on group effectiveness. Their Model of Leadership and Group Effectiveness (Figure 9.2) is based on a systems model of group behavior with inputs (individual, group, and organizational), throughputs (processes), and outputs (accomplishment of objectives, results of group work). The model is based on the functional leadership claim that the leader's function or job is to determine the team or group's needs and then to take care of these needs to ensure team effectiveness.

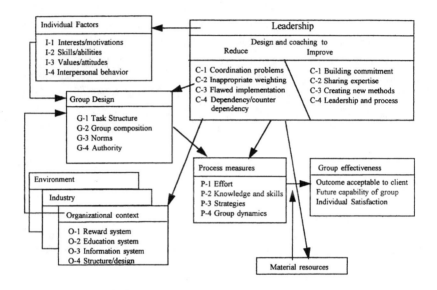

Figure 9.2. A Model for Group Leadership and Group Effectiveness
SOURCE: Taken from R. L. Hughes, R. C. Ginnett, & G. J. Curphey, *Leadership: Enhancing the Lessons of Experience*, 1993, Homewood, IL: Irwin. p. 429. Used with permission.

The model can be used by the leader or team members to determine the best course of action to take. The leader must observe ongoing group processes to see if there is a problem and to determine if there is some input problem that might be contributing to this process problem. If the diagnosis reveals that all the inputs are satisfactory, then the leader's role is to engage in "coaching" behaviors within the team's processes to improve the team's functioning.

In terms of Inputs (see figure 9.2), the model demonstrates that various *individual factors* such as members' interests, skills, values, and behavior can affect the *design* of the group as can various external *context* factors such as the systems of reward, information, or education surrounding the group. The *group design* itself can also affect performance in terms of how the task is structured, how the group is composed, what authority relations exist, and what norms are developed.

In terms of Process, the model lists four levels of process: (1) effort, (2) knowledge/skills, (3) strategies, and (4) group dynamics. The model further suggests how each of these four levels of process might interact with the corresponding levels within the inputs. You will notice in the model that within the group design box at level G-1 is task structure; this corresponds to level P-1 (effort) in the process measures box. Such a level-by-level analysis can be used by team leaders to understand the complexity of team functioning and to diagnose team problems. For example, if you were a leader and observed that your team was not showing much effort (process P-1) in accomplishing its tasks, you could look to group design at level one (G-1) and see task structure. You might find that the task is poorly structured and is so confusing that no one knows how to work on it effectively, which makes it look like the team is not putting forth effort. But maybe you do not find anything wrong with the task structure, and you continue in your problem analysis across level one by also looking at level I-1 for individual factors (interests/motivations). Perhaps the lack of group effort can be traced to the fact that team members are not interested in the project or the task at hand. But again, you might not find any problems with interests/motivations and so you continue your level-one analysis by looking at organizational context factors at level O-1 (Reward system). Such a cross-level comparison with organizational context might suggest that one of the reasons your team is not showing any effort is because the members are not being satisfactorily rewarded for their efforts, so they do not bother to work hard. Hughes et al. (1993) feel that these "key leverage points" predict the "most likely problem areas," but these authors also point out that other relationships across levels can also occur (p. 426). To continue with the above problem of a lack of team effort, you might find that norms (Level G-3) are at the bottom of the problem with an unstated group norm that no one should work hard and make others look lazy. Or you might find that the effort problem is actually a combination of several of these factors, such as no rewards, confusing task, and lazy norms.

In terms of leadership, the model demonstrates how the leader can serve as a medium by using the model to process information that would help to identify team problems and solve them. Hughes et al. (1993) suggest that the leader study the team to find any process problems, conduct a levels analysis with possible contributing inputs, and then take the necessary action steps to remedy the diagnosed problems.

In terms of material resources, the model lists these necessary ingredients separately and indicates that without them excellent leadership and design will have little impact.

Group effectiveness is the final element of this model, which demonstrates the outcomes necessary for a successful work group or team. Three elements determine whether or not a group has been effective. First, is the outcome acceptable to the client, the people who will use the outcome (output quality)? Second, is the group still able to function effectively as a group ("teamness")? Third, are the individual members of the group satisfied with their outcomes and performance (satisfaction)?

The model provides a framework upon which to build a theory of the complex phenomenon of team leadership. The model can help the leader as a "medium" to process the information regarding the team's current state of health and well-being and to diagnose the contributing problems and take the corrective actions to improve the team's health. By comparing their team to established standards or criteria of team excellence, leaders can determine the team's areas of greatest weakness, which might need critical intervention. The leader's two primary functions are to monitor and to take action. By using the model to guide the inquiry into whether or not the team is performing in an effective manner, a leader can diagnose the areas of concern. The leader can then take corrective action outside the team by ensuring necessary resources and contextual supports as well as take corrective action inside the team by strengthening the design of the team and by providing process coaching to the team (Hackman & Walton, 1986).

How Does the Leadership and Group Effectiveness Model Work?

Team leaders can use the group effectiveness model to help them make decisions about the current state of their teams and what, if any, specific actions they need to take to improve a team's functioning. The model portrays leadership as a group oversight function in which the leader's role is to help the group achieve effectiveness. The model provides the leader with a cognitive map to identify group needs and offers suggestions to the leader for how to take appropriate corrective actions. The model helps the leader make sense of the complexity of groups and offers practical suggestions based on theory and research as to what actions to take to make the group more effective.

In using the model, the team leader would monitor the team's processes and determine if there were any problems with the team's (1) effort, (2) knowledge and skills, (3) strategies, or (4) group dynamics. If the leader diagnoses a problem in one or more of these areas, then he or she needs to track across the appropriate levels (1-4) to determine if individual factors, contextual factors, or group design factors might be contributing to the particular process problem. The four levels used consistently throughout the model point the leader to the most likely "cause" of the team's problem. If, for example, team members are in conflict and always fighting for control and power, then the leader might see this as a process problem of group dynamics (level 4). By looking to the group design box the leader could see that perhaps the authority base of the group is contributing to the problem. Maybe the roles and responsibilities of group members are unclear or maybe the authority is not vested in the appropriate individuals. The leader might also need to look to context boxes or the individual factors box to see if these factors are also contributing to the constant group struggle for power. Maybe the interpersonal behavior of one group member (Individual, Level 4) is so authoritative and autocratic that he or she is the main source of the team's problem in group dynamics.

Once the leader has diagnosed the problem(s), he or she needs to take the appropriate action to reduce or remedy the diagnosed problem(s). For example, if the leader has found a problem with the process measure of effort, then the leader would reduce coordination problems and improve commitment by redesigning the task structure, by motivating team members, by providing more organizational rewards, or by any combination of these.

If, in the analysis of the team, the leader finds that inputs and process factors are operating satisfactorily, then the leader can turn his or her attention to coaching and improvement. As in sports teams, the coach does not stop working just because the team is currently winning. For example, a football coach keeps working to build commitment, share expertise, create new methods, and improve group and leadership processes. The effective football coach never rests on past success but works to improve the team's functioning for the future. Organizational team leaders could learn a great deal from sports team coaches. The leadership and group effectiveness model helps point the way for such constant analysis and improvement.

Strengths

One of the model's strengths is that it is designed to answer many of the questions not answered in earlier small group research by focusing on the real-life organizational work group and the leadership needed therein. The model places the work group or team in context within the organization, industry, or environment and also takes into account the accessibility of material resources. In addition, the real-life focus on performance and group effectiveness is also one of the strengths enabling leaders and members to diagnose and correct team problems. By learning what constitutes excellent teams and applying these criteria to team performance, leaders can better learn how to lead teams to the highest levels of excellence. This is very important if organizations are to stay competitive in the global economy.

A second strength of the model is that it provides a complex and cognitive guide that helps leaders to design and maintain effective teams, especially when performance is below standard. Such an approach is consistent with the emerging theoretical notions of leader as a medium whose job is to process the complex information inherent within teamwork. "Leadership is a complex process; complexity of actions is thus identifiable as leadership" (Fisher, 1985, p. 185). Any model or theory that would try to simplify such a complex process would be inappropriate and inadequate. The group effectiveness approach is not simplistic, and it integrates in a manageable and practical form many complex factors in a way that can help leaders be good "mediums" or processors of information.

Another strength of the model is that it takes into account the changing role of leaders and followers in organizations. The model does not focus on the "position power" of a leader but instead focuses on the critical functions of leadership as diagnosis and action taking. The critical leadership functions can be implemented by any team member to assess the current effectiveness of the team and then take appropriate action. This approach is consistent with the current movement in organizations to rethink leadership responsibilities in work groups. The responsibilities or functions of team leadership—such as setting goals, coaching, or rewarding—have historically rested with the group's formal leader, but now with organizational restructuring these duties and responsibilities are frequently shared and distributed across team members.

In addition, this approach to team leadership can help in selecting team leaders. If you have to select a team leader, it might be best to select someone who is perceptive, open, objective, analytical, and a good listener and who has good diagnostic skills. You might also want to select a leader who has a wide repertoire of action-taking skills, that is, one who is comfortable intervening in the group process in such ways as negotiation, conflict resolution, problem solving, goal focusing, influencing upward, and more. A good leader not only can diagnose the team's problem but can reach into a personal bag of tricks and pull out the corresponding appropriate action or actions (requisite variety). For example, if I diagnose that two members of my team are in conflict with one another, I need to be able to determine the root cause of that conflict and select the most appropriate behavior (or nonbehavior) to deal with this problem.

The final strength of the model is that it is *heuristic*, which means it suggests ideas for future research and study. The feature of the model that shows the inputs, process, and leadership factors across the four levels suggests many new areas to investigate. We could test various effects across any level in the model. For example, What is the relationship between group dynamics (process 4), interpersonal behavior (individual 4), authority (group design 4), and structure (organizational context 4)? Under what conditions are each of these factors most influential? When do other levels intervene? How can negative effects across levels be reduced, improved (leadership C-4), or both? Following such a model can help organize and direct future studies in leadership so that this complex phenomenon might not appear so complex.

Criticisms

One of the weaknesses of the present approach is that the entire model is not completely supported or tested. The applied focus on group effectiveness and the organizational work group is a relatively new approach to studying teams. Much of the earlier research on small groups did not directly apply to understanding real-life organizational teams. Many questions still need to be answered regarding team patterns over time, self-fulfilling group cycles, authority issues, and content issues (Hackman, 1990). Do these theoretical relationships hold true in new groups, mature groups, and deteriorating groups?

Do these theoretical notions hold true across all types of groups? Research also needs to focus more on organizational rewards. How can the leadership reinforce the values and behaviors that will perpetuate the functioning of the team rather than rewarding the individual members of the team (Ilgen et al., 1993)?

Although one of the strengths of this model is that it takes into account the complex nature of team leadership, this very complexity is also one of this approach's greatest weaknesses. The model is very complicated to understand, and it does not provide easy answers to difficult decisions for the leader. With so much distributed and shared leadership in organizations today, such a complicated approach to leadership might not be practical for the growing number of team leaders.

This theoretical approach, in addition to being highly complex, does not offer on-the-spot answers to specific situations for the team leader. What should the leader say to a team member who is crying? How do you deal with team members who are screaming at each other? What do you do when the organization refuses to reward team performance? The group effectiveness approach seems to be best suited to diagnosis and long-range planning but does not seem to provide much guidance for the everyday interactions and complications of team management. The leadership portion of the model needs to be expanded to learn more about specific skills and interventions that could help the group deal with the more immediate critical incidents that arise on a daily basis.

Finally, the fact that the group effectiveness approach suggests new and creative directions for leadership training could be construed as a strength. However, these directions for leadership training are currently vague, complex, and somewhat overwhelming. Monitoring skills such as data gathering, diagnosis and forecasting, hypothesis testing, and learning skills are advocated along with various action-taking skills such as envisioning, inventing, negotiating, decision making, teaching, and implementing (Hackman & Walton, 1986). Such a long list of team leadership skills makes it very difficult to know where to start. This is compounded by the fact that many teams are empowered and self-directed, necessitating that these skills be taught to everyone who serves in the role of team leader, sometime, somewhere. The roles of leaders and followers can change over time in a planned organizational restructuring or can even change within the course of a day, making it very important for the leader to understand the follower roles and vice versa. More focus and attention need to be given as to how to teach and provide skill development in the areas of diagnosis and action taking so that such leadership skill develop-ment can be implemented easily within all levels of the organization.

Application

There are many ways to apply the group effectiveness approach to leading organizational teams. One way to use the model itself would be to analyze the team by using the various boxes and levels in the model to attempt to diagnose the location of any team problem you might have. For example, if the group was not performing effec-tively (group effectiveness), then the leader could see if there were appropriate material resources or if there was a problem with one of the process measures. If a process problem were noted, then the leader could do a levels analysis to determine what inputs might be contrib-uting to the process problems. The leader (leadership) could take corrective action in the form of design changes or coaching to reduce the problems and improve the working conditions.

The leader might also choose to use a survey or questionnaire, like the one included later in this chapter, to help conduct the team's diagnosis and set the steps needed for action. The instrument devel-oped by LaFasto and Larson (1987) can measure a team's health in terms of the eight criteria of team excellence discussed above. The team members are asked to complete the questionnaire, as is the team leader. Then the results of this information are fed back to the entire team, allowing the team members to compare their performance on each of these criteria to a normative data bank of organizational teams. Such a normative comparison can suggest to the team leader and members just which areas are most in need of improvement. The team then can work to prepare action plans to correct the highest priority problems in the team. This team assessment approach is very helpful in determining the complex factors affecting team excellence and building a committed team involved in action planning.

Case Studies

To help you better understand how the group effectiveness approach can be used to lead organizational work groups or teams, you can refer to the case studies below. For each case, you will be asked to put yourself in the role of team leader and apply the group effectiveness approach in analyzing and offering solutions to the team problems.

Case 9.1

Jim Towne is the head of computing in a major utilities company and reports to the vice president of Administration. This vice president has asked him to develop a plan for a common approach to future computing activities in the company. Historically, each unit of the company has had its own approach to computing services. The other two members of the team are Jay Jefferson, who is head of engineering, and Sally Monroe, who is head of production. They report to the vice presidents of Production and of Engineering, respectively, and are consistently rewarded by these vice presidents for cost containment decisions. Towne does not have any direct authority over Jefferson and Monroe in terms of the team's decision making. He has been given the role of facilitator of the team. All of the team members are quite competent technically in their respective areas and have a long and valued history with the company. They have never previously worked together on any projects.

Shortly after beginning to work together, it became obvious to all involved that something was wrong with the group dynamics of this team. The team members would have discussions in which they would agree on a solution. Yet when Towne would report upward to the vice president of Administration, he would change the wording and information contained in the report so that he could exert more control over the decision-making process.

He felt frustrated over not having any direct authority over the other team members and felt blocked by their unwillingness to go with any decisions that might cost money. Towne's sneaky actions caused the other members to distrust him, and in future meetings they became quite argumentative and resistant to his ideas and suggestions.

Questions

Please refer to Figure 9.2, Model for Leadership and Group Effectiveness, when answering these questions.

* What Individual factors seem to be contributing to the P4-group dynamics problem on this team?
* What interpersonal behaviors by team members have contributed to the problem?
* What are the authority problems in this team?
* How should this team be restructured or designed from an organizational context perspective?

Case 9.2

The local cancer center has a health team designed to coordinate the care of children with cancer. The team is composed of a physician, Dr. Raymond Rose (a clinical oncologist); a radiologist, Dr. Wayne Linett; a nurse practitioner, Sharon Whittling; a social worker, Cathy Stone; a physical therapist, Nancy Crosby; and a child life worker, Janet Lewis. The team meets on a weekly basis to discuss the 18 children under their care and to come to agreement about the best course of treatment for each child. Cathy Stone, the social worker, is the head of the team and is responsible for the case management of each child. When the team meets, however, Drs. Rose and Linett dominate the conversation. They feel that their medical background gives them greater knowledge and skill in the area of treatment of cancer in children. They welcome input from the women in the group, but when it comes to making a decision they insist on doing it their way for the good of the patient. The social worker, child life worker, physical therapist, and nurse resent this behavior because they are the ones who spend the most time with the children and feel that they know best how to handle the children's long-term care. The group effectiveness or outcomes of this group are such that the patients feel no one cares about them or understands them. The team is also having trouble working together, and no one on the team is feeling satisfied with the outcome.

Questions

Please refer to Figure 9.2, Model of Leadership and Group Effectiveness, to answer these questions.

* How was the process measure of knowledge and skills (P-2) affecting the process of this health team?

- In terms of the group composition (G-2), how did gender affect this group?
- How did status of medical specialty?
- Were authority issues also involved in this case (G-4)?
- How?
- As the leader of this group, what could you do to make it more effective?

Case 9.3

A faculty member, Kim Green from the Management Department, was asked to chair a major university committee to plan the mission of the university for the next 25 years. Three other senior faculty and seven administrators from across the campus were also asked to serve on this committee. The president of the university, Dr. Sulgrave, gave the committee its charge: "What should Northcoast University be like in the year 2020?" Dr. Sulgrave told the committee that the work of this task force was of utmost importance to the future of the university and the charge of the committee should take precedence over all other matters. The task force was allowed to meet in the president's conference room and use the president's secretary. The report of the committee was due in 2 months.

The task force members felt very good about being selected to such an important team. The team met on a weekly basis for about 2 hours. At first the members were very interested in the task and participated enthusiastically. They were required to do a great deal of outside research and gathering of information. They would return to the meetings proud to demonstrate and share their research and knowledge. After a while, however, the meetings did not go well. The members could not seem to agree on what the charge to the group meant. They argued among themselves about what they were supposed to accomplish and resented the time the committee was taking from their regular jobs. Week after week the team met and got nothing accomplished. Attendance began to become a problem, with people skipping several meetings, showing up late, or leaving early. Group members stopped working on their committee assignments. Kim Green didn't know what to do, because she didn't want to admit to the university president that the committee members didn't know what they were doing. She just got more and more frustrated. Meetings became sporadic and eventually stopped altogether. The president got involved in a "crisis" in the university and seemed to lose interest in Kim Green's committee. The president never called for the report from the committee, and the report was never completed.

Questions

Refer to the eight characteristics of team excellence to answer these questions—clear elevating goal, results driven structure, competent team members, unified commitment, collaborative climate, standards of excellence, external support and recognition, and principled leadership.

- What characteristics of excellence were lacking in this task force?
- Which characteristics of excellence were evident in this task force?
- What would be the most important change you would make if you were the leader of this task force?

Leadership Instrument

Several different instruments have been used to assess team effectiveness and the leadership within those teams. Larson and LaFasto (1989) have developed a survey to assess a team's health. They developed this survey after studying many different types of excellent organizational teams. Their research has demonstrated eight criteria or factors that are consistently associated with team excellence and high performance. The complete survey contains more than 40 questions across the eight factors that are used to diagnose a team's performance level and to suggest which areas might need corrective action. The team members are given the questionnaire, and their scores are combined and averaged to obtain a group view. At the same time, the leader of the team fills out the survey. The responses from the team leader are then compared with the team members', and the areas of greatest weakness, if any are diagnosed. Then the team, along with the leader, plans action steps to correct and improve these weak areas.

The survey is designed as a diagnostic tool for teams to help them sort through the complex maze of issues and problems confronting them and to pinpoint areas for action taking. The team's results on these items can be compared with scores from many other teams to provide some normative information about a team's current level of performance.

As you fill out the sample questionnaire, think about a group or team to which you belong either as a member or as the leader. The items that you score "False" (either a 1 or a 2) are the areas of team weakness from your personal perspective. To obtain a team assessment you would need to compare your scores on this instrument with the scores of the other group members. For example, if almost everyone on the team scores "False" to Item 3: "Team members possess the essential skills and abilities to accomplish the team's objectives," then the team leader might need to provide training to increase the competence of team members. An instrument like this one that assesses team effectiveness is particularly helpful to the team leader in diagnosing the area(s) of team weakness and suggesting solutions to improving team effectiveness.

Team Effectiveness Questionnaire

INSTRUCTIONS: This questionnaire contains questions about your team and the leadership within this team. Indicate whether you feel each statement is true or not true of your team. Use the following scale.

KEY: 1 = False, 2 = More False Than True, 3 = More True Than False, 4 = True

__4__ 1. There is a clearly defined need—a goal to be achieved or a purpose to be served—that justifies the existence of our team. (clear elevating goal)

__2__ 2. We have an established method for monitoring individual performance and providing feedback. (results driven structure)

__3__ 3. Team members possess the essential skills and abilities to accomplish the team's objectives. (competent team members)

__3__ 4. Achieving our team goal is a higher priority than any individual objective. (unified commitment)

__3__ 5. We trust each other sufficiently to accurately share information, perceptions, and feedback. (collaborative climate)

__3__ 6. Our team exerts pressure on itself to improve performance. (standards of excellence)

__3__ 7. Our team is given the resources it needs to get the job done. (external support/recognition)

___4___ 8. The team leader provides me the necessary autonomy to achieve results. (principled leadership)

___3___ 9. Our leader is willing to confront and resolve issues associated with inadequate performance by team members. (principled leadership)

___4___ 10. Our leader is open to new ideas and information from team members. (principled leadership)

___3___ 11. Our leader is influential in getting outside constituencies—industry, board, media, the next level of management—to support our team's effort. (principled leadership)

SOURCE: Adapted from Team Excellence Survey (Copyright 1987 LaFasto and Larson. Portions reprinted with permission of authors).

Scoring Interpretation

In addition to such targeted questions on each of the eight criteria of excellence, the survey also asks open-ended questions to allow team members the opportunity to comment on issues that might not be specifically covered in the directed questions, such as strengths and weaknesses of the team and its leadership, changes that are needed, norms that are problematic, or issues that need to be addressed. The complete version of the survey is given to team members and the team leader, and all are involved in the diagnosis and in the resulting action planning. Such a method is clearly consistent with the empowerment movement in organizational teams and helps deal with the enormous complexity involved in making teams effective.

Summary

The increased importance of organizational teams and the leadership needed within them has produced a renewed interest in team leadership theory. The leadership and group effectiveness model provides a framework within which to study the systematic factors that contribute to a group's outcomes or general effectiveness. Within this approach, the leader's critical function is to assist the group in accomplishing its goals by monitoring/diagnosing the group and taking the requisite action.

A systems model has been developed to display the various components and elements within this effectiveness approach. The model portrays the relationship between inputs (individual factors, context factors, group design, material resources) and outputs (group effectiveness measures) and process measures (effort, knowledge, strategies, and group dynamics). In addition, the model demonstrates the role the team leader can play in monitoring and taking the appropriate action relative to these factors.

A questionnaire has also been developed to ascertain a team's general level of effectiveness. Eight criteria have been found to be present in highly effective teams. The survey, filled out by team members as well as the team leader, can aid in diagnosing specific areas of team problems and suggesting action steps to be taken by the team.

One of the strengths of this approach is that it focuses on real organizational work groups and what makes them effective. The model also emphasizes that much of team leadership is shared and can be distributed within the work group.

The model offers help in selecting leaders and team members with the appropriate diagnostic and action-taking skills. Furthermore, the model is also appropriately complex, providing a cognitive model for understanding and researching organizational teams.

One of the weakness of this approach is that it is new and not much research exists to support the many connections and claims made by the model. The analytical and action-taking leadership skills prescribed by the model need further development. Also, for pragmatists who want immediate answers to every question, this model might be frustratingly complex and long term.

Hackman (1990), in support of this approach, suggests that those who lead organizational teams need to recognize that team effectiveness is a complicated process and that the factors involved are complex and interrelated and must not be studied in isolation.

The team leader needs to learn to create the conditions that support team excellence by allowing the team to thrive. Such an approach recognizes that there is no one best way for a team to function and allows each team to create its own norms and structure.

References

Barge, J. K. (1989, Fall). Leadership as medium: A leaderless group discussion model. *Communication Quarterly, 37*(4), 237-247.

Barge, J. K. (1994). *Leadership: Communication skills for organizations and groups.* New York: St. Martin's.

Drecksel, G. L. (1991). Leadership research: Some issues. In J. A. Anderson (Ed.), *Communication Yearbook* (Vol. 14, pp. 535-546). Newbury Park, CA: Sage.

Fisher, B. A. (1985, May). Leadership as medium: Treating complexity in group communication research. *Small Group Behavior, 16*(2), 167-196.

Fleishman, E. A., Mumford, M. D., Zaccaro, S. J., Levin, K. Y., Korotkin, A. L., & Hein, M. B. (1991). Taxonomic efforts in the description of leader behavior: A synthesis and functional interpretation. *Leadership Quarterly, 2*(4), 245-287.

Hackman, J. R. (1990). Work teams in organizations: An orienting framework. In J. R. Hackman (Ed.), *Groups that work (and those that don't): Creating conditions for effective teamwork* (pp. 1-14). San Francisco: Jossey-Bass.

Hackman, J. R., & Walton, R. E. (1986). Leading groups in organizations. In P. S. Goodman & Associates (Eds.), *Designing effective work groups* (pp. 72-119). San Francisco: Jossey-Bass.

Hughes, R. L., Ginnett, R. C., & Curphey, G. J. (1993). *Leadership: Enhancing the lessons of experience.* Homewood, IL: Irwin.

Ilgen, D. R., Major, D. A., Hollenbeck, J. R., & Sego, D. J. (1993). Team research in the 1990's. In M. M. Chemers & R. Ayman (Eds.), *Leadership theory and research: Perspectives and directions* (pp. 245-270). San Diego, CA: Academic Press.

LaFasto, F. M. J., & Larson, C. E. (1987). *Team Excellence Survey.* Denver, CO: Authors.

Larson, C. E., & LaFasto, F. M. J. (1989). *Teamwork: What must go right/What can go wrong.* Newbury Park, CA: Sage.

Parker, G. M. (1990). *Team players and teamwork.* San Francisco: Jossey-Bass.

Wellins, R. S., Byham, W. C., & Wilson, J. M. (1991). *Empowered teams: Creating self-directed work teams that improve quality, productivity, and participation.* San Francisco: Jossey-Bass.

CHAPTER 10

Psychodynamic Approach

ERNEST L. STECH

Description

Our first experience with leadership occurs the day we are born. Mom and Dad become our leaders, at least for a few years. That is the most basic premise of the psychodynamic approach to leadership. Our parents create, particularly in the early years of childhood, deep-seated feelings about leadership. The parental image is highlighted in business when we refer to a corporation as "paternalistic." Hill (1984) has written on "the law of the father," a psychodynamic examination of leadership. Members of the U.S. Air Force sometimes refer to their service as the "Big Blue Mother," referring of course to the color of the uniforms and the "wild blue yonder." The familial metaphor is used frequently in organizations that term themselves "one big happy family," with the natural consequence that the leaders are the parents. Childhood and adolescent experiences in the family are reflected in reactions to paternalistic, maternalistic, and familial patterns of leadership and management. Some people respect and respond to authority figures. Others rebel. Most important, however, psychological development produces personality types, and the key to effective leadership is to understand these types and their differences.

The emergence of the psychodynamic approach to leadership has its roots in the works of Sigmund Freud in his development of psychoanalysis (Freud, 1938). Freud was attempting to understand and help patients who had problems that were not responding to the conventional kinds of treatments of that day. So he moved to hypnosis and found that he could help some of his patients, who were suffering from what was then known as hysterical paralysis, to overcome their difficulties. Later he discovered that hypnosis was not necessary. Simply having patients talk about their pasts was enough to effect a cure.

Freud's work spawned a large number of offshoots. One of his well-known disciples was Carl Jung, who eventually developed his own body of psychological writings. Today Jungian psychology is well accepted, whereas classical psychoanalysis has found less acceptance in recent years. Yet it is from the works of both Freud and Jung that the psychodynamic approach to leadership has been constructed.

A leading proponent of the psychodynamic approach to leadership is Abraham Zaleznik (1977), a management professor at Harvard. The psychodynamic approach is also behind much of the writing about charismatic leaders (Hummel, 1975; Schiffer, 1973; Winer, Jobe, & Ferrono, 1984-1985). One branch of psychodynamic theorizing is termed *psychohistory* and consists of attempts to explain the behavior of historical figures such as Lincoln and Hitler. These studies review the historical record of the leader and delve into the familial background as well. There are some basic general ideas underlying the various psychodynamic approaches to leadership.

Important concepts in the psychodynamic approach to leadership include the family of origin, maturation or individuation, dependence and independence, regression, and the shadow self. Each of these plays a unique role in the leadership process.

Family of Origin

The first concept, the *family of origin*, underlies any understanding of the behavior of adults. Each of us is born into a family. The traditional family consists of two parents and one or more children. Today, of course, there are numerous single-parent families as well. No matter which type of family, the role of the parent is to socialize the child into society. The psychodynamic view is that the child begins life essentially as a very self-centered being, more animal than human. The parent's role in early infancy is to meet the needs of the child. In one sense, the parent has control over the very dependent child, but at the same time the child has an equal degree of control, through his or her needs, over the parent. Every time the baby cries, the parent responds with food, touch, or a clean diaper.

Maturation or Individuation

As time goes on, the child becomes more independent of the parent, needing less direct satisfaction of needs. This goes on through the preschool, kindergarten, and elementary and secondary school years. With each succeeding stage of development, the child drifts farther from the parental home. However, the child, properly socialized, carries a parent inside constantly supervising, analyzing, and judging.

All through the process of *maturation*, which psychologists call *individuation*, a key issue is the relationship of the child to authority figures, which, in turn, is related to how the parent acts in her or his role. Highly authoritarian parents may induce either a very submissive or a very resistant attitude in the child. A laissez-faire parent, on the other hand, can create a confused child who has trouble defining boundaries and limits. When such an individual does confront an authority figure, the reaction can be difficult to predict. (There are various other issues that develop in the family of origin, for example, the issue of intimacy. For the purposes of dealing with leadership, however, the authority figure theme is our focus here.)

Dependence and Independence

Adults may find themselves in a relationship with an authoritarian leader or one with a more participative style, and the reaction of the adult team member to the leader will be a function of the way authority figures, parents in particular, behaved and were dealt with in the past. Psychodynamically, an individual may react to a leader in a *dependent, counterdependent,* or *independent* manner. Dependency is self-explanatory. The counterdependent reaction is rebelliousness, rejecting the directives of the leader. Independence occurs when the subordinate assesses leadership attempts by doing reality testing, that is, by assessing the relative probabilities and merits of various courses of action. Such an individual will accept directives that make sense and question those that do not.

Similarly, the way a leader behaves toward his or her subordinates is related to the way in which the leader was raised. Strict authoritarian parenting can create an equally strict and authoritarian leader. Individuals who react against that kind of upbringing tend to take on a more laissez-faire style.

It is possible for an adult to study and be trained in the proper ways of behaving as a leader. By reading books and going to training seminars, the leader can learn the appropriate behaviors for handling a variety of subordinates in a wide range of situations. This is overlaid on the individual's personality. Yet when placed in a very stressful situation, the leader may revert to more basic patterns of behavior. This is termed *regression* in the psychodynamic approach and is a concept found in at least one other chapter in this book.

Repression and the Shadow Self

A difference between the psychodynamic approach and that of others described in this volume is found in the idea of depth psychology. Behavioral psychology takes the position that only behaviors, which can be seen, heard, or felt, are worth studying. Another version of psychology holds that we can also study what people think and feel, the ideas and emotions of which we are conscious. But depth psychology says that some of what impels us to certain acts and feelings is below the conscious level, that is, resides in the subconscious.

Parents, to bring that theme back into the discussion, are charged with the responsibility of socializing the child. That means teaching the young person the difference between right and wrong, between what is acceptable and unacceptable in society. Behaviors that are wrong and unacceptable are punished. For example, most parents teach their child that it is wrong to hit someone and particularly to hit a parent. Yet the child still has the impulse to strike out at someone who has just inflicted pain. Punishment by the parent—which may be a verbal rebuke or some "time out" in a corner—teaches the child not to hit but may, eventually, even teach the child not to feel the anger.

The technical term for the result of this process is *repression*. We put into deep recesses of the mind those thoughts and feelings that

are deemed unacceptable by society. Yet when a person is hurt by someone, the physiological reaction still occurs. Something will eventually
happen. It may be in the form of an ulcer. It may be in the form of a
sarcastic remark to a friend. Depth psychology says that at least some
of our behavior cannot be understood simply in terms of the immediately preceding stimulus or even of a verbal explanation offered by
the individual. To get at the underlying reason for some actions, the
person must sit down and talk, try to remember past experiences, and
dredge up the feelings associated with those experiences. Then she
or he can begin to "explain" why current actions occur.

Jungian psychology introduces the *concept of the shadow* (Jung,
1923). This is somewhat related to the idea of repression. An individual's shadow is that part of the personality that is unacceptable consciously and the existence of which is therefore denied. For example,
a leader may pride herself on very high ethical standards and impec-
cable integrity. Yet that woman may also be a very politically astute
individual who is able to survive in a complex array of relationships
in a corporation by carefully wording her statements and remaining
ambiguous on some issues. This side of her personality does not fit
with her self-image and will be denied, yet others will see that she is
politically adroit and even admire her for it. The shadow is often
evident to others although denied by the person.

Concepts such as individuation, counterdependence, and repression come out of the highly technical literature of psychoanalysis,
psychiatry, and psychological counseling and are used by professionals to discuss their clients and clinical techniques. Such discussions
can be abstruse and not easily understood by the lay person. There
have been attempts to make psychodynamic theory more accessible.

Relational Analysis

A popularized and popular psychodynamic model was created
by Eric Berne and titled "transactional analysis" (Berne, 1961; Harris,
1967). It could also have been called "relational analysis." Berne labeled three ego states: *parent, adult,* and *child.* These terms obviously
relate to family roles. In Berne's view, the parent ego state tends to be
one that is either controlling or nurturing. The child ego state can be
either playful or rebellious. Finally, the adult ego state is one in which
the individual engages in reality testing, finding out what the situation is really like, the options available, and the likely results of any

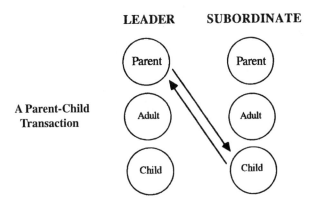

Figure 10.1. Ego States of Leader and Subordinate

particular action. The important point in this form of analysis is in the transactions between persons that are shown in Figure 10.1.

A leader acting out of the parent ego state is likely to get a reaction from a follower that is out of the child ego state. This is a parent-child transaction and relationship. Similarly, a subordinate who acts in a dependent and therefore childlike way will tend to draw out the parental response of the leader. The technical term in psychoanalysis for this is *cathecting*. Each person tends to cathect or pull out of the other person a matching response pattern. In other words, leaders and followers—as well as friends, spouses, lovers, and relatives—create relationships with each other, and it is not enough simply to look at the personality of the leader or of the subordinate.

How Does the Psychodynamic Approach Work?

From its inception with Freud, the psychodynamic theory and method were intended to produce change in the client. This underpinning has continued throughout the history of the field of psychology, including the advent of social work and pastoral counseling of individuals. In the 1960s, procedures were developed to apply these methods to people without serious mental disturbances and came to be known as the human potential movement and subsequently as personal growth or personal development. This spawned a whole series of books, seminars, workshops, and lectures so that today there are entire sections of bookstore shelves devoted to the subject.

One assumption underlies all of these psychodynamic and personal growth techniques. The clinician, workshop facilitator, and writer assume that insight into the psychological past of the individual will result in changes in feelings, attitudes, and behaviors. For example, a person who was raised in an authoritarian family of origin can recognize that pattern of child rearing and through understanding it overcome the tendency to become either dependent or counterdependent in relationships with authority figures. Similarly, an individual may have a shadow self that tends to be nurturing and kind, yet the work situation encourages that person to take on a tough, even critical, demeanor. If insight about the shadow self can be brought about, that individual may find it easier to express the nurturing side at work or may wish to find employment in a situation where kindness is accepted as a norm.

The development of insight is a long-term proposition. Adherents to the psychodynamic model would say, in fact, that it is a continuing life-long endeavor.

Many healthy and "normal" people see counselors, therapists, and guides regularly. These people attend seminars, workshops, and retreats. They read extensively on the subject and continually assess and reassess their own life history, values, emotional reactions, and relationships.

From the viewpoint of the psychodynamic model, all of the various tests and evaluations of leadership style are useful for the insights they produce. A leader who understands his or her style will be more effective than one who is blind to it. Even more important, however, is the leader's ability to understand how that style came about, from the family of origin, from dealings with authoritarian or laissez-faire teachers and coaches, or from social interactions that encouraged the repression of some feelings.

Strengths

The greatest strength of the psychodynamic approach is that it results in an analysis of the relationship between the leader and the follower.

This transactional emphasis is important, and it should be emphasized that it is a transaction between the two persons. In some models of leadership, the leader is supposed to exhibit certain appropriate behaviors that will create the desired response in the subordinate. The leader, in that kind of model, is not really an ordinary mortal but someone who can always act in the most appropriate way. The psychodynamic approach takes the position that both leader and subordinate have needs and feelings, not all of which are consciously available, and their relationship will be a result of the mix of those needs and feelings.

A second strength is the universality of the psychodynamic approach. Much of the theory underlying this approach, in contemporary times, is based on a search for a universal truth in human existence, and this is done through a reliance on a study of myth. Jung (1923, 1961), as well as Freud, relied heavily on Greek myths to label psychological actions and reactions such as the Oedipus complex. Subsequently, Joseph Campbell (1949, 1988) spent his lifetime studying mythic stories from cultures around the world, and he was able to show that there are basic themes underlying all of the stories from all of the cultures he studied. This work has been related to the concept of psychological archetypes that presumably are applicable cross-culturally.

Another strength of the psychodynamic approach is that it emphasizes the need for insight on the part of the leader. Insight into self is obtained by bringing into consciousness and dealing with issues from childhood and the family of origin. By talking and writing about these issues, the leader obtains insight that then permits her or him to understand the feelings that emerge in present situations. In turn, the ability to monitor those feelings and the behaviors they produce allows the leader to override them. The leader is also encouraged, in this approach, to gain insight into the reactions of subordinates. Rather than taking their responses at face value, the leader is able to understand why a particular action is taken. This should permit the leader greater tolerance of follower actions.

The psychodynamic approach, following from the preceding comments, encourages the leader to pursue a course of personal growth and development that can result not just in better leadership but also in a more rewarding life. The leader may find satisfaction in more than just the acquisition of power or accomplishment of great goals.

Lastly, the psychodynamic approach, at least in its most modern form, discourages manipulative techniques in leadership. This is discussed more fully in the section on applications. Effective leadership using the psychodynamic approach is based upon self-understanding and empathy with the feelings and reactions of the follower. Ultimately, the effective leader, using this approach, becomes a teacher and counselor as well as a goal setter, directive giver, and all of the other traditional leader roles.

Criticisms

There are, of course, criticisms of the psychodynamic approach. One, clearly, is that much of the early work on this approach was based on clinical observation and treatment of persons with serious difficulties. This was a psychology of the abnormal rather than the normal. Psychiatrists work, for the most part, with people who are having problems. Thus the observations they make are probably biased by the troubles of their clients. In recent times, there has been more emphasis on the psychodynamics of the everyday individual, particularly in the humanistic psychologies and personal growth realm, but the academic and clinical bias is still toward the dysfunctional and problematic.

Even more telling is the subjective nature of the findings of clinical psychologists. The insights obtained by a particular psychiatrist or psychologist will depend, obviously, on the information brought forth by the client or set of clients, but those insights will also be colored by and may even be directed by the unconscious predispositions of the clinician. These professionals prepare for their work by going through a process of insight development, usually by working with a previously trained individual. In other words, every psychoanalyst has undergone psychoanalysis. Every counselor should have undergone rigorous counseling. Those processes do not guarantee that the individual is without biases and predispositions. We all see what we want or need to see, and that includes even the most highly trained and experienced clinician.

Research in the psychodynamic area tends to consist of case study reports from individual psychiatrists. If applied to leadership, such insights may be colored by the biases of the psychiatric observers. A psychiatrist who is herself somewhat counterdependent may describe effective leadership in laissez-faire or democratic terms and denigrate more authoritarian forms.

Closely related to the issue of subjectivity and probably more important are the cultural biases carried by the individual psychologist. Freud's early work was based on the treatment of upper-middle-class Viennese women in a society that was extremely patriarchal. Freud himself, of course, was male and he associated with well-educated and affluent men. Virtually all psychologists over the years, by definition, are well educated and relatively well off financially. Their patients, for the most part, come from similar backgrounds, particularly the patients who pay for their own treatment. Most of those patients, in the past, have been white and at least middle class, with a Judeo-Christian background. We simply do not know to what extent the picture we have of the human psyche is equally valid for persons with a Hispanic, African-American, or Asian cultural background. Thus any leadership model developed out of the psychodynamic literature or practice is likely to be most applicable to the white middle-class individual with a Judeo-Christian upbringing.

Further, much of the early work in psychodynamics was based on the traditional two-parent family of origin. Today many children are growing up in single-parent families and, perhaps even more common, in families composed of step-parents and step-siblings. Divorce and remarriage create complex sets of relationships.

The psychodynamic approach is also limited in that it focuses primarily on the psyche of the leader and on the psychological factors that dictate the nature of the relationship between the leader and follower. In other words, it does not take into account organizational factors. These could include the culture of the organization, its structure, and the particular kinds of challenges and tasks it faces.

A final limitation is that the psychodynamic approach does not lend itself to training in any conventional sense. The leader has to undergo a process of personal growth and insight development, and, ideally, continues that process for as long as he or she is in the leadership position.

Application

The psychodynamic approach to leadership is unique in that it is not specifically addressed to the question of leadership but rather to the larger issues of human existence and relationships. As noted previously, the concepts that make up this approach arose out of clinical practice rather than through the standard social science quantitative and qualitative research methods. This approach places a great emphasis on personal growth for leaders. For example, the work of the humanistic psychologists (Maslow, 1962, 1971; Rogers, 1961; Shostrom, 1967) has spawned a wide variety of seminars, workshops, and training sessions devoted to providing individuals with the opportunity to learn about human behavior and experience.

Clinical work and the personal growth movement both emphasize the development of insight by the individual. The foundation of psychodynamics is based on the unconscious and the development of emotional response patterns in early childhood within the family of origin. People who become aware of these learned patterns and who are able to articulate them can then choose to behave differently. First comes insight, then behavior change.

Therefore, the application of the psychodynamic approach to leadership involves the development of insight by the leader into her or his own emotional responses and their genesis. The leader may also become somewhat educated in psychodynamics and attempt to understand and empathize with the reactions of subordinates. Ideally, the follower is able to gain insight in his or her feelings and behaviors. These statements do not imply that either the leader or the subordinate must engage in psychotherapy. The options available for insight development range from reading some of the numerous books available on personal growth to attending workshops and seminars that provide feedback from other persons or through psychological test results.

One of the methods currently used to develop better relationships between leaders and subordinates, particularly in business organizations, is to have individuals assess their personal styles through a personality inventory. It is not uncommon to have all of the personnel involved, whether managers, professionals, staff, or line employees, take a standard psychological inventory such as the Myers-Briggs Type Indicator™ that results in scores on four dimensions of personality. The test outcomes are then made available and discussed by the participants. Each person becomes aware of every other individual's "type." Generally, this results in greater understanding of and tolerance for the way the people work together. The leader is included in this process so that he or she becomes aware of the types of each of the members of the team and they, in turn, are able to see the leader's "type." There are no evaluative features to the Myers-Briggs results. They simply represent different ways of psychological functioning. Kroeger and Thuesen (1992) have written a book on the psychological types and their implications for people at work.

The use of test results to understand and compare styles suggests the ultimate goal of the psychodynamic approach to leadership in practical terms. Humans are able to use language, and one of the more important uses is to talk about relationships. Effective human relationships evolve when the parties are able to talk about the relationship as well as about themselves as individuals and about the work they do. Yet most people find it difficult to bring up this kind of relational communication. The use of the Myers-Briggs or similar questionnaire outcomes is one way to encourage people to discuss their relationships.

Case Studies

In this section, case studies (Cases 10.1, 10.2, and 10.3) of leadership in organizations are provided that can be explained using the psychodynamic approach. The questions provided at the end of each case will help you analyze the situations.

Case 10.1

Jim Ferris is the president and CEO of a small manufacturing company that produces metal and plastic components for larger local businesses. Eight months ago, Jim hired an operations manager who was given responsibility over all of the fabrication, inventory, quality control, and associated functions on the shop floor. Hal, the operations manager, stepped right in and was very effective in improving the efficiency of the whole shop.

Several months after Hal was hired, Jim began having a weekly formal review meeting that included Hal and the supervisors under his direction. The first few meetings went very well. Recently, Hal has begun to act in a very reserved manner in contrast to his very enthusiastic and energetic behavior in the prior months. Jim is smart enough to realize that the change in behavior began just a month or so after he started having the review meetings.

Because Hal was an important factor in the company's current profitability and growth, Jim wanted to identify the problem and deal with it. He retained an industrial psychologist as a consultant who then came into the plant and interviewed Hal and all of the production supervisors. The psychologist's report pinpointed the problem. Hal had difficulty working for authoritarian leaders. Jim did not see himself that way, but the psychologist pointed out that Jim had shifted from letting Hal go his own way to instituting the review meetings.

Questions

* What intervention could the industrial psychologist make to minimize the problem?
* What can Jim do to take Hal's reactions into account and still maintain some control over operations?
* What would help Hal see, understand, and change his behavior?

Case 10.2

Jenny Folsom is the manager of a group of marketing specialists. She has good relationships with most of her team except for Connie Perez. Jenny is on the verge of letting Connie go. Connie just cannot seem to work up to the expectations that Jenny has. Over the past year, Jenny had four quarterly review sessions with Connie. In each one Jenny pointed out her expectations and where Connie was falling short. Connie continued to act in much the same way even though she felt she was trying to improve.

Before going to the drastic and final step of dismissing an employee, Jenny has gone to the Personnel Department and specifically to the Training and Development Group. She has presented her problem to two training and development specialists. This is what she said: "Connie seems to get bogged down in details. I give her a project to work on and a set of overall objectives. Then, when I talk to her, I find that she is buried in some minor issue, getting all the information she can, talking to other people about that issue. It drives me crazy. I need to get the project completed and have her move on to something else. I want her to see the big picture. We have a lot to do, a whole strategy to implement. I can't afford to have someone getting hung up on minor details."

The training and development specialists sense that there is a big difference in personal styles between Jenny and Connie. They invite Jenny to come back the next day, at which time she is given a briefing on personal styles. It quickly becomes evident that Jenny is an NT (the code is explained later in this chapter) temperament, an "intuitive thinker," in the Jungian personality types. She is good at conceptualizing and systematic planning. She can see the underlying principles of organizations and systems.

With each accomplishment of her group, Jenny can see three or four new big challenges. When the training and development specialists talked this way to Jenny she agreed readily with their description of her.

Connie, on the other hand, seems to be an SF (sensor-feeler) temperament based on Jenny's description. Connie is very practical and down to earth. She actually is quite good at problem solving in an immediate way. And she is highly resourceful, able to find information and answers. Unfortunately, she simply is not the type to see the "big picture."

Jenny's question to the training and development specialists is: So what do I do?

Questions

- Should Jenny have a session with Connie on her own?
- Should she have the session with the training and development specialists?
- Should Connie be given the results for herself and for Jenny?
- What kinds of issues should the two women discuss?
- What kinds of tasks should Jenny assign to Connie in the future?

Case 10.3

Gerry heads up a team of personnel who staff a large retail copy center. He has an assistant manager, two shift leaders, and a staff of 16 well-trained team members. The store is open 7 days a week and 24 hours a day. Gerry is proud of the way his team functions. There is some turnover because the team members are paid a relatively low hourly rate. However, the store engages in a profit-sharing plan that supplements the team members' paychecks fairly well each month. Gerry thought they could do better.

In the prior 6 months, Gerry has tried all of the standard motivational techniques spelled out in textbooks and seminars. Now he decides to take a bold step. On a Sunday afternoon, Gerry holds a team meeting. He talks about their current sales and profitability level and points out that he thinks they could do better. The team members do not respond one way or another to this statement. Gerry then tells them that he wants to do two things that day. First, he wants them to write down, anonymously, their impression of him as a leader and how he could improve his performance. After that is done, he opens up the floor to discussion of how they could improve their overall performance. At first there is some reluctance on the part of the team members to offer anything beyond the usual suggestions, most of which had been tried at one time or another. Then Gerry says: "Let's be bold. Let's go out on a limb and try some things that we haven't tried before. Does anyone have any ideas?" At first there is silence. Then one team member offers the suggestion that each person be given the opportunity to do some sales work in addition to running the copy machines and staffing the front counter. Some of the people express their doubts, particularly about their own ability to do sales. Gerry points out that whoever wanted to do sales could do it, and others could figure out other ways to find more interesting tasks.

Questions

- What should Gerry do next in the meeting?
- What should he do with the suggestions produced by the team?
- What should he do with the feedback he received?
- How should he react to anything that he considers negative? Should he compile the feedback and show it to the team members at the next meeting?
- If so, how should it be handled?

Leadership Instrument

The Myers-Briggs Type Indicator, based on Jung's psychological types, is a multiquestion instrument that is usually administered by a clinician or research worker. The test is copyrighted and its use is limited to persons who have the professional qualifications to administer it and interpret the results. There is another psychological test, the Jungian Type Survey (Gray, Wheelwright, & Wheelwright, n.d.), that is also copyrighted but not restricted to certified practitioners in use. The format of the questions on the Myers-Briggs Type Indicator and Jungian Type Survey is like this:

> In solving a personal problem, do you prefer:
>   a. Reading a book on the subject
>   b. Consulting a trusted friend

Each question poses a situation and provides two alternative responses. There are four basic dimensions to the Myers-Briggs, and 16 personality types. (The types are identified by a series of four letters, for example, ISFJ, and the letter designations will be described briefly below.) The Jungian Type Survey deals with three dimensions and eight personality types instead of the four and 16 in the Myers-Briggs version. Neither questionnaire is a leadership instrument in the usual sense. However, they do provide a way for the leader to evaluate her or his personal style and thus gain insight. In addition, they permit the leader to compare his or her style to those of subordinates.

The first dimension is composed of two terms that have found their way into our everyday language: *extraverts* (E) and *introverts* (I). This scale covers the source of a person's energy. The introvert is a reflective, internally focused, and deep person who likes to think things through before speaking, whereas the extravert is much more sociable, externally focused, and gregarious and tends to speak before thinking.

The second dimension is labeled "sensors versus intuitors." Before proceeding, note that the terms used should not be interpreted literally and in a commonsense way. The Jungian typology and nomenclature are unique. This first dimension of personality types relates to how people gather information. *Sensors* (S) tend to be practical, realistic, factual, and specific in their information gathering whereas *intuitors* (N) are more conceptual, theoretical, general, and random in the same function. There are now four possible combinations: ES, EN, IS, and IN.

The third dimension relates to decision making, and the two types here are labeled as *thinkers* (T) and *feelers* (F). The former are firm, just, clear, and detached in their approach to decision making. Feelers, on the other hand, lean more toward human, harmonious, subjective, and involved decision making. The number of combinations is now up to eight: EST, ESF, ENT, ENF, IST, ISF, INT, and INF.

The fourth and last dismension distinguishes between *judgers* (J) and *perceivers* (P), the difference in how people deal with their environment and create their lifestyles. Judgers emphasize control, planning, structure, and schedule in their lives. Perceivers tend more toward adaptability, flexibility, spontaneity, and openness. Adding this distinction to the 8 types listed above produces the final 16 personality types. This dimension is not used in the Jungian Type Survey.

A crude first approximation to finding a personality type can be obtained by reviewing the four descriptors under each dimension and circling the ones that seem to apply to an individual, oneself or a subordinate. A checklist for assessing your own psychodynamic styles is provided in this section.

Remember that there is no intent or any hidden agenda as to which of each of these pairs is better than the other. If you make a judgment toward one or the other, that is probably because it matches your own style. If you are a feeler, the traits of that style will look and sound better to you.

Keep in mind that the results of the Jungian type analysis and the Myers-Briggs instrument do not suggest that one style is more appropriate than another for the leader. Rather, the significant point is that the leader should compare her or his style to that of each subordinate in order to understand where the relationship may go smoothly or may require some work. If there is a style match, little difference and conflict will result. An INTJ leader dealing with an INTJ follower will find a generally compatible relationship. That same leader, in dealing with an ESFP, might find it difficult to understand how and why the subordinate was performing certain tasks, and the subordinate would have some problems in working for that leader. Yet if the two persons were to bring out their styles and the differences in those styles, they would have a better chance for working together in spite of the differences. The key to the psychodynamic approach is not to attempt to match leaders and followers, a virtually impossible task in real-life situations, but rather to bring to the surface and discuss personality types (or psychological issues) openly. The assumption is that such a process will permit any two people to work together effectively.

Psychodynamic Styles Checklist

EXTRAVERT	versus	**INTROVERT**
sociable		reflective
gregarious		deep
externally focused		internally focused
speak before thinking		think before speaking

SENSOR	versus	**INTUITOR**
practical		conceptual
realistic		theoretical
factual		random
specific		general

FEELER	versus	**THINKER**
humane		firm
involved		detached
subjective		objective
harmonious		just

PERCEIVER	versus	**JUDGER**
adaptable		controlled
flexible		planned
spontaneous		scheduled
open		structured

Summary

The psychodynamic approach to leadership arose out of the development of methods for dealing with emotionally disturbed individuals and out of psychological theories of personality development. Freud and Jung were two of the pioneers in this effort.

Clinical work and theorizing led to the development of the concepts of the family of origin, individuation, dependence, counterdependence, independence, regression, repression, and the shadow self.

Popularized versions of the psychodynamic approach were devised, the best known being transactional analysis.

The essential assumption of the psychodynamic approach is that an individual can change behaviors and feelings by obtaining insight into his or her upbringing, prior relationships, and psychological development. The key is to provide mechanisms such as workshops, counseling sessions, or personality assessments that lead to insight.

The strengths of the psychodynamic approach include the emphasis on analyzing the relationship of the leader to the subordinate, an attempt at universality of human experience, the need for insight development by the leader, the encouragement of personal growth, and a rejection of manipulative techniques in dealing with other humans including subordinates.

A major criticism is that much of the theory is based upon the treatment of persons with serious emotional difficulties or crises. A major portion of the psychodynamic theory arises out of the subjective impressions of clinicians and the uses of one-person case studies. There is also a potential for cultural bias in the creation of psychodynamic explanations of behavior, including an assumption of a family of origin consisting of two parents. A limitation also occurs in that the psychodynamic approach focuses on the psychology of the individual leader and ignores the culture and social norms of the organization. Finally, this approach limits the ability to train individuals because it emphasizes the need for insight rather than skill development.

In application, the psychodynamic approach suggests that the leader with insight into her or his own personality and into those of the subordinates will function effectively. This is put into practice when the members of an organization are given a personality inventory and the results are shared among all. The participants are then more readily able to understand and accept their differences.

There are numerous personality inventories used in the application of the psychodynamic approach to leadership, but the most common is the Myers-Briggs Type Indicator. Results of this assessment instrument provide distinctions on four dimensions: extravert or introvert, sensor or intuitor, thinker or feeler, and judger or perceiver. As result, there are 16 potential personality types. Sharing of the leader's personality type and those of the members of the team is assumed to improve understanding among the participants.

Thus, the psychodynamic approach is unique because it focuses on the basic personality of the leader and subordinates and not specifically on leadership traits, behaviors, or processes.

References

Berne, E. (1961). *Transactional analysis in psychotherapy.* New York: Grove.

Campbell, J. (1949). *The hero with a thousand faces.* Princeton, NJ: Princeton University Press.

Campbell, J. (with Moyers, B.). (1988). *The power of myth.* Garden City, NY: Doubleday.

Freud, S. (1938). *The basic writings of Sigmund Freud* (A. A. Brill, Ed.). New York: Modern Library.

Gray, H., Wheelwright, J. H., & Wheelwright, J. B. (undated). *Jungian Type Survey.* San Francisco: Society of Jungian Analysts.

Harris, T. A. (1967). *I'm OK—You're OK.* New York: Harper & Row.

Hill, M. A. (1984). The law of the father. In B. Kellerman (Ed.), *Leadership: Multidisciplinary perspectives.* Englewood Cliffs, NJ: Prentice Hall.

Hummel, R. P. (1975). Psychology of charismatic followers. *Psychological Reports, 37,* 759-770.

Jung, C. J. (1923). *Psychological types.* New York: Harcourt & Brace.

Jung, C. J. (1961). *Memories, dreams, and reflections.* New York: Vintage.

Kroeger, O., & Thuesen, J. M. (1992). *Type talk at work.* New York: Delacorte.

Maslow, A. (1962). *Toward a psychology of being.* New York: Van Nostrand.

Maslow, A. (1971). *The farther reaches of human nature.* New York: Penguin Books.

Rogers, C. R. (1961). *On becoming a person.* Boston: Houghton Mifflin.

Schiffer, I. (1973). *Charisma: A psychoanalytic look at mass society.* Toronto: University of Toronto Press.

Shostrom, E. L. (1967). *Man, the manipulator.* Nashville, TN: Abingdon.

Winer, J. A., Jobe, T., & Ferrono, C. (1984-85). Toward a psychoanalytic theory of the charismatic relationship. *Annual of Psychoanalysis, 12-13,* 155-175.

Zaleznik, A. (1977, May-June). Managers and leaders: Are they different? *Harvard Business Review, 55,* 67-68.

CHAPTER 11 | # Women and Leadership

DAYLE M. SMITH

The topic of gender and leadership has fascinated the popular press in the past two decades. Hundreds of recent magazine and newspaper articles discuss "breaking the glass ceiling," "women and the 50-cent dollar," "the queen bee syndrome," and "women's alternative leadership styles." The purpose of this chapter is to explore what we know related to gender and leadership. Questions to be addressed include such issues as: How far have women advanced into leadership roles in the latter part of the 20th century? Does a glass ceiling still exist, if it ever did? Do men and women have different leadership styles? Are there specific strategies that help women become leaders? Whereas previous chapters in the book addressed leadership as singular theories, this chapter will explore leadership from the multifaceted dimensions of women's and feminist theory. Although the chapter focuses on women in general, it should be pointed out that the issues surrounding the study of women and leadership have implications for others as well. Women of color, the disabled, and other diverse

AUTHOR'S NOTE: The author would like to acknowledge the following people for their valuable input in the drafting of this chapter: Art Bell, Sean Taylor, and Alissa Hauser.

populations face many of the same and in some cases greater barriers to "breaking the glass ceiling" and assuming leadership roles.

A Historical Overview

The facts of women's leadership roles throughout history have often been obscured by highly charged political screens. Too often, the status of women leaders in former decades has been distorted, by diminution or augmentation, to serve as part of a rhetorical argument for the contemporary progress or regress of women in leadership. In truth, women in this century have worked and taken leadership roles in virtually all sectors of government, business, the nonprofit community, and social movements. At the same time, these women in leadership roles tended to be the exception, far out of proportion to their numbers in the general population.

During the decades of World War I and World War II, women were drawn into business and government positions by circumstance as much as by choice. The early draft in World War I conscripted white American males into service; women and African Americans were left to make up the workforce.[1] Women proved essential in running businesses, working in the manufacturing and service sectors, and in keeping American business alive. Yet when World War II ended and men returned to "their" jobs, women found themselves displaced from business and government positions. With many exceptions, of course, women tended to return to their more traditional roles: mothers, homemakers, school teachers, nurses, and secretaries.

The 1950s saw a surge in marriages and a renewed search, in earnest, for the suburban American dream. House, family, cars, vacations, and domestic luxuries were the dreams of the booming population. Because a family could survive and even prosper on one income, the "baby boom" kept millions of women in the nursery rather than the boardroom.

By the early 1960s, however, more challenging economic conditions and the growing popularity of birth control pills sent women once more into the workforce. The ability to do family planning allowed women to exercise career choices and make decisions regarding the types of contributions they might make to society. Many women were also opting not to marry or were postponing marriage and childbearing in pursuit of careers. The mid-1960s saw an increase in the divorce rate. As single parents with few resources and/or skills to enter the workforce, women found what work they could, often at low levels and on part-time schedules.

Largely in response to women's frustrations in their professional and domestic situations, the women's movement took a powerful hold on the popular imagination and, eventually, public policy beginning in the late 1960s. The women's movement in the United States was composed of two groups (Carden, 1974; Freeman, 1975; Hole & Levine, 1971).[2] One group emerged from President Kennedy's establishment in 1961 of the Commission on the Status of Women (1961). Later, a second and more radical group, often referred to as the "women's liberation" segment, emerged in 1967 from civil rights activism and peace movements. Although their methods and political theories may have differed, both groups were significant in bringing attention to women's rights and increased opportunities for women in the workforce.

The Commission's 1963 report and committee publications documented discrimination against women. The Equal Employment Opportunity Commission (EEOC), whose task it was to enforce antidiscrimination law (primarily the 1964 Civil Rights Act), failed miserably at first in taking action on discrimination claims. This inaction galvanized women in their resolve to have sex discrimination complaints taken seriously by the EEOC. They formed the National Organization for Women (NOW) to put political and legal pressure on government agencies to eliminate legal and economic discrimination in the workplace (Carden, 1974; Freeman, 1975). Many other organizations of professional women developed during this time as well.

These early feminists believed that (a) individuals should have equal opportunities regardless of gender, (b) the criteria used to evaluate job performance should be gender-blind, and (c) perceived differences in abilities and interests between genders are not innate but rather are the result of socialization and the general lack of equal opportunity for women (Jaegger, 1983).

In addition to the recognition of women's rights and their abilities to make significant contributions to society, economic necessity continued to change the makeup of the family and the work environment. Rising inflation and interest rates in the 1970s made it clear that living the American dream required dual incomes, especially in major urban centers. More and more women entered the workforce, this time in search of not only a job but a job that paid well.

Although women made up an increasing percentage of the workforce during the 1980s, they continued to be excluded from most leadership positions (see, e.g., Morrison, White, Van Velsor, & the Center for Creative Leadership, 1992). Even in occupations such as school teaching in which women dominated the workforce, leadership roles (principal, headmaster, department chair) were still given almost exclusively to men. Although women were trained as doctors and engineers, these fields admitted even the most qualified women with reluctance, and seldom into leadership positions. Harvard Business School, for example, did not admit women to an entering class until 1974. The Air Force Academy, West Point, and other service academies did not admit women until 1976. More recently, 1996 saw the Virginia Military Institute and the Citadel still fighting to keep women from entering their programs, even with the United States Supreme Court mandate. Thus, opportunities for men and women in the workforce remain unequal, whether by law or practice.

The women's movement, which spawned so many groups and professional organizations, continued to apply pressure to place laws on the books that prohibited discrimination (e.g., Title VII, which prohibits sex discrimination in employment). At the same time, the mood of the country was changing. The baby boomers were growing up and had a different set of expectations for themselves and their children. Men and women were going to college in approximately equal numbers. Women felt free to put off marriage and childbearing if they chose, as they defined a career for themselves and acquired the technical skills to succeed in it.

This trend has accelerated to the present. Whether motivated by economic necessity or by choice, women are competing in the workforce for the same jobs and opportunities as men. The workforce of the 1990s not only accepts but depends upon these contributions. As the baby bust generation enters the workforce, "help wanted" opportunities will open to women as never before due to a shrinking labor pool. U.S. Department of Labor (1988) statistics for Workforce 2000 suggest that 80% of all new entrants to the workforce will be women and other minorities. But even when women workers exceed the number of male workers, it is likely that women will still lag far behind in achieving equal positions in leadership.[3]

This gap between the quantity of female labor versus the hierarchical quality of those positions has been explained by the fact that women have had a later start in making these inroads into corporate and governmental levels of power. Women have made inroads into the business world with women composing nearly half of the U.S. workforce by 1991 (Morrison et al., 1992). Yet these inroads are not at the top. Career development and climbing a corporate ladder takes time, often as long as 20 years in some studies (Kotter, 1990). Is it just a question of time? Or does a woman's style of leadership explain the gap? Are there organizational barriers to women becoming leaders—in effect, a glass ceiling? These are the questions that face the huge corps of women now in the workforce.

Leadership Style: Does Gender Make a Difference?

Contemporary feminist leadership theory views the nature of leadership differently than does more traditional leadership and management theory. Rosener, in a study of women leaders, found that socialization and career paths explain why women lead differently. Although women can lead in ways more similar to the traditional approach of corporate hierarchy (command and control) that men in organizations may take, women in the study described a leadership style innately different. The women interviewed said that their leadership style came to them naturally. Rosener (1990) explains:

> Although socialization patterns and career paths are changing, the average age of the men and women who responded to the survey is 51—old enough to have had experiences that differed because of gender. Until the 1960's, men and women received different signals about what was expected of them . . . women [as] wives, mothers, volunteers, teachers, nurses. . . . In all of these roles they are supposed to be cooperative, supportive, understanding, gentle, and to provide service to others . . . men have had to appear to be competitive, strong, tough, decisive and in control. . . . This may explain why women today are more likely than men to be interactive leaders. (p. 124)

In other words, women described a leadership style that was succeeding "because of—not in spite of—certain characteristics con-

Feminist Leadership Characteristics

- Uses consensus decision making
- Views power in relational terms as something to be shared
- Encourages productive approaches to conflict
- Builds supportive working environments
- Promotes diversity in the workplace

Figure 11.1. A List of Characteristics Considered to Be Feminine That Help to Distinguish Between "Male" and "Female" Ways of Leading

sidered to be 'feminine' and inappropriate in leaders" (Rosener, 1990, p. 120).

These findings are not surprising. Feminist leadership perspectives have viewed organizational leadership as having similar characteristics to the style of leadership women leaders described in their interviews with Rosener. Griggs (1989), in a study of university women's centers and women's study programs, articulated these similarities, which are summarized in the chart in Figure 11.1.

Reviewing these characteristics suggests that women are more comfortable in work environments that are not "boss centered" and therefore develop distinctly adaptive leadership styles. Rosener describes this style as an "interactive" or more transformational style of leadership. The behaviors exhibited in each of these areas help distinguish between traditional "male" and "female" ways of leading.

Consensus Decision Making/ Participatory Structures

Men, traditionally, have viewed leadership as a top-down hierarchy of power. Pecking orders with top-down management styles have been construed in the research literature as more "masculine" in nature (Helgesen, 1990; Maier, 1992; Rosener, 1990). Masculine approaches to leadership from this perspective capture a vertical division of labor in which managers tell subordinates what to do. The style is much more oriented toward an authoritarian approach with respect to organizational structure and decision making. In contrast to this leadership paradigm is Helgesen's (1990) concept of the Web. Drawing from her own research and the work of Gilligan (1982), Helgesen describes women's leadership practices as leading from the center of the organization whereas males tend to lead from hierarchies. Leadership from the center is similar to the way a spider web is formed. The goal is to form interrelated teams linked by the central leader. A web brings people together, whereas a hierarchy is related to looking out for one's own best interests—protecting the power base. By leading from the center, a leader can get information from a variety of sources rather than depending on a chain of command. The leader has more input because the leader is not "out of the loop" and simultaneously gains more input from teams around her (Helgesen, 1990).

Power

Traditional definitions of power see it as something that is zero-sum in nature—the more power one person has, the less another has. Other "masculine" conceptualizations of power depict power as something you have "over" other people, something you control. In analyses of this masculine perspective, power has been seen as a scarcity model based on domination and control of others (Schaef, 1981). Feminists have critiqued this definition of power and have reframed it in a way that does not require domination of others. A related view of power suggests that it can be defined as energy and strength rather than domination and control (Carroll, 1984; Hartsock, 1979; Maier, Ferguson, & Shrivastava, 1993; Schaef, 1981). Power is viewed as a source of synergy—something to be taught and shared. Whereas the masculine view might look at power *over* others, a feminine perspective would see power *with* others (Maier et al., 1993). Power, from this feminine perspective, is understood not in hierarchical terms but in relational terms. Talking about power in relational terms suggests a power model with attributes such as cooperation and interdependence rather than a model of competitiveness and dominance (Hartsock, 1979).

Information and Skill Sharing

In organizational life, information and expertise have often been perceived to be a source of power; in fact, French and Raven's classic work on bases of power identifies expert power as a significant source. The feminist perspective recognizes this power base, but what distinguishes this perspective from more masculine approaches is how this information and expertise are shared in the organization. Feminist leadership tends to be more educational in nature with leaders making a commitment to share information and expertise so that others can become effective as organizational participants and leaders as well. A focus on personal self-development (Griggs, 1989; O'Sullivan, 1976), or as Maslow has described self-actualization, is a significant characteristic of a feminist perspective on leadership. Rosener (1990), in her classic *Harvard Business Review* article, "Ways Women Lead," describes what the women leaders she interviewed had to say about sharing power and information:

> Sharing power and information accomplishes several things. It creates loyalty by signaling to coworkers and subordinates that they are trusted and their ideas respected. It also sets an example for other people and therefore can enhance the general communication flow. And it increases the odds that leaders will hear about problems before they explode. Sharing power and information also gives employees and coworkers the wherewithal to reach conclusions, solve problems and see the justification for decisions. (p. 123)

These women leaders went on to say that one of the advantages of sharing information and encouraging employees to take a more active role in participation is that the employees feel important—their self-worth is enhanced, which improves the organization overall.

Conflict Management

The masculine view of conflict tends to see conflict as threatening and negative. Conflict should be suppressed "under the assumption that it poses a problematic threat to the group or organization" (Maier et al., 1993). The feminist perspective views conflict as an important interaction for getting issues out on the table and resolved. Compromise and win-win conclusions are possible. Conflict can be cooperative in nature—a group concern. Developing methods to work through conflicts is of primary concern from the feminist leader's perspective. The process is just as important as the conflict itself. Feminist theorists write of the importance of conflict environments in which trust is present and participants are committed to resolving conflicts in a nonconfrontational way (Griggs, 1989). Thomas and Kilmann's (1978) conflict management grid captures this process well by articulating different ways of resolving conflict by balancing cooperativeness (attempting to satisfy the other party's concerns) with assertiveness (attempting to satisfy one's own concerns). On the grid there are five different strategies identified: avoidance, competition, compromise, accommodation, and problem solving. Compromise and problem solving are two strategies that the feminist perspective embraces. The heart of the feminist perspective on leadership could, perhaps, be captured with Thomas and Kilmann's definition of problem solving, which is to seek true satisfaction of everyone's concerns in the conflict by working through the differences and developing consensus on how to solve a problem so that, in essence, everyone wins.

Supportive Work Environment

Of all the components of feminist leadership style, this factor— building supportive work environments—is a significant strength for women in management. The feminist perspective argues that leadership practiced from a feminist point of view creates work settings characterized by warmth, understanding, encouragement, support, nurturance, listening, empathy, and mutual trust (Griggs, 1989; St. Joan, 1976). Carr-Ruffino (1993), writing in her book *The Promotable Woman*, makes the case that women have a significant advantage with this leadership skill in that they possess, as women, the ability to inspire loyalty and to understand worker needs based on how they, as women, have been socialized. Research on how boys and girls learn and are socialized in classrooms also suggests that women have developed natural supportive, people-oriented skills and function best in those environments (Sadker & Sadker, 1994).

Organizations in the 90s are finding themselves moving in this direction as well. To compete globally, businesses are finding that they require the type of leadership that builds effective work teams and capitalizes on people skills to really move organizations forward and meet the challenges of continuing change (Naisbett & Aburdene, 1990). Skills that reflect this feminine perspective can be summarized as more facilitative and consultative in nature. These skills might include the ability to empower others, coaching, sharing information, building trust and loyalty, cooperation, consensus building, inspiring, being tuned in to employees' needs and desires, compassion, being both task and people oriented, and so on (Carr-Ruffino,

1993; Glaser & Smalley, 1995; Skopec & Smith, in press; Smith, in press).

Commitment to Diversity

This final component, a commitment to diversity, has been a mainstay of the feminist movement since the early 19th century. As discussed earlier in this chapter, feminists have taken a stand against oppression related to gender, race, and sexuality. They have, by their different leadership styles, demonstrated that diversity of skill, thought, and management approach is valuable. Women have been instrumental, when taking leadership roles, in changing workplaces and the work environment through a number of initiatives, including the adoption of work and family balancing strategies, getting a parental leave act passed in the United States, and advocating alternative work arrangements to create workplace flexibility and increased productivity (see, e.g., Smith, 1991). Different leadership styles can be effective. Valuing diversity in these different ways implies that differences in leadership style create more opportunities for ladder climbing for both men and women.

In many ways, the characteristics articulated above demonstrate how leadership skills that are drawn from the feminine perspective create a new style of leadership for both men and women that is more appropriate for the way businesses are being managed in the competitive 90s. Maier (1992), in an article on evolving paradigms of management in organizations, drew from a survey of the literature to provide a useful analysis showing how assumptions about men and women leaders have changed over the years to reach this new style (see Figure 11.2).

Figure 11.2 highlights several benchmarks of perceptions of women in the workplace. Although the basic assumptions about female versus male managers have come full circle (i.e., that men and women are similar), the implications of the current theoretical trend in management styles suggest that men and women can learn from each other's unique leadership traits and incorporate the positive aspects of each into a more androgynous style. This style results in a work environment in which "men and women can both be 'like women' and 'like men' " (Maier, 1992, p. 31). The effective leadership style is one that captures the best of both styles of leading.

Evolution of Theoretical Perspectives on Women in Management, 1955-1990

Assumptions About Men and Women	Implications for Managerial Women	Type of Change
I. Essentially Different (1950s-1960s)	Sex-Based Exclusion "A woman's place is in the home"	Maintenance of status quo
"Masculinism" (Sexism)	Women and men contribute to society in separate, role-differentiated ways	No individual or structural change. Independence of work and family assumed.
II. Essentially Similar (1970s-present)	Role-Based Inclusion Assimilation to masculine role	Individual change (women). No structural change. Independence of work and family assumed.
"Equal Opportunity" (Feminism)	"A woman can manage just as well as a man" Value women's ability to contribute "like a man."	
III. Essentially Different (1980s-present) "Feminine-ism"	Sex-Based Inclusion Integration-diversity "Vive la difference!" Value women qua women's "unique" contributions.	No individual change. Some structural change. Independence of work and family is still assumed.
IV. Essentially Similar (1990s - ?) "Transformative Feminism"	Role-Based Inclusion Androgyny-Diversity Men and women can both be "like women" and "like men."	Individual and structural change. Interdependence between work and family is acknowledged.

Figure 11.2. Changes in Assumptions About Men and Women in the Workplace and the Implications for Managerial Women
SOURCE: M. Maier, 1992, "Evolving Paradigms of Management in Organizations: A Gendered Analysis." *Journal of Management Systems*, 4(1), p. 31. Used with permission.

Glaser and Smalley (1995) make the point clearly in their book *Swim With the Dolphins*, using a metaphor to compare workplace behaviors of "sharks, guppies, and dolphins." Sharks capture the "command and control" model. Tough, arrogant, ruthless, cold-blooded sharks run the business. The guppy metaphor is used to capture the ineffective, weak applications of management. The dolphin, on the other hand, excels at communication and is warm-blooded and friendly.

Dolphins, like sharks, are concerned with profitability and the balance sheet, but choose an alternative style to maximize an organization's effectiveness. They are true leaders—not bosses, in Glaser and Smalley's terminology. Both men and women can be dolphins, yet a woman's style of leadership, influenced by years of socialization in feminine traits, positions her well to take this dolphin role and become an effective leader.

Given these new theoretical perspectives, why haven't women reached the top of Corporate America? The Feminist Majority Foundation (1991) reported that, based on how long it has taken women to advance, another 475 years would be required to reach parity with men in the executive ranks. The barriers that women face are the focus of the following section.

The Glass Ceiling

Former Secretary of Labor Lynn Martin wrote in *A Report on the Glass Ceiling Initiative,*

> Ample evidence has been gathered to show that minorities and women have made significant gains in entering the workforce. But there is also significant evidence from research conducted by universities, non-profit organizations, executive recruiters, and the Department of Labor that documents a dearth of minorities and women at management levels—the so-called "glass ceiling." (U.S. Department of Labor, 1991, pp. 1-2)

The glass ceiling phenomenon describes an invisible barrier to advancement opportunities. Women and minorities "hit" the ceiling when they find they can't seem to rise any higher in the organization, yet the executives running the organization won't admit the barrier exists. In a survey of women managers, 90% of those surveyed felt that the glass ceiling is the most significant problem facing women managers; 80% said that women were underrepresented at the executive level. Pay inequities exist as well. Several studies have indicated that women find themselves in positions with little line authority and relatively low pay (Cook, 1987; Salmans, 1987). In 1995, the Bureau of Labor reported that women earned approximately 74% of what men earned for doing the same work. A report on salaries in *Working Woman Magazine* (February 1996) revealed that women were earning 85%-95% of what men earn in the same positions, depending on the profession. Although the ratio continues to increase, the barriers to pay equity are attitudinally ingrained.

Some studies have indicated that women earn, on average, one half of what men earn for the same type of work, particularly at higher levels. How have women responded when faced with these barriers? One hypothesis suggests dropouts. Women are dropping out of the corporate ladder-climbing game. More than 4.5 million women in America run their own businesses, and it is predicted that nearly half of all the small, more entreprenurially based businesses will be owned by women by the year 2000 (Nelton, 1990). While these statistics are exciting and demonstrate the opportunity for women-owned and -run businesses, the barriers to advancement, promotion, and pay equity in existing organizations still plague women in the workforce.

Both internal and external barriers present obstacles to women who want to break the glass ceiling. Consider the following:

1. Women managers tend to be clustered in the lower-paying entry levels of management, such as working supervisor and first-line supervisor.
2. Women managers' pay lags behind men's at every level.
3. When women move into an occupation in significant numbers, the occupation loses status and decreases in pay, and men tend to move out of it. Conversely, if an occupation loses status and pay for other reasons, women are more likely to be hired into it.
4. Women are likely to hit the glass ceiling to top-level and even middle-level positions, according to a 1991 Labor Department study. (Carr-Ruffino, 1993, p. 12)

Other factors include:

1. a continued reliance on "old-boy" networks (relying on word-of-mouth referrals instead of recruiting and hiring from a diverse labor pool as legally required by EEO/AA guidelines; using executive search firms without stressing the need for diversity)

2. a skewed appraisal and compensation system (in which bonuses, perks, and favorable performance reviews were most frequently given to white men)

3. a lack of corporate responsibility or executive accountability (top executives made no effort to give high-visibility, career-enhancing assignments to women and minorities and failed to keep records of their informal hiring and promotion systems, with the end result that they reportedly were oblivious to the gender and racial disparities they were creating. (Office of Federal Contract Compliance Programs Data, cited in Maier, 1993, p. 289)

Stereotypes about women also hinder their ability to move ahead. Research abounds with studies reporting on the stereotyping and negative preconceptions about the abilities of women (and other minorities) to lead (e.g., Cook, 1987; Fierman, 1990; Owen & Todor, 1993; McIntosh, 1988). Work and family conflicts may also contribute to career path halts, but perhaps more important is the inflexibility of organizations to help women (and men) better balance work and family issues. Whereas corporate child care, flexible work arrangements (e.g., compressed work weeks, job sharing, flextime, telecommuting, etc.), resource and referral support, vouchers, dependent care assistance plans, the new Family and Medical Leave Act, and other strategies have eased work-family struggles, the majority of organizations are not truly family friendly. Even in *Working Mother's* list of top companies to work for, the men and women in these organizations often indicate that a company is only as family-friendly as an employee's immediate supervisor (Smith, 1991, 1992). Without flexibility and support, it is often difficult for women (and men) to have both families and fast-track careers (see, e.g., Schwartz, 1992).

Breaking the glass ceiling is a significant challenge for women, especially given that the "gatekeepers and power brokers" in companies tend to be white males. Maier (1993), in his analysis of how to reduce sex stereotyping and promote egalitarian male-female relationships in management, indicates what must occur for women to advance: "men, . . . by virtue of their status as the gatekeepers and power brokers in organizations, possess, as a group, inherent structural advantages over women" (p. 290). Citing other research (Acker, 1990; Lorber, 1983; Schwartz & Rago, 1984) that makes the case, Maier continues,

And for women, as a group, to break the glass ceiling depends on the extent to which men are prepared to work with them as equals, offering them the same types of informal as well as formal supports that men have themselves historically relied on for advancement. For this to happen, men have to assume an active role as equal teammates and allies of women, which requires identifying compelling reasons to do so. (p. 290)

In other words, breaking the glass ceiling requires a major commitment on the part of organizations to take action in promoting and advancing people regardless of their gender or ethnicity and for men to take an active role as partners in implementing this change. Some of this work has already begun with major corporate efforts in diversity training, recognition of the strengths related to how women lead, formal mentoring programs, and implementation of work/life human resource management strategies. In the final analysis, however, women will have to overcome the external barriers and manage their own internal barriers as well. Carr-Ruffino (1993), citing a 1990 Gallup Poll, found that traits most admired in men include the ability to be aggressive, independent, objective, dominant, unemotional, not excitable in a crisis, active, logical, worldly, and competitive. Respondents also associated many of these traits more closely with men than women. Not surprisingly, these traits are also expected of a strong leader. In a discussion of the "male" and "female" qualities that androgynous managers should develop, Sargent (1981) makes the case that women can learn the skills that are typical male strengths, such as becoming more focused on task and regarding it just as important as relationships. They can also enhance their more feminine traits, such as the ability to accept task failure and not take it as personal failure. Other strengths that can be developed, expanded, or both, are outlined in Figure 11.3.

The advice presented in Figure 11.3 describes how women might begin to think through developing more masculine-oriented traits, and enhancing their feminine-oriented strengths to become more successful managers. These strategies may significantly impact both promotability and advancement opportunities.

What can women in leadership and in line for leadership expect in the next decade? Clearly, many changes are taking place in the work environment that may lessen the impact of the glass ceiling. In an era of downsizing, restructuring, and reengineering, new para-

Typical Masculine Strengths Women Can Develop	Typical Feminine Strengths Women Can Expand
• Learn how to be powerful and forthright.	• The ability to recognize, accept, and express feelings.
• Become *entrepreneurial*.	
• Have a direct, visible impact on others, rather than just functioning behind the scenes.	• Respect for feelings as a basic and essential part of life, as guides to authenticity and effectiveness, rather than as barriers to achievement.
• State your own needs and refuse to back down, even if the immediate response is not acceptance.	• Accept the vulnerability and imperfections of others.
• Focus on a task and regard it as at least as important as the relationships with the people doing the task.	• A belief in the right to work for self-fulfillment as well as for money.
• Build support systems with other women and share competence with them, rather than competing with them.	• A belief in the value of nonwork roles as well as work identity.
• Build a sense of community among women instead of saying, "I pulled myself up by my bootstraps, so why can't you?"	• The ability to fail at a task without feeling failure as a person.
• Intellectualize and generalize from experience.	• The ability to accept and express the need to be nurtured at all times.
• Behave "impersonally," rather than personalizing experience and denying another's reality because it is different.	• The ability to touch and be close to both men and women without necessarily experiencing or suggesting sexual connotations.
• Stop turning anger, blame, and pain inward.	• Skill at listening empathetically and actively without feeling responsible for solving others' problems.
• Stop accepting feelings of suffering and victimization.	
• Take the option of being invulnerable to destructive feedback.	• The ability to share feelings as the most meaningful part of one's contact with others, accepting the risk and vulnerability such sharing implies.
• Stop being irritable, a "nag," and/or passive-resistant about resentments and anger.	• Skill at building support systems with other women, sharing competencies without competition, and feelings and needs with sincerity.
• Respond directly with "I" statements, rather than with blaming "you" ones ("*I'm* not comfortable with that" rather than "*you* shouldn't do that").	• The ability to relate to experiences and people on a personal level rather than assuming that the only valid approach to life and interpersonal contact is an abstract, rational, or strictly objective one.
• Become an effective problem solver by being analytical, systematic, and directive.	
• Change self-limiting behaviors, such as allowing interruptions or laughing after making a serious statement.	• Acceptance of the emotional, spontaneous, and irrational parts of the self.
• Become a risk-taker (calculating probabilities and making appropriate trade-offs).	

Figure 11.3. List of Typical Masculine and Feminine Strengths Related to Effective Androgynous Styles of Management

SOURCE: Adapted from *The Androgynous Manager* by Alice G. Sargent (New York: Amacom, 1981). Cited in N. Carr-Ruffino, *The Promotable Woman* (Belmont, CA: Wadsworth, 1993).

digms for leading in organizations are emerging. The necessary skills to lead in these organizations, as discussed earlier, are those that women may bring to the organization innately. Beyond the advice suggested in Figure 11.3, what else can explain how gender may impact leadership? Where can women, with their "interactive" style of leadership (Rosener, 1990), make great advances? This last section explores one of the significant new paradigms in leadership and provides some strategic directions for women in leadership to pursue.

Women as Leaders in a New Century

One significant way to break the ceiling is to analyze how leadership in organizations has changed in recent years and to foresee women's meaningful place in those changes. The most significant leadership challenge facing organizations in the 1990s is the ability to find leaders equipped to work in an environment made up of *self-directed teams*. In the future, the best leaders may be those who make themselves eventually unnecessary or at least relatively invisible to self-directed teams. That paradox—that leading often means giving up power rather than accumulating it—lies at the heart of the leadership challenge for the next century, and, ironically, stems from early feminist thought on what makes for an effective organization. This approach to leadership, frankly, has been difficult for traditional male leaders to learn. It's hard for them to imagine that the band may be able to play quite well without the conductor.

The more participatory, networking style of women leaders may make them better candidates, on balance, to lead teams, whereas the leadership skills for traditional, and largely male, team management are essentially directive in nature and include such skills as maintaining control, focusing and directing member activities, accepting responsibility for final decisions, setting and enforcing work and quality standards, distributing rewards and sanctions according to member performance, and motivating team members.

For some business situations and purposes, this set of leadership skills is well suited, at least for attaining short-term organizational goals. Yet it may fail to serve organizations well in the longer term. Traditional leadership approaches to team management exercise the talents of the leader but do little to encourage independent thinking, innovation, team spirit, and accountability among team members. Women leaders have been at the forefront of organizational efforts to reengineer the leadership functions necessary for team-based work. What are these functions that, arguably, are well suited to "women's way of leading"?

Delegated Leadership

A small step toward less directive leadership involves the delegation of selected leadership tasks to team members. In this leadership style, the team is hardly self-directed, of course. The leader is still pulling most of the strings under the guise of giving team members a chance to perform as designated leaders-for-a-day.

Let's say, for example, that a leader asks team members John, Alice, Ruth, and Bill each to serve in turn as meeting leaders for weekly team meetings. To some extent, this option does serve to develop these individuals' leadership skills. But the whole arrangement may come to look and feel like a training exercise—preparing for independent initiative rather than practicing it. A lockstep rotation of meeting leaders may also tend to defuse any team action agendas. What seemed important in John's meeting may not be important when Alice, Ruth, or Bill take their turns at bat.

Elected Leadership

A supervisor can turn the selection of leaders over to the team itself. This option certainly empowers team members and underlines their responsibility for independent problem solving. Interpersonal relations on the team, however, must be sufficiently developed for consensus selection of leaders. Close votes, with a significant minority left grumbling on the sidelines, can sabotage any elected leader's efforts.

In addition, elective leadership can sometimes lead to the "slaves creating the master." There is no guarantee that a leader elected from the ranks won't quickly fall into the role of traditional taskmaster. A team empowered to select its own leadership can be disempowered by selecting the wrong leader. This undesirable result is all the more likely if team members have no training or experience in team leadership. Old leadership styles may crop up not because they are preferred by the team but because they are familiar.

Shared Leadership

In this leadership approach, the nature of leadership itself undergoes a marked transformation. From the supervisor's point of view, shared leadership means redefining the leader's role in five ways:

- The old leader displays greater knowledge, experience, and wisdom in decision making than that possessed by team members. The new leader shows others how knowledge, experience, and skill in decision making can be acquired.
- The old leader tells team members what to do. The new leader participates in deciding with team members what courses of action to take.
- The old leader talks most of the time. The new leader listens most of the time.
- The old leader discourages risk taking and punishes missteps on the part of team members. The new leader encourages team initiative and accepts risk and occasional failure as part of the learning curve.
- The old leader has a relatively low opinion of the intelligence, motivation, and trustworthiness of team members. The new leader respects team members and values their contributions.

Shared leadership, in effect, removes many of the boundaries between the leader and those who are led. The supervisor given responsibility for the team and its results blends in as a team participant. This approach to leadership resolves the problem of "talent divorce," in which one particularly skilled individual (the supervisor) is summarily excluded from team processes. Empowerment of the team by the supervisor, in other words, does not have to mean walking out of the meeting room and hoping for the best. It does mean climbing down from the traditional leadership pedestal.

Once "in the trenches" with the rest of the team, the supervisor exerts *developmental leadership* by three strategies:

1. The supervisor *gets to know* team members and lets himself or herself be known. All team successes will depend directly upon the degree of interpersonal trust shared by team members. The supervisor can begin to build that trust by modeling sincere interest in others.
2. The supervisor *raises process questions* without dictating answers. In early meetings, the supervisor can ask the team such questions as
   - what do you think is our purpose as a team?

- what are our individual roles?
- what norms can we agree upon for our discussions? (For example, we can agree to welcome divergent opinion and seek consensus whenever possible.)

3. The supervisor *interprets organizational politics*. In their formative meetings, team members understandably have many "what ifs" about their degree of support in the organization, performance expectations from top management, and their vulnerability if results aren't immediately forthcoming. The supervisor needs to be a channel for whatever assurance and support top management is willing to give to the team. It is crucial that a supervisor's words of encouragement on the part of top management be sincere and trustworthy. A team can be quickly destroyed by reassurances that turn out to be false.

Leadership at a Distance

This final leadership option is practiced most often with executive teams made up of experienced team players. Once given their charter, these self-directed teams are free to achieve their goals (and often define or refine them along the way) in any way that makes sense to the team as a whole. The leader is available to the team for counsel, access to resources, and other forms of support. But, day to day, the leader's contact with the team is minimal. The team reports its results to the organizational leader. If the results meet or exceed expectations, both the organizational leader and the team members are rewarded. If not, the team is put on notice by the leader to "hit the numbers" or face dissolution as a group.

This leadership style downplays the potential contributions of the leader to the team in favor of ultimate empowerment for the team itself. For such empowerment to draw the best from team members, it must be *real* in the organization. In the words of one director of a Fortune 100 company, "Around here, the authority of our project teams is, at best, ambiguous. We are told 'you can make decisions.' But, in reality, if senior management doesn't like it, it won't fly." In this situation, teams are not really empowered to do their own best thinking and acting, but instead play an expensive guessing game called What Does the Boss Want?

The qualities of the leadership style described in this section support the points raised by the feminist leadership perspective. That this perspective can readily link with the needs of organizations in the 90s and beyond is a compelling argument for embracing a model of androgynous leadership that is gender-blind.

Strengths

This chapter has identified several ways to think about the issue of leadership and gender through both a feminist perspective and a skill-based orientation. There are several strengths in this particular approach.

First, this approach takes into account a salient body of research on women and management that dovetails nicely with the new emphasis on teamwork in organizations. As organizations place more and more of their efforts on team-based work environments, the skills required to succeed in these structures stem from an understanding of women's managerial skill base. Rather than a traditional perspective that may capture leadership skills from a vertical or top-down division of labor, the feminist perspective centers on consensus decision making, participation, and the sharing of power and information. These skills are all integral to creating high performance work teams. Women, historically, have been socialized in such a way that these skills may come to them more naturally (see, e.g., Carr-Ruffino, 1993; Helgesen, 1990; Rosener, 1990).

Second, this approach offers a means of exploring leadership from the best of both "masculine" and "feminine" styles of leadership. The literature in this area suggests that an "androgynous" style of leadership, capturing the best of both women's and men's ways of leading, offers the leader a set of behaviors that can be effective in a variety of situations.

Third, this approach embodies the principles that are valued in the diversity literature. As organizations compete in the global environment, face shortages in skilled labor, and recognize the changing demographics of the American workforce, diversity of skill and thought through race, gender, and culture become competitive advantages.

Finally, this approach attempts to answer the question: Does gender make a difference? In explaining what makes leaders successful and effective, research that investigates alternative causality for explaining leadership success is additive to the body of knowledge in the field. In the leadership and gender studies, for example, researchers have been able to demonstrate different attitudes toward women as managers that may explain why women have faced barriers to hierarchical positions of leadership (see ATWAM Scale at the end of the chapter).

Criticisms

The primary criticism of this approach has been that it may have focused too much on the question: Is there a difference between men and women? Although men and women may lead differently, it is important to recognize that this conclusion may, in fact, be a significant generalization with many exceptions. Unfortunately, the research exploring this question has been largely anecdotal in nature. The field suffers from a dearth of well-designed empirical research.

A second criticism is that this approach, in general, focuses almost exclusively on the experience of white women and should therefore not be generalized to all women. The experiences of African American women and women of other ethnicities differ significantly. The barriers faced by these women may be more akin to a "brick wall" than a glass ceiling. Thus, the strategies of "androgyny" (Glaser & Smalley, 1995; Sargent, 1981) or team-oriented opportunities may be limited due to stereotypes, ingrained attitudes, and blatant discrimination.

A final criticism is that the focus on gender as a separate leadership variable may result in emphasizing differences rather than embracing inclusion. If we look to gender as a way to explain why women have not gotten ahead, we lose sight of the focus on leadership strategies that can be implemented regardless of gender and do much for the personal management development of both men and women.

Case Studies

The following three case studies (Cases 11.1, 11.2, and 11.3) are about women and leadership. The first describes a leader who sets up a web-like team structure, the second deals with a leader who is "fast tracked," and the last addresses issues of trust that arise when an organization makes a transition to a team environment. At the end of each case, you will find questions that can be used in doing an analysis of the case.

Case 11.1

The Arizona Student Leadership Conference holds an annual summer camp for 200 high school student leaders. Joellen Fernandez is the executive director of the organization and is an expert in quickly building effective teams. She plays the role of facilitator, as opposed to "master."

This year she has hired a team of 15 counselors to supervise and carry out the conference activities. Traditionally, she asks counselors to arrive a week early to help her plan the conference program. Rather than coming to the conference with a preplanned agenda for the counselors, Joellen begins the first meeting with the team by asking them two questions:

1. What activities do you want to do this year?
2. Why do you think these activities would fit the goals of the conference?

Joellen facilitates discussions among the counselors and leads some of the chosen activities but leaves all decision-making power to the team. This year, the team decides to do a series of activities that illustrate that all people have leadership capabilities, but that sometimes one must look beyond the traditional view of the "leader" to find them.

The conference designated one of the days a silent day. A wide range of activities was planned, during which none of the counselors or students could talk. Students who were considered "quiet" and often got lost in the shuffle suddenly stood out and started to take charge of several of the activities.

Questions

- Why did this team work so well together?
- Why was the conference considered to be successful?
- Would you find it difficult to relinquish control of a project like this one if the ultimate responsibility for it rested on your shoulders?
- Do you think Joellen gave up too much power?

Case 11.2

Robin Martin-Jones graduated with a business degree in finance from a mid-sized state university. In her last semester of her senior year, Robin began meeting with and interviewing with the college recruiters from a variety of financial service institutions. Although she was most interested in working with a small, more entrepreneurial-type firm, Robin was very impressed with one large Fortune 500 organization. The recruiter shared with her the many advantages of working with his firm. The training programs, future educational opportunities, career development options, and mentoring programs all sounded too good to pass up. When the recruiter mentioned how far women had advanced in his organization, Robin was sold. She accepted the job offering and looked forward to starting with the firm.

As a "fast tracker," Robin joined 15 other men and women in an intense 18-month training program. These organizational newcomers learned many facets of the business. The best and brightest of these young people were told that 5 of them would be chosen to continue their studies in an MBA program with the firm picking up all the costs. With excellent recommendations from her supervisor, Robin was selected to receive this educational support along with 1 other woman and 3 of the men.

Robin applied and was accepted in a top MBA program and, again, excelled. She worked part-time for the firm and attended classes full-time. Two years later, Robin graduated near the top of her class. She returned to the firm full-time and quickly received a promotion from financial analyst to assistant branch manager. The other MBA graduates received similar opportunities in other locations of the firm. Over the next 2 years, Robin continued to receive strong performance reviews and was given the opportunity to relocate and learn other facets of the business. Although reluctant to leave the branch, she knew that to advance in the company she could not afford to turn down this offer. After a successful stream of different positions, each one building upon the skills of the others, Robin settled into a mid-level management position with responsibility for 10 financial analysts. She enjoyed this position and noted that others who had gone through the same fast-track program were at the same level in the organization and could liaison with her on a number of special projects.

During this time, Robin married and began to balance her career with her family life. When she decided to take advantage of the family leave policy that gave her 6 weeks paid leave after the birth of a child, she congratulated herself on choosing a family-friendly company that accommodated both her family goals and career aspirations. After the birth of her child, she returned to work on an 80% flexible work arrangement with full management support from her superiors. Her performance was consistently rated outstanding, and in her last performance review her manager noted that although she worked the 80% option, she was accomplishing the objectives of other managers who worked a full-time schedule. Pleased with this track record, Robin began taking notice of the opportunities to advance in the job. Several possibilities emerged, for all of which she was qualified. Her counterparts in other areas assured her that she was just perfect for several of these positions and would recommend her highly for advancement. Robin knew she had the support of her immediate boss as well. She indicated in all of her interviews that she was looking forward to coming back full-time now that her baby was a year old. In three of the promotion opportunities that Robin was up for, she was passed over.

Robin noted that the 3 men with whom she had "fast tracked" were rising steadily in the organization, while management seemed to support her only in the mid-level roles. Her discouragement at being passed over, despite her track record, motivation, commitment, and training, left a bad taste in her mouth. Top management told her that her time would come. After 3 more years of "star" performing and no further advancement in the firm, Robin left to form a start-up with a colleague from graduate school.

Questions

- Did Robin fall victim to a glass ceiling?
- Is the "fast track" an option for women who want time off for children?
- Should it affect how their career paths are treated?
- Do you think the firm would have passed over one of the men who took time off (encouraged by the firm)?
- What advice would you give to Robin and other men and women in this firm, and to the firm itself?

Case 11.3

Ana Cortes worked as a new team leader in a distribution center for a major retailing organization. She was 27 years old with a high school education, an Associate of Arts degree in management from the local community college, and approximately 6 years of experience both part-time and full-time in retail operations (customer service, inventory control, and distribution operations). Her promotion to team leader was in recognition of her motivation, dedication to the organization, and demonstration of management potential. Whereas supervisors managed between 15 and 20 individuals in a variety of distribution operations, the teams were designed to be more specialized and consisted of 5 to 7 team members who were responsible to a team leader. As the distribution center moved increasingly to a team environment, with less emphasis on traditional "supervisor" and job foreman type structures, those individuals promoted to team leaders found themselves facing many challenges. Many members of the teams had been used to having a supervisor and, in most cases, these supervisors, as well as the workers, tended to be men.

Ana was one of five women who held these new slots. All team leaders were considered to be equal in organizational levels. One of the supervisors left upon hearing of the new arrangement. The other four became team leaders. Ana was excited about the new responsibility and motivated to implement the team skills she had learned both on the job and in the company-provided training. She thought that given her camaraderie with the employees prior to the restructuring, the transition would be smooth. It appeared to be just the opposite.

During the transition to teams, Ana found herself frustrated by the lack of respect she garnered in this new position. Previously, she had considered herself and was treated as "one of the guys." Now she was a "leader." She perceived that her team members did not trust her and felt that they were being "spied on" while on the job. Several of the team members were insistent on "testing her" by stretching the limits on what they could get away with in terms of lower productivity. Ana learned that the other women team leaders were experiencing similar problems. The supervisors who were now team leaders offered little support. Ana, along with one of her counterparts, went to the vice president of human resources and asked for her support.

Questions

- What leadership skills might Ana employ to turn around team member attitudes?
- What support does Ana need from other team leaders and the organization?
- How might Ana become a more "interactive" leader?

Leadership Instrument

Questionnaires, surveys, and tools used to assess gender and leadership are not widely available. Many of the tools used throughout the book, designed to measure leadership in general, certainly apply to women as well as men. Several instruments that look at leadership style, learning style, or decision-making style are available that do take into account that gender differences may be present. The MBTI, or Myers-Briggs Type Indicator instrument, for example, specifically calls for respondents to identify gender in order to account for potential differences in the way certain personality traits may be explained. Yet there is a lack of literature on measurement and gender with respect to leadership practices. The most common survey-type material is designed to increase self-awareness about gender differences and tends to be found in popular women's magazines, professional women journals, and the like.

The Attitudes Toward Women as Managers Scale, (ATWAM) which appears in this section is a useful tool for assessing the attitudes, biases, and approaches that both men and women have when working with women in the workplace. This scale is useful when thinking about glass ceiling issues because it helps to identify latent stereotypical thinking that may explain the attitudinal barriers that exist in the work environment. What is particularly surprising is that when groups of people take the instrument and interpret their results, they find that women as well as men hold attitudes that can be detrimental to women's career advancement. In other words, this instrument is not for men only.

Identifying these attitudes toward women in leadership roles and recognizing how socialization may have impacted the way we respond to the questions in the survey is a useful first step in sensitizing us to how we act toward women, both directly and in more subtle ways. The results you obtain from filling out the survey should be used to develop your own awareness of your subconscious as well as conscious attitudes toward women in leadership roles. Knowing how these attitudes play out in the way we behave in the workforce can be the next step in breaking the glass ceiling.

As you fill out the survey, be sure to think through how you honestly would answer these questions as you really are, not as you would like others to perceive you. Then follow the directions at the end of the survey to score and interpret your results. You may be surprised with the findings. This instrument is an effective tool for all employees to begin the discussion on valuing the contributions of men and women in management regardless of gender and in breaking down the stereotypes that may explain why women managers have not advanced in the organization as quickly as men.

Attitudes Toward Women as Managers (ATWAM) Scale
EDWARD B. YOST and THEODORE T. HERBERT

INSTRUCTIONS: From each *set* of three statements below, select the one state-ment with which you *most agree* and place an M (for "most agree") in the blank to the right of that statement.

For each *set,* also select the one statement with which you *least agree* and place an L (for "least agree) in the blank to the right of that statement.

Note that one statement in each set will not be chosen at all.

1. A. Men are more concerned with the cars they drive than with the clothes their wives wear. _____

   B. Any man worth his salt should not be blamed for putting his career above his family. _____

   C. A person's job is the best single indicator of the sort of person he is. _____

2. A. Parental authority and responsibility for discipline of the children should be divided equally between the husband and the wife. _____

   B. It is less desirable for women to have jobs that require responsibility than for men. _____

   C. Men should not continue to show courtesies to women such as holding doors open for them and helping them with their coats. _____

3. A. It is acceptable for women to assume leadership roles as often as men. _____

   B. In a demanding situation, a woman manager would be no more likely to break down than would a male manager. _____

   C. There are some professions and types of businesses that are more suitable for men than for women. _____

4. A. Recognition for a job well done is less important to women than it is to men.   _____

   B. A woman should demand money for household and personal expenses as a right rather than a gift.   _____

   C. Women are temperamentally fit for leadership positions.   _____

5. A. Women tend to allow their emotions to influence their managerial behavior more than men.   _____

   B. The husband and wife should be equal partners in planning the family budget.   _____

   C. If both husband and wife agree that sexual fidelity is not important, there is no reason why both should not have extramarital affairs.   _____

6. A. A man's first responsibility is to his wife, not his mother.   _____

   B. A man who is able and willing to work hard has a good chance of succeeding in whatever he wants to do.   _____

   C. Only after a man has achieved what he wants from life should he concern himself with the injustices in the world.   _____

7. A. A wife should make every effort to minimize irritations and inconveniences for the male head of the household.   _____

   B. Women can cope with stressful situations as effectively as men can.   _____

   C. Women should be encouraged not to become sexually intimate with anyone, even their fiancés, before marriage.   _____

8. A. The "obey" clause in the marriage service is insulting to women.   _____

   B. Divorced men should help support their children but should not be required to pay alimony if their wives are capable of working.   _____

   C. Women have the capacity to acquire the necessary skills to be successful managers.   _____

9. A. Women can be aggressive in business situations that demand it.   _____

   B. Women have an obligation to be faithful to their husbands.   _____

   C. It is childish for a woman to assert herself by retaining her maiden name after marriage.   _____

10. A. Men should continue to show courtesies to women such as holding doors open for them or helping them with their coats.   _____

    B. In job appointments and promotions, females should be given equal consideration with males.   _____

C. It is all right for a wife to have an occasional, casual, extramarital affair. _____

11. A. The satisfaction of her husband's sexual desires is a fundamental obligation of every wife. _____

B. Most women should not want the kind of support that men traditionally have given them. _____

C. Women possess the dominance to be successful leaders. _____

12. A. Most women need and want the kind of protection and support that men traditionally have given them. _____

B. Women are capable of separating their emotions from their ideas. _____

C. A husband has no obligation to inform his wife of his financial plans. _____

SOURCE: Reprinted with permission from E. B. Yost and T. T. Herbert, *Attitudes Toward Women as Managers (ATWAM) Scale.* Copyright © 1985 Pfeiffer, an imprint of Jossey-Bass Inc., Publishers, all rights reserved.

Scoring:

1. Record your response for the indicated items in the spaces provided.
2. On the basis of the information provided below, determine the points for each item and enter these points in the space provided to the right. For example, if, in item 3, you chose alternative A as the one with which you *most* agree and alternative B as the one with which you *least* agree, you should receive 3 points for item 3.

Note that items 1 and 6 are "buffer items" and are *not* scored.

3. When you have scored all 10 scoreable items, add the points and record the total at the bottom of this page in the space provided. This is your total ATWAM score.

Your Response	Item No.	Points per Item Response*						Points
		1		3		5		7	
	1	Not Scored						
M ____ L ____	2	C(M) B(L)	A(M) B(L)	C(M) A(L)	A(M) C(L)	B(M) A(L)	B(M) C(L)	
M ____ L ____	3	A(M) C(L)	A(M) B(L)	B(M) C(L)	C(M) B(L)	B(M) A(L)	C(M) A(L)	

(continued)

M ___	4	C(M)	C(M)	A(M)	B(M)	A(M)	B(M)
L ___		B(L)	A(L)	B(L)	A(L)	C(L)	C(L)
M ___	5	C(M)	C(M)	B(M)	A(M)	B(M)	A(M)
L ___		A(L)	B(L)	A(L)	B(L)	C(L)	C(L)
	6	Not Scored					
M ___	7	B(M)	B(M)	C(M)	A(M)	C(M)	A(M)
L ___		A(L)	C(L)	A(L)	C(L)	B(L)	B(L)
M ___	8	C(M)	C(M)	A(M)	B(M)	A(M)	B(M)
L ___		B(L)	A(L)	B(L)	A(L)	C(L)	C(L)
M ___	9	A(M)	A(M)	C(M)	B(M)	C(M)	B(M)
L ___		B(L)	C(L)	B(L)	C(L)	A(L)	A(L)
M ___	10	B(M)	B(M)	C(M)	A(M)	C(M)	A(M)
L ___		A(L)	C(L)	A(L)	C(L)	B(L)	B(L)
M ___	11	C(M)	C(M)	B(M)	A(M)	B(M)	A(M)
L ___		A(L)	B(L)	A(L)	B(L)	C(L)	C(L)
M ___	12	B(M)	B(M)	C(M)	A(M)	C(M)	A(M)
L ___		A(L)	C(L)	A(L)	C(L)	B(L)	B(L)

NOTE: * M indicates item chosen as "most"; L indicates item chosen as "least."

Scoring Interpretation

The total score that you have received from the ATWAM (Attitudes Toward Women as Managers) provides an indication of your feelings about women in managerial roles. The higher your ATWAM score, the more prone you are to hold negative sex-role stereotypes about women in management. Possible total scores range from 10 to 70; a "neutral" score (one that indicates neither positive nor negative attitudes about women as managers) is in the range of 30 to 40.

Summary

This chapter has explored the relationship between gender and leadership, providing both historical and theoretical perspectives. In addition to looking at theory behind women in leadership, the chapter also investigated the impact of leadership styles, analyzed barriers to promotion and advancement opportunities for women, and suggested some avenues for women to develop further their leadership potential. A case was made for using a feminist perspective in meeting the new leadership challenges associated with the widespread changes being made in today's business organizations. Such progress notwithstanding, women and other minorities will continue to face stereotypes and negative preconceptions as they seek advancement opportunities. To that end, an instrument is provided that helps to survey attitudes toward women in management roles. The results of the survey should provide for a provocative discussion of gender and leadership.

There are several strengths to viewing leadership from the feminist perspective. First, organizations are moving toward team-based environments, and this approach highlights the importance of understanding women's managerial skills (e.g., building consensus, participating, and sharing of power), most of which are critical in the development of effective teams. Second, this approach underscores the importance of androgynous leadership, incorporating the best of both "masculine" and "feminine" styles of leadership. Third, the values of the feminist approach are congruent with the current emphasis on recognizing diversity in the workplace. Lastly, this approach adds to our understanding of how differing attitudes toward women and men have created barriers to the advancement of women in the workplace.

On the negative side, this approach may focus too much on the question: Is there a difference between men and women? and not enough on well-designed studies to explore the explanations for and implications of these perceived differences. Second, because this approach draws from studies that focus almost exclusively on white women and ignore the experiences of African American women and women of other ethnic groups, the generalizations made from this approach are limited. Finally, by focusing on gender as a separate leadership variable, this approach emphasizes differences between men and women rather than leadership strategies that can benefit both men and women in management settings.

Despite these criticisms, the issues outlined in a discussion of leadership and gender offer managers a strong perspective on the skills, attitudes, and beliefs necessary to lead others in successful, high-performance work environments. Awareness of the internal and external barriers that women of all races face is the first step in breaking the glass ceiling and valuing diversity in leadership.

Notes

1. Small units of African American men served in the military but widespread segregation of units characterized the armed services during the First and Second World Wars.

2. The popular women's movement of the 60s and 70s was primarily engineered by and focused on white women. In 1974, the Combahee River Collective, a group of African American women, began talking about the place of women of color within "feminism." By the late 1970s, popular feminist discourse began to discuss women of color and their glaring absence from the earlier feminist movement. For more information and perspectives on women of color and feminism, refer to Combahee River Collective, "A Black Feminist Statement"; Mitsuye Yamada, "Asian Pacific American Women and Feminism"; and Cherrie Moraga, "La Guera," all reprinted in Moraga and Anzaldua (Eds.), *This Bridge Called My Back: Writings by Radical Women of Color.* New York: Kitchen Table Press, 1993.

3. For a more comprehensive discussion of the history of women in the workforce, see Susan Householder Vanhorn, *Women, Work & Fertility, 1900-1986,* New York: New York University Press, 1988; Alice Kessler Harris, *Out to Work: A History of Wage Earning Women in the U.S.,* New York: Oxford University Press, 1982; Alice Kessler Harris, *Women Have Always Worked: A Historical Overview,* New York: Feminist Press, 1981.

References

Acker, J. (1990). Hierarchies, jobs, bodies: A theory of gendered organizations. *Gender & Society, 4*(2), 139-158.

Carden, M. L. (1974). *The new feminist movement.* New York: Russell Sage.

Carroll, S. (1984). Feminist scholarship on political leadership. In B. Kellerman (Ed.), *Leadership: Multidisciplinary perspectives* (pp. 139-156). Englewood Cliffs, NJ: Prentice Hall.

Carr-Ruffino, N. (1993). *The promotable woman: Advancing through leadership skills.* Belmont, CA: Wadsworth.

Cook, K. (1987, August 17). Why aren't women in top jobs? *USA Today,* p. 2D.

The Feminist Majority Foundation. (1991). *Empowering women in business.* Washington, DC: Author.

Fierman, J. (1990, July). Why women still don't hit the top? *Fortune,* p. 40.

Freeman, J. (1975). *The politics of women's liberation*. New York: David McKay.

Gilligan, C. (1982). *In a different voice*. Cambridge, MA: Harvard University Press.

Glaser, C., & Smalley, G. (1995). *Swim with the dolphins: How women can succeed in corporate America on their own terms*. New York: Warner Books.

Griggs, C. S. (1989). *Exploration of a feminist leadership model at university women's centers and women's studies programs: A descriptive study*. (Unpublished doctoral dissertation, University of Iowa; UMI Dissertation Services).

Hartsock, M. (1979). Feminism, power, and change: A theoretical analysis. In B. Cummings & V. Schuck (Eds.), *Women organizing: An anthology* (pp. 2-24). Metuchen, NJ: Scarecrow.

Helgesen, S. (1990). *The female advantage: Women's ways of leading*. Garden City, NY: Doubleday.

Hole, J., & Levine, E. (1971). *Rebirth of feminism*. New York: Quadrangle/New York Times Book Company.

Jaegger, A. (1983). *Feminist politics and human nature*. Brighton, Sussex; UK: Rowman & Allanheld.

Kotter, J. P. (1990). *A force for change: How leadership differs from management*. New York: Free Press.

Lorber, J. (1983). Trust, loyalty, and the place of women in the informal organization of work. In J. Freeman (Ed.), *Women: A feminist perspective* (pp. 370-378). Palo Alto, CA: Mayfield.

Maier, M. (1992). Evolving paradigms of management in organizations: A gendered analysis. *Journal of Management Systems, 4*(1), 29-45.

Maier, M. (1993). The gender prism: Pedagogical foundations for reducing sex stereotyping and promoting egalitarian male-female relationships in management. *Journal of Management Education, 17*(3), 288-317.

Maier, M., Ferguson, K., & Shrivastava, P. (1993). *Organizational dysfunction as gendered practice: The Space Shuttle Challenger disaster.* (work in progress).

McIntosh, P. (1988). *White privilege and male privilege* (Working Paper Series #189). Wellesley, MA: Wellesley College, Center for Research on Women.

Morrison, A., White, R., Van Velsor, E., & the Center for Creative Leadership. (1992). *Breaking the class ceiling: Can women reach the top of America's largest corporations?* Reading, MA: Addison-Wesley.

Naisbett, J., & Aburdene, P. (1990). *Megatrends 2000: Ten new directions for the 1990's*. New York: William Morrow.

Nelton, S. (1990, July). A nearly fearless forecast. *Nation's Business*, p. 45.

O'Sullivan, L. (1976). Organizing for impact. *Quest, 2*(3), 69-80.

Owen, C. L., & Todor, W. D. (1993). Attitudes toward women as managers: Still the same. *Business Horizon, 36*(2), 12.

Rosener, J. B. (1990, November/December). Ways women lead. *Harvard Business Review*, pp. 119-125.

Sadker, M., & Sadker, D. (1994). *Failing at fairness: How America's schools cheat girls*. New York: Scribner.

Salmans, S. (1987, August 17). Top tiers still elude women. *New York Times*, p. B4.

Sargent, A. (1981). *The androgynous manager.* New York: American Management Association Communications.

Schaef, A. W. (1981). *Women's reality: An emerging female system in a white male society.* Minneapolis, MN: Winston Press.

Schwartz, F. (1992). *Breaking with tradition: Women and work, the new facts of life.* New York: Warner Books.

Schwartz, F., & Rago, J. (1984). Beyond tokenism: Women as true corporate peers. In J. B. Ritchie & P. Thompson (Eds.), *Organization and people* (3rd ed.; pp. 420-428). St. Paul, MN: West.

Skopec, E., & Smith, D. M. (in press). *The practical executive and team building.* Lincolnwood, IL: NTC.

Smith, D. M. (1991). *Kincare and the American corporation: Solving the work-family dilemma.* Homewood, IL: Business-One, Irwin.

Smith, D. M. (1992, March). Company benefits and policies only a start to becoming family friendly. *Employee Plan Benefit Review.*

Smith, D. M. (in press). *Leadership.* Lincolnwood, IL: NTC.

St. Joan, J. (1976). Who was Rembrandt's mother? *Quest,* (2), 67-79.

Thomas, K. W., & Kilmann, R. H. (1978). Comparison of our instruments measuring conflict behavior. *Psychological Reports, 4*(2), 1139-1145.

U.S. Department of Labor. (1988). *Workforce 2000: Work and workers for the 21st century* (Document #029-014-00240-2). Washington, DC: Government Printing Office.

U.S. Department of Labor. (1991). *A report on the Glass Ceiling Initiative.* (Document 92052275). Washington, DC: Government Printing Office.

Yost, E. B., & Herbert, T. T. (1985). Attitudes toward women as managers (ATWAM) scale. In *The 1985 annual developing human resources* (pp. 123-127). San Francisco: Pfeiffer.

| Popular
Approaches to
Leadership

MARY ANN BOWMAN

As Peter Northouse noted in the introduction to this book, leadership has become a highly popular topic, with numerous new books appearing regularly in bookstores across the United States. Some of the authors whose books sell well become household names, appearing frequently on television talk shows, having their books excerpted in popular magazines, producing video- and audiotapes, and being cited often in print and electronic media. As a result, they often develop enormously successful consulting practices as well. Among those whose books on leadership have been widely read in the 1990s are Stephen Covey (1989, 1991), Peter Senge (1990, Senge et al., 1994), Max Du Pree (1987), James Kouzes and Barry Posner (1993, 1995), Peter Block (1993), and Ronald Heifetz (1994).

Popular Versus
Theoretical Approaches

Several characteristics distinguish these popular approaches to leadership from the theories presented earlier in this book. First, most of these authors are writing primarily for a general or leadership-practitioner audience, rather than a strictly academic one (Heifetz is perhaps an exception). Although they may include the facts, figures, and footnotes that buttress most scholarly works, their writing is more "user-friendly," making their books more readable and easily accessible. In other words, no scholarly background is assumed on the part of the reader, nor is one required to understand the ideas presented, although the level of difficulty varies from author to author. An additional difference is that some of the popular authors include a religious orientation that would be unacceptable in more academic writing.

These leadership authors also tend to have a more pragmatic, applied orientation to leadership. Unlike the authors who discuss theoretical approaches that seek to explain which, how, and/or why leadership behaviors occur within organizations, the majority of these writers tend to focus on what *should* occur to make leadership effective. They often include informal case studies, along with anecdotes about the authors' own experiences in working within or for organizations. They tend to be advice giving and future oriented, with the intention of having an influence on the way organizations actually function.

In addition, the popular writings on leadership tend to define leadership broadly. Rather than focusing solely on CEOs or top-level executives, they often present leadership as a behavior that applies in many life contexts—at work and at home. For this reason, readers are able to generalize many of the authors' concepts to their own situations. Even those who are not working in positions typically thought of as leadership or managerial in nature can easily find useful ideas in these books.

This pragmatic approach to leadership, when presented in a readable style for a wide, general audience, has proven again and again to be a formula for success for the authors who do it best.

Common Themes

The characteristics described above apply to the popular leadership books of any period, but the most successful books of the 1990s have several recurring themes in common, themes that distinguish them from most of the previous writings on leadership.

Servant-Leader Paradigm

First, many of these authors tend to be influenced by the idea of the leader as a servant, a concept first presented in terms of modern leadership in a work written by Robert K. Greenleaf in 1977, *Servant Leadership: A Journey Into the Nature of Legitimate Power and Greatness.* His ideas were strongly biblical in their foundation, as are some of the other authors' (e.g., Covey, 1991; Du Pree, 1987). Greenleaf (1996) noted that the "way some people serve is to lead" (p. 112). The servant-leader concept focuses on the idea that leaders have the obligation to pursue service to others, rather than their own self-interest (Block, 1993; Covey, 1991; Du Pree, 1987; Greenleaf, 1996; Kouzes & Posner, 1993). Thus, leaders whose primary concerns are their own professional advancement, personal gain, satisfaction of power needs, or a combination of these are failing to meet the basic requirement of servant leadership. Leaders must shift the focus of attention from their own needs and interests to the needs and interests of others (Kouzes & Posner, 1993, p. 91), believing that "serving others is the most glorious and rewarding of all leadership tasks" (p. 185).

Peter Block (1993) uses the term *stewardship* for this concept, noting that "when we choose service over self-interest, we say we are willing to be deeply accountable without choosing to control the world around us" (p. 6). Stewardship holds authority without using punishments, rewards, or directive power to get things done (p. 32). Block notes that partnership (which requires balancing power and accountability) is the better approach to service, rather than patriarchy.

Stewardship requires humility and the desire to make a contribution (Block, 1993, p. 41). Servant-leaders or stewards are motivated not by what they can get from their positions but by what their roles as leaders allow them to give to others (within the organization, and in society as a whole). Block provides detailed suggestions for defining a stewardship contract (pp. 63-74) through which one might transform an organization into one based on stewardship principles.

Spiritual-Ethical Orientation

Most of the popular leadership authors write from a spiritual perspective, rather than solely from a business or managerial one. Less attention is paid to bottom-line or profit issues, and more to issues of character, integrity, trust, honesty, and the like. Yet the assumption is that following spiritually oriented principles will lead not only to happier employees but also to more productive workers and more effective organizations. Covey (1991) describes principles on which leadership should be based, including trustworthiness, character, competence, maturity, self-discipline, and integrity. He also emphasizes the seven habits of effective people: being proactive; beginning with one's personal mission in mind; putting first things first; thinking win-win; seeking first to understand, then to be understood; using synergy by valuing the opinions, values, and perspectives of others; and engaging in continuous improvement of all dimensions of one's life (Covey, 1989).

Keeping promises—doing what you say you'll do—recurs as a significant way for leaders to demonstrate their character and credibility (Block, 1993; Covey, 1991; Kouzes & Posner, 1995, 1993). Listening is also frequently mentioned as an important way in which leaders demonstrate their openness to and acceptance of their followers (Covey, 1991; Du Pree, 1987; Greenleaf, 1996; Heifetz, 1994; Kouzes & Posner, 1993).

Work is viewed as an activity that has the potential to provide life meaning—but not the only activity. Covey, in particular, includes chapters about family life and relationships in his writings. In writing about work, however, he notes a common theme—that people want more from work than many of them are currently getting. He says:

> People want to contribute toward the accomplishment of worthwhile objectives. They want to be part of a mission and enterprise that transcend their individual tasks. They don't want to work in a job that has little meaning, even though that may tap their mental capacities. They want purposes and principles that lift them, enable them, inspire them, empower them, and encourage them to be their best selves. (Covey, 1991, p. 180)

Empowerment of Followers

The popular approach to leadership emphasizes the importance of the leader's relationship with followers. A leader's power is granted from those below (Block, 1993). Leadership is a reciprocal relationship, and being a leader means being "a part of, not apart from" (Kouzes & Posner, 1993, p. 2). Leaders build credibility when they appreciate their constituents and develop the capacity to liberate leadership in others. The new work relationship is one in which authority is shared, which means that "leaders and constituents are mutually responsible for the same effects, with or without explicit shared decision making" (Senge, Kleiner, Roberts, Ross, & Smith, 1994, p. 72).

This approach also shifts attention from the decision-making behaviors of individual leaders to what leaders do to enable followers to grow, learn, and engage in collaborative, team-oriented decision making. Empowerment makes members responsible for creating the organization's culture (Block, 1993, p. 49) and creates a kind of shared leadership among all organizational constituents. Kouzes and Posner (1993) state, "Leadership is a set of skills and practices that can be learned regardless of whether or not one is in a formal management position" (p. 156). Kouzes and Posner (1995) also refer to the leadership principle of enabling others to act, and they emphasize the importance of fostering collaboration and cooperation.

Block (1993) notes that the kind of fundamental change needed in organizations today cannot be accomplished by strong leadership. Because of various scandals that continue to occur at the highest levels of leadership, many people have become cynical and suspicious of leaders in general. To effect critically needed change, followers must become part of the leadership process—there must be an exchange of purpose between leader and constituents. In Block's (1993) view, everyone at all levels must define the organization's vision, goals, and purpose (p. 29).

Heifetz (1994), analyzing various historical examples of political leadership, notes the human tendency to seek answers from a single authority, something he calls "maladaptive" (p. 73). Block (1993) also notes the danger of human dependency on authority. Heifetz calls for a kind of leadership without authority, saying that the "leader has to engage people—in facing the challenge, adjusting their values, changing perspectives, and developing new habits of behavior" (p. 276). Heifetz's work in particular suggests the complexity of some leadership issues, and also calls into question the ease with which team leadership can be applied in all situations.

Du Pree (1987) embraces the team approach to leadership, describing several rights of team members, including to be needed, involved, understood, and accountable. He notes that the members of an organization need to "become learners together" (p. 66).

Although Peter Senge's works are considered highly influential contributions to the discussion about leadership, in a sense he spends little time addressing the behaviors of top leaders. Instead, his focus is more on the creation of learning organizations—those work environments in which individuals at all levels are enabled to acquire the disciplines that will allow them to continue learning and growing. The disciplines identified by Senge are systems thinking, developing personal mastery, working with mental models, building shared vision, and team learning.

In this approach, the team, not the individual, is the fundamental learning unit within the organization. Developing an environment that encourages learning is the "primary task" of the leader, and "perhaps the only way that a leader can genuinely influence or guide others" (Senge et al., 1994, p. 65). It thus makes sense that Senge focuses more on leadership at the systemic level rather than at the individual level.

Strengths

As discussed above, the common themes of these popular approaches to leadership are the servant-leader paradigm, a spiritual-ethical orientation, and the empowerment of followers. Among the strengths of these approaches are the following:

These approaches are humanistic and positive in their orientation, focusing attention on the employees of any organization as human beings with individual needs and concerns that should be taken into account when decisions are made. The authors tend to assume that the motives and behaviors of leaders and followers can and will be based on such positive characteristics as unselfishness, honesty, trust, need for personal growth, and more. Implicit throughout these writings is the assumption that what is good for individuals is ultimately also good for the organization.

A second strength is that these approaches provide a spiritual perspective missing from most of the leadership literature. Both the servant-leader paradigm and the spiritual-ethical orientation are congruent with and reflect a societal preoccupation with spiritual issues and concerns throughout the 1990s. The growth in New Age philosophical/spiritual orientations and the resurgence of interest in more traditional religions suggest that many people are interested in discussing values, examining ethical/moral issues, and looking for deeper meanings in their daily lives than can be found in simple materialism or consumerism.

This spiritual orientation provides the perspective of a higher purpose to leaders and their constituents. It reminds leaders of their responsibilities to others and their obligation to make a contribution. The purpose of leadership is to serve others, whether individuals or society-at-large, rather than to advance leaders' own needs and interests. These approaches are not intended to keep leaders from paying attention to the bottom line, but rather to remind them of the consequences in human terms of their leadership. They suggest that it is actually possible for organizational life to include a spiritual dimension, for both leaders and followers.

A third strength is that these approaches are easy to understand, both in terms of usefulness and in terms of application. They make intuitive sense, and readers can see how they might apply the approaches in their professional lives—and often in their personal lives as well.

A final strength is that these approaches are also consistent with accepted managerial principles, particularly those of Total Quality Management. They promote the value of an empowered workforce working cooperatively with leaders. Although the importance of the individual leader is not denied in these theories, the value of teamwork among individuals who are continually learning and growing receives greater emphasis. The success of the organization depends on not just who is at its helm but also the collaborative efforts of all its workers. The importance of creating a working environment in which individuals can thrive is presented as a key to organizational success.

Criticisms

Despite the popular appeal of these approaches and their admitted strengths, they do have limitations. One criticism is that many of the theories presented have not been tested by published, well-designed, empirical research. Although many examples may be provided of how the ideas have been used in organizational settings, the majority of these tend to be anecdotal in nature.

A second criticism is that, despite the pragmatic orientation of the approaches, the theories may actually be quite difficult to apply in real-life settings. Application could be difficult for one significant reason—the underlying assumptions of some of the theories do not take into account the complexity of individual motivation and behavior within organizations. At times the authors appear to be out of touch with the day-to-day reality of the working world. Not only do they tend not to acknowledge that human behavior may not always be positive or constructive, but they also do not offer specific strategies for applying these approaches when circumstances are less than ideal.

For example, the belief that all organizational members want to and will behave in an ethical way seems naive. The servant-leader paradigm may be spiritually sound in principle, but one might question if it could actually be applied to the corporate world reported by the media, in which CEOs are paid (and accept) enormous bonuses even as they cut their own workforce because their companies are not making a profit. These leaders do not seem to see service toward others as a driving purpose.

Approaches emphasizing spiritual and ethical concerns may simply appear to be too idealistic to be practical. Honesty, integrity, trustworthiness, and compassion are not always the principles by which many organizations are being led—even if most people would agree that they should be. One has only to read a few of the e-mail messages from frustrated employees in *The Dilbert Principle* (Adams, 1996) to know that leadership isn't necessarily being conducted by these standards.

The empowerment of employees is also an idealistic concept that may be difficult to implement. Although this approach has received a great deal of discussion in the popular media and lip service from many organizations, anecdotal evidence suggests that employees may not always feel as empowered as their bosses say they are. Of the popular leadership authors, only Heifetz and Block suggest that some individuals may actually have dependency needs that make them prefer to rely on the authority of autocratic leaders. Collaboration is difficult to implement in settings where employees would rather be told what to do than accept shared responsibility for leadership.

Some organizations have indeed truly adopted and continue to use successfully such concepts as team learning and collaborative decision making. Nevertheless, it appears that true learning organizations are still in the minority, whereas traditional, hierarchical, autocratic organizations are quite common.

Essentially, it may be accurate to say that the limitations of these approaches are inherent in the nature of human beings themselves. The concepts in theory appear to be valid and valuable; it is their implementation that creates barriers for the achievement of a true change in leadership. Human leaders are, like all human beings, a paradoxical mixture of idealism and pragmatism, high ideals and unethical behavior, altruism and ambition, generosity and greed. It will always be easier to send employees to workshops on effectiveness or learning organizations than it will be to integrate the principles of the workshops into the everyday lives of those who attend—including those in leadership positions.

Despite these limitations, the popular approaches described here make a positive contribution to the literature by presenting a more humanistic, spiritual, and idealistic model of leadership that recognizes the value of individual contributions through the active involvement of all followers in organizational decision making.

Application

The common conceptual themes found in the popular leadership literature may be applied to any organizational setting and to all levels of leadership through the perspective of the approaches advocated by the authors. Many of them can be applied to the interpersonal realm as well.

Case Studies

The case studies presented here (Cases 12.1, 12.2, and 12.3) provide an opportunity for you to consider how these approaches might be applied in the situations described. Questions following each case will assist you in analyzing these situations from the perspective of these popular approaches to leadership.

Case 12.1

Thea Burnett assumes her position as the vice president of a large company (employing more than 2,000 persons) with high hopes. Bright, hard-working, and idealistic, she is eager to implement ideas that will make a difference in her new organization. She is committed to the belief that the purpose of leadership is to make a meaningful contribution, and she is committed to maintaining high ethical standards in all aspects of her life. The company president and CEO is a brilliant and talented executive who has publicly expressed pleasure at having a woman in this high-level position of leadership. He has been cordial and supportive throughout the interview and hiring phases of her employment.

Because Thea has a strong interest in the empowerment of employees and total quality management (TQM), she is pleased when she realizes that the president has made many public statements about the value of TQM, created an office to support it, and supported the funding of several TQM projects within various departments of the company. She looks forward to creating an initiative within her own area that will implement collaboration and teamwork among employees. Thea strongly supports the idea of the learning organization and the creation of an environment in which employees can continually grow and learn.

As Thea begins her work, she decides to talk with all of the managers in charge of the TQM projects already ongoing within the organization. She invites each of them to individual meetings in her office, and after she has completed a number of private interviews with them, she begins to notice a disturbing trend. First, she observes that the managers feel extremely frustrated about the usefulness of their TQM efforts, each noting in turn that higher administration really has no commitment to shared, collaborative leadership. They feel that their work in this direction is being thwarted because decisions will ultimately always be made at the top of the organization. The employees on their teams are becoming increasingly cynical about the time and energy being put into shared decision making that will go nowhere, and the managers are having a hard time explaining to employees why they should be optimistic about the process.

Another disturbing trend that Thea notes is that the managers seem to be quite fearful of retribution for honestly sharing their views. Each person is very careful to make clear that his or her statements are "off the record," and each hints at dire consequences if true opinions were to be known. The managers seem to be suggesting a climate of fear within the organization that causes employees to be quite reluctant to express their thoughts and feelings on any but the most innocuous topics. Statements are made about "killing the messenger" and a desire to hear only good news. Thea wonders how problems can be addressed if this is indeed the case—and she wonders exactly what form the retributions have taken. As a new vice president, it has not always been easy for her to gather information about the "story behind the story" that helps with understanding of an organizational culture.

In terms of her own relationship with the president, lately Thea has noticed a lack of respect in his communications with her. He doesn't solicit her opinion, seems to focus his attention elsewhere when she is speaking, and often interrupts her with topics unrelated to those she is addressing. Lately, he has begun to deal with her mainly through e-mail or through his low-level assistants, and she is becoming increasingly paranoid about his real perceptions regarding women leaders—and the level of authority she actually has in the organization. Thea wonders whether any attempt to implement collaborative decision making within her area will result only in her feeling as frustrated as the managers—and possibly cause her authority to be eroded by having decisions reversed by the president.

Thea's discussions with managers and her own experiences have now led her to have several areas of concern:

- The perception that organizational decision making is autocratic, not collaborative
- The perception that telling the truth will be punished
- The perception that her authority may be in jeopardy because of a lack of respect from the president, perhaps because of her gender

Questions

- How well does Thea's leadership philosophy fit with the assumptions of the popular approaches to leadership?
- What about the company president's?
- The managers'?
- If you were Thea, and you needed to stay in this position for some time, what actions would you take to address your concerns?

Case 12.2

Samuel Sada is a new international faculty member at a medium-sized university in the southeastern United States. Although he attended graduate school in this country, his native accent is still quite strong, and he tends to speak quickly. Quite a few of his students (and some of his colleagues) are having a hard time understanding him, and he is not always good about slowing down or repeating himself. Thus, his customers (i.e., students) are unhappy with the services he is providing them (i.e., his teaching).

Samuel's situation is further complicated by the fact that he lacks much understanding of some fundamental concepts of providing good service to his students. He frequently comes late to class; he fails to return projects until weeks after they were turned in; his explanations of concepts and principles are not always clear; and he tends to blame poor student attitudes for his troubles. He is hurt by the fact that students do not show him respect, and he wonders if his black skin could bias their perceptions.

The supervision of Samuel's work in the classroom is affected by the fact that his department has no one in charge at the moment. The performance of the previous chairperson was deemed inadequate and after some departmental restructuring, the position has remained unfilled. Consequently, Dean Margaret Patterson has taken over the job of managing the department, along with her regular duties. Thus, no middle manager stands between Samuel and his top supervisor.

A disturbing pattern has begun to develop. Students almost never take their complaints to Professor Sada; instead, they go directly to the dean. Soon the students recognize that they have easy access to the dean and there is a steady flow of students into her office, filling her ears with complaints about Samuel's general inadequacy as a teacher.

Because Dean Patterson has in the past had some difficulties with other international faculty members, she is eager to prevent further problems from developing. When she had to deal with such a situation previously she tried to be patient, compassionate, and understanding, and it did not work. The faculty member made no effort to change (at least from the dean's point of view), and ultimately he had to leave the university. Now the dean fears this scenario is happening again, and she believes her "soft" approach was ineffective—so she has decided to turn tough.

Whenever the students come to Dean Patterson, she is available to listen to them. Yet she almost never speaks directly to Samuel about the complaints she is hearing except to report them. Samuel feels that she does not ask for his opinions or explanations—that he has been judged guilty without a trial. According to his view, she has already decided that in all regards Samuel is wrong and the students are right. Because Dean Patterson is very unhappy about the complaints she hears, she sends Samuel a strongly worded letter that tells him he must improve immediately—or else.

Questions

- How well does the dean's leadership philosophy fit with the assumptions of the popular approaches to leadership?
- Could the dean have handled this situation differently from the start?
- How?
- What are some ways that Samuel, in the leadership position of teacher, could use the principles of the popular leadership approaches to provide better service (a more meaningful learning experience) to his students?

Case 12.3

Judith Duncan has just completed her Ph.D. at the age of 45. Her area of expertise includes program and performance evaluation, performance assessment, and the implementation of quality measures. She worked for several years in a grant-funded position for which the grant abruptly ended, largely due to internal political reasons. Having been out of work for some time, she is thrilled when she is hired by a governmental mental health agency for a job that seems to be perfectly aligned with her doctoral training.

Judith's previous job provided a high degree of flexibility in terms of scheduling, dress, and behavior in general, so the rigidity in place at her new position comes as something of a shock. Time clocks are punched, every minute must be accounted for, informal chats with co-workers are discouraged, and in general her supervisor, Bob Voight, seems to be keeping a very tight rein on the way the office functions. She adjusts to her new working environment, however, and believes that things are going relatively well, despite the fact that she finds the atmosphere negative and constricting. Perhaps because of the nature of the environment, or perhaps because of her own personality, Judith has not made many new friends in her job.

Because she has been hired specifically to evaluate quality and determine ways to implement quality measures, she closely observes the way things work in the office—both the good and the bad. In her view there is more bad than good, but she is reserving judgment to some extent because she is relatively new to the position. However, at team meetings, when members are asked for their views, Judith expresses her opinions about the topics under discussion. Having come from a team-oriented working environment in the past, she understands the purpose of a meeting as the gathering of team members' views. The longer she is in the position, the more open she is about expressing her perspectives about the way things work, could be improved, or both, in the office. Sometimes Judith can be more blunt than diplomatic in her comments, but she is usually credited for her intelligence and honesty.

One Thursday when Judith arrives at work, Bob Voight calls her into his office. He tells her that he is requesting that she collect her belongings and leave the building. She will be allowed to resign, but if she returns the next day, she will be fired. He really provides no adequate explanation of this decision. Although Judith leaves the office, she decides to return the next day and be fired. Bob Voight is furious when he sees that she has returned to the office on Friday morning. They have an angry exchange in which he makes statements that reveal that numerous lies have been spread about her in the office. He fires her on the spot. Seeing that there is no longer any way to defend herself, Judith leaves the building.

Questions

- What is going on in this organization?
- How well does Bob Voight's leadership philosophy fit with the assumptions of the popular approaches to leadership?
- Assuming Judith's performance was inadequate, how could Bob have handled this situation differently?
- What ideas from the popular leadership approaches could Judith herself have used more effectively to ensure a different outcome in this situation?

Leadership Instrument

The following instrument is designed to allow the respondent to reflect on a variety of leadership situations and consider what leadership behaviors would be most congruent with the principles found in the popular approaches to leadership. These situations describe what could occur in many different types and sizes of organizations.

Popular Leadership Approaches Questionaire

INSTRUCTIONS: Evaluate each of the situations described below to determine which of the responses—a, b, c, d, or e—is most congruent with the leadership principles of the popular approaches described in this chapter.

1. What should a leader do when the organization is having trouble meeting its bottom line?
    a. Call employees together and announce the need for downsizing.
    b. Meet individually with employees whose jobs will be eliminated.
    c. Ask managers to immediately organize problem-solving teams to brainstorm solutions.
    d. Cancel executive bonuses and all pay raises.
    e. c and d

2. How should a leader handle a situation in which a newly hired executive isn't performing up to expectations in her position?
    a. Do a reality check by talking with others about their perceptions of the situation.
    b. Invite the executive for a private discussion about what she needs to do to meet the demands of the position.
    c. Send the executive a memo of warning in which the person's failure to perform up to expectations is clearly defined.
    d. Try to be patient and ignore the performance until the person has been in the job longer.
    e. b and c

3. How should a leader respond when a study of staff morale suggests that several problem areas are affecting employee satisfaction?
    a. Call in top management and demand to know why their staff members aren't happy.
    b. Organize informal meetings with small, representative groups of staff from affected areas and listen to their views.
    c. Organize meetings of small, representative groups of staff from affected areas and have them generate solutions to the problems.
    d. Implement the most feasible solutions generated by problem-solving teams, monitor the success of these efforts, and reexamine staff morale in 6 months.
    e. c and d.

4. What would be the best way for a new leader to start his job?
   a. Visit every department in the company, ask employees to share their perceptions of the strengths and weaknesses of the company, say little, and actually listen.
   b. Assemble an all-company meeting in the auditorium and present a formal address.
   c. Visit department meetings and do a presentation to the employees.
   d. Invite department managers to a lunch meeting where he does most of the talking.
   e. Have a private meeting with each manager and ask them to tell him how things are going.

5. What should a leader do when the organization seems to need a new vision?
   a. Invite managers to tell her what the vision should be.
   b. Tell managers what the vision *will* be.
   c. Assemble an all-company meeting in the auditorium and, in a formal address, tell them what the new vision will be.
   d. Ask managers to organize teams to work collaboratively on developing a shared vision.
   e. Decide that vision is highly overrated in determining organizational effectiveness and forget about it.

6. What should a leader do if employees have been promised that their views will be a major influence in the choice of the next vice president, but the candidate employees overwhelmingly prefer turns out not to be the leader's choice?
   a. Delay a decision and do more information gathering about the employees' candidate.
   b. Delay a decision and conduct a public relations campaign for the leader's preferred candidate.
   c. Hire the person employees prefer.
   d. Hire the person the leader prefers.
   e. Hire neither candidate and reopen the search for a vice president.

Discussion of the Questionnaire

Each situation described in the leadership questionnaire offers the possibility of many leadership responses, each of which may be valid, depending upon the organizational context and the leadership philosophy in place. In each case, however, certain behaviors appear to be far more consistent with the principles of the popular approaches to leadership.

Situation 1: The Organization
Is Not Meeting Its Bottom Line

Answer (e) is the optimal choice, because not only does the leader involve employees in shared problem solving and decision making, but he also includes executives in the sacrifices required to address the problem. Thus, the leader's credibility as a trustworthy individual is reinforced because he has demonstrated a concern for the best interests of the organization and of the individuals who work within the organization. This is consistent with the values of the servant leader or steward who sees his primary purpose as to serve.

The other approaches, Answers (a) and (b), appear to be firmly entrenched in more traditional leadership models in which decisions are made and delivered autocratically. Meeting individually with employees, as in Answer (b), at least demonstrates greater sensitivity to and respect for the feelings of the persons in question. But in general, the automatic solution of downsizing seems to be a strategy in which employees are viewed as part of the problem, not part of the solution.

Situation 2: A New Executive
Isn't Measuring Up to Expectations

Answer (b) is the optimal answer, because this response treats the individual with respect and demonstrates trust in the possibility of a positive outcome to the problem. These behaviors typically reflect a concern for high ethical standards. Such a session would, of course, require positive mentoring on the part of the leader, clear criteria for expectations, and specific suggestions about how to improve.

Although Answer (a) has the potential to provide some useful information to the leader, it would need to be considered very carefully because standards of privacy, confidentiality, and personal respect could easily be breached. A more effective strategy might be for the leader to encourage the executive to solicit feedback directly from those in the organization who are in the best position to evaluate her performance. Answer (c), sending a memo of warning, would clearly be a punitive, autocratic response that could destroy a sense of trust and trustworthiness. This does not seem to be a situation in which Answer (d), ignoring the problem, would be particularly useful. Personnel problems tend to get worse, not better, when ignored.

Situation 3: A Study of Staff
Morale Reveals Problem Areas

Answer (e) is the optimal choice because it demonstrates trust in the perceptions of staff members, makes them partners in decision making by implementing some of their suggestions, and shows a commitment to addressing staff concerns by building in an ongoing assessment process.

Answer (a), demanding that top managers explain why employees aren't happy, shows both an autocratic leadership style and a distrust of the validity of employee opinions. Answer (b), although not a bad step in principle, is helpful only if followed with real action. The employees' views have already been reported in the study; listening to them further is only a delaying tactic at this point. If that meeting should occur without any further follow-up, leader credibility is likely to be negatively affected.

Situation 4: A New Leader Starts His Job

Answer (a) is the optimal choice, because it involves employees, shows humility and self-discipline on the part of the leader (keeping quiet is not easy for most leaders), and communicates a powerful message about the value of individual employees to the organization.

Answer (b), presenting a formal address to the assembled company, is a traditional approach for those whose focus is on the individual leader—and it could be effective as either an introduction or a follow-up to Answer (a). If the formal address made the promise to conduct the sessions described in Answer (a), and those sessions occurred, this would communicate the leader's commitment and trustworthiness. If the address were made as a follow-up to the sessions, it would allow the leader to reflect on all he had learned from the sessions, thank employees for their contributions, and make a public pledge to continue involving staff in shared leadership.

Answer (c), presentations to department meetings, is a traditional, leader-centered approach, with communication flowing in one direction to a captive audience. Answer (d) has the same weakness and narrows the audience to managerial-level employees. Answer (e) has the virtue of one-on-one sessions, but again is restricted to managers. Keeping these kinds of sessions reserved only for those in formal leadership positions sends the cultural message that the leader intends to keep a hierarchical structure that does not necessarily value the contributions of employees.

Situation 5: The Organization Needs a New Vision

Answer (d) is the optimal choice, because employees are going to work collaboratively in teams to develop a vision for the organization. The leader has clearly demonstrated her willingness to share leadership with employees and her appreciation of employees' ideas and insights.

Answer (a), inviting managers for their views, has the virtue of asking for some suggestions from others; but it is once again limited by relying only on the voices of those at formal leadership levels. Answers (b) and (c), telling managers or simply announcing to the entire company what the vision will be, are traditional, autocratic approachs. Approach (c) could be used, however, after the vision has been developed from the activities of Answer (d). Answer (e), deciding to forget about a vision, is likely to be an ineffective strategy that will demonstrate only the leader's lack of imagination and leadership skills.

Situation 6: The Employees' Choice Is Not the Leader's Choice

Answer (c) is the optimal choice, although a difficult one. This situation provides a perfect opportunity for the leader to demonstrate that he will keep the promise that he made to employees; that he has trust in the ability of employees to share in leadership decisions; and that he has the humility to accept a decision made by others. Through this decision, the leader can clearly show that his purpose is to serve the organization, not to gratify his own ego.

Answer (a) only postpones the decision, which is likely to please no one and will clearly be perceived as a stalling tactic. Answer (b), conducting a public relations campaign for the leader's choice, is a cynical response intended to brainwash employees into changing their minds. Answer (d) is the traditional, autocratic response that demonstrates that leadership begins and ends at the top. Answer (e), reopening the search, is a compromise tactic likely to please no one. All of these less desirable responses have the potential to destroy any sense of trustworthiness that the leader may have earned.

Summary

The popular approaches to leadership typically are found in writings that are intended for a general or leadership-practitioner audience; have a pragmatic, applied orientation to the topic; and define leadership broadly. Because of their readability and appeal to a wide audience, such books often end up on the best-seller list.

The approaches to leadership in the 1990s have several common themes. First, many of the authors have been influenced by the servant-leader paradigm, a concept that emphasizes the need for leaders to be motivated by the desire to serve others rather than by their own self-interest. Second, a majority of the popular authors write from a spiritual-ethical orientation, focusing on issues of character, ethical behavior, and life meaning. Third, almost all the popular leadership approaches emphasize the importance of the empowerment of followers. According to this view, leadership should be shared with employees in a way that incorporates collaborative teams in cooperative decision making. Attention shifts from a focus on the individual leader to the creation of an environment in which employees can grow and learn together—the learning organization.

One of the strengths of the popular leadership approaches is that they have a humanistic, positive orientation that focuses on employees as human beings with individual needs and concerns. A second strength is that they provide a spiritual perspective that is missing from most of the leadership literature. This perspective is congruent with a contemporary interest in spiritual issues. A third strength is that the approaches are easy to understand and make intuitive sense. A final strength is that the approaches are consistent with accepted managerial principles, especially total quality management. They promote the value of an empowered workforce working cooperatively with leaders and sharing in decision making.

These approaches have limitations as well. One criticism is that many of the theories presented have not been tested by published, well-designed, empirical research. Much of the evidence presented to support the ideas is anecdotal in nature. A second criticism is that, despite their pragmatic orientation, these theories may actually be difficult to apply in real-life settings. The highly idealistic underlying assumptions of the approaches often do not take into account the complexity of individual motivation and behavior within organizations. The authors tend not to acknowledge these more troubling aspects of employees and tend not to provide suggestions about how their ideas might be applied in negative situations.

In addition, not all employees may wish to be involved in a collaborative work setting; some may prefer to be in an authoritarian setting where they can simply be told what to do. The limitations of the approaches seem to be inherent in the nature of human beings themselves, a paradoxical mixture of highly positive and very negative characteristics.

Despite their limitations, as noted earlier, the popular approaches presented here have made a positive contribution to the literature of leadership. They appear to have met a need for a more humanistic, spiritual, and idealistic vision of leadership, and in doing so have clearly captured the imagination of many. In emphasizing the importance of treating all employees as valuable individuals with significant contributions to make, they encourage leaders to develop a model for the future that incorporates the collaborative strength of many, rather than the isolated power of one.

References

Adams, S. (1996). *The Dilbert principle*. New York: Harper Business.

Block, P. (1993). *Stewardship: Choosing service over self-interest*. San Francisco: Berrett-Koehler.

Covey, S. R. (1989). *The seven habits of highly effective people: Restoring the character ethic*. New York: Simon & Schuster.

Covey, S. R. (1991). *Principle-centered leadership*. New York: Summit Books.

Du Pree, M. (1987). *Leadership is an art*. East Lansing: Michigan State University Press.

Greenleaf, R. K. (1977). *Servant leadership: A journey into the nature of legitimate power and greatness*. New York: Paulist Press.

Greenleaf, R. K. (1996). *On becoming a servant leader*. San Francisco: Jossey-Bass.

Heifetz, R. A. (1994). *Leadership without easy answers*. Cambridge, MA: Belknap Press of Harvard University Press.

Kouzes, J. M., & Posner, B. Z. (1993). *Credibility: How leaders gain and lose it, why people demand it*. San Francisco: Jossey-Bass.

Kouzes, J. M., & Posner, B. Z. (1995). *The leadership challenge: How to keep getting extraordinary things done in organizations* (2nd ed.). San Francisco: Jossey-Bass.

Senge, P. M. (1990). *The fifth discipline: The art and practice of the learning organization*. New York: Doubleday Currency.

Senge, P. M., Kleiner, A., Roberts, C., Ross, R. S., & Smith, B. J. (1994). *The fifth discipline fieldbook: Strategies and tools for building a learning organization*. New York: Doubleday Currency.

Author Index

Subject Index

About the Author

Peter G. Northouse (Ph.D., University of Denver, 1974) is Professor of Communication at Western Michigan University. For more than 20 years he has been involved in curriculum development and in teaching leadership and organizational communication on both the undergraduate and graduate levels. In addition to several book chapters, he has published many articles in professional journals and is coauthor of *Health Communication: Strategies for Health Professionals* (2nd ed.). He is currently Chair of the Health Communication Division of the International Communication Association and serves on the editorial board of the *Journal of Health Communication*. His research interests include communication in leader-member relationships, transformational leadership, and conflict resolution. He has worked as a consultant in a variety of areas, including leadership, conflict management, and organizational communication.

About the
Contributors

Mary Ann Bowman (Ed.D., Western Michigan University, 1991) is Director of Faculty Development Services at Western Michigan University. Her background includes 14 years of university teaching, focusing on communication, leadership, and public speaking. She has authored several books and publishes regularly on a variety of issues in regard to professional development in higher education.

Susan E. Kogler Hill (Ph.D., University of Denver, 1974) is Associate Professor and Chair of the Communication Department at Cleveland State University. Her research and consulting has been in the areas of interpersonal and organizational communication, specializing in group leadership, teamwork, empowerment, and mentoring. She is author of a text titled *Improving Interpersonal Competence*. In addition, she has published in many professional journals and has written chapters in several books.

Dayle M. Smith (Ph.D., University of Southern California, 1986) is Professor of Management at the University of San Francisco. She currently teaches leadership, organizational behavior, and human resource management. She has published many articles and several books, including *Kincare and the American Corporation: Solving the Work/Family Dilemma,*

Motivating People, Leadership, and *Team Management.* Her research focuses on work/life management and leadership topics. She is also an active consultant to industry on a variety of human resources-related areas.

Ernest L. Stech (Ph.D., University of Denver, 1970) is President of Chief Mountain Publishing, Inc., and Chairman of the Board and Chief Executive Officer of Documents on Demand, Inc. He has authored numerous articles in professional journals and several textbook chapters. He is author of *Leadership Communication* and coauthor of *Working in Groups* and *Effective Group Communication.* His research interests have concentrated on the analysis of human interaction in various business and social settings.